OUR
EQUINE
FRIENDS

OUR
EQUINE
FRIENDS
STORIES OF HORSES IN HISTORY

GRANT MacEWAN

FIFTH
HOUSE

The publisher gratefully acknowledges the support of The Canada Council for the Arts and the Department of Canadian Heritage.

THE CANADA COUNCIL | LE CONSEIL DES ARTS
FOR THE ARTS | DU CANADA
SINCE 1957 | DEPUIS 1957

We acknowledge the financial support of the Government of Canada through the Book Publishing Industry Development Program for our publishing activities.

Printed in Canada by Transcontinental

02 03 04 05 06 / 5 4 3 2 1

National Library of Canada Cataloguing in Publication Data

MacEwan, Grant, 1902–2000.
  Our equine friends
  Previous ed. has title: Hoofprints and hitchingposts.
  ISBN 1-894856-01-5

  1. Horses—History. I. Title.
SF283.M32 2002   636.1'009   C2002-910568-4

Published in Canada by   First published in the U.S. in 2002 by
Fifth House Ltd.   Fitzhenry & Whiteside
A Fitzhenry & Whiteside Company 121 Harvard Ave.
1511 - 1800 4th Street SW   Suite 2
Calgary, Alberta, Canada   Allston, Massachusetts
T2S 2S5   01234

TABLE OF CONTENTS

Foreword

Writing about horses is a labor of love. It's like writing about an old friend who has lived long and dangerously and gained in personality and attractiveness. It's also like portraying a friend for whom the author feels a great sense of indebtedness and gratitude.

Clearly, the extremes of fortune experienced by horses over a very long period set the race apart. It's a forty million year association with North American soil and just about everything conceivable has happened to horses: spectacular, evolutionary changes, extinction of the wild race in this Western Hemisphere, re-introduction in a domesticated state, inheritance of an essential place in agriculture and industry, decline in the face of mechanization and, finally, return to popularity for the light breeds.

Inevitably, the story intrudes upon geology, archaeology, history, agriculture, recreation and art.

Horse fortunes rose and fell in spectacular ways but, throughout history, one quality remained remarkably constant: the human fondness for good and beautiful and reliable horses. For no other animals—unless they be dogs—has man displayed such feeling and attachment.

It was with this hope of capturing some of this sentiment for horses—western horses in particular—that these chapters were undertaken. It is left to other books to convey instruction about feeding, breeding, management and other matters of a technical nature; this one attempts to record what an ever-widening circle of horse lovers—young and old, male and female, rural and urban—might wish to remember about Canadian horses. The horse, having served Canadians well, has a story to tell. We should not forget our equine friend.

Grant MacEwan

CHAPTER 1

Mainly Sentiment

Without the warm and majestic presence of the horse, the course of world history would have been strangely different—and immensely more dull. Genghis Khan and Alexander The Great and a host of others with familiar names might have been no more than home-town heros. As a common pedestrian, Ben Hur would have performed no exploits worthy of memory. Attila The Hun, fighting on foot, would be forgotten quickly. For Napoleon there'd be no grand campaigns and, in the Crimea—no Charge of the Light Brigade.

Even in the New World it is difficult to think of progress in the absence of Mounted Police, cowboys, stage-coaches, covered wagons, school ponies and millions of draughters in farm fields.

Some of history's mounts became as well known as the human leaders who rode them. The spotted war horse, Rakush, sharing the glory of ancient victories with the immortal Rustem, inspired the poets. Foaled on the grasslands of Interior Asia, the colt's pedigree, allegedly, was as unusual as later successes—a man-killing mare of Ferghana for a dam and something described as a "demon" for sire. Only when Rustem slew the wild mare was he able to capture and break the colt, ultimately the swiftest and most courageous warhorse of his time. The conquering Rustem would ride no other.

No less famous was Bucephalus, dashing steed of Alexander The Great, and Greek writers, inspired by the animal's speed and graceful shape, left something for the record. Bucephalus, a black with white star on his forehead, offered support for an old maxim that "the wildest colts make the best horses." Hoping for a rewarding sale, the Thessalian owner displayed the untamed colt before King Philip of Macedonia, father of the 12-year-old Alexander. At first the King was unimpressed by the beautiful and unmanageable brute, but Alexander was captivated. No doubt there were some classical horse trading negotiations and, finally, the King condescended to buy the spirited colt if Alexander believed he could master the outlaw.

Nobody, unfortunately, recorded details about the bronk-riding performance in which the young man succeeded in riding and partially taming the savage animal. King Philip, having settled at a high figure, was overjoyed and between Alexander and Bucephalus there grew understanding and attachment. None but Alexander ever rode the horse; none but Alexander wanted to try riding him. Inseparable, man and horse went through the long and dangerous war campaigns in Persia and India, making history as they travelled. The horse died in 339 B.C. but whether it was the result of a war wound in Northern India or simply death by natural causes at the age of thirty years is not clear. One story has it that when mortally wounded in battle, Bucephalus carried Alexander to safety and then expired. In any case, on Alexander's orders, a city bearing the horse's name was built near the River Hydraspes, a monument to a great horse and a great loyalty between a man and his horse.

Napoleon's white Arabian stallion, Marengo, and the Duke of Wellington's Copenhagen—both ridden in the Battle of Waterloo—are other examples of horses sharing their master's fame. Generals for hundreds of years, like cowboys and outlaws of more recent times, had to be able horsemen. Napoleon rode various horses but favored Marengo, the one on which he appears in the familiar painting, Retreat From Moscow. Marengo was wounded at Waterloo but after the battle was taken to England where he lived to an unusual age, reported as thirty-seven years.

Canada, too, produced warhorses, agile, faithful and worthy of honor. Large numbers of native remounts were taken to the South African War and the First World War, some to inspire lines like those penned by Saskatchewan's Stanley Harrison when his trusted horse was killed at Passchendale in November, 1917: "Never shall I forget the first time I saw him there in the hills at home. Head uplifted, his brilliant eyes regarded me with kindly dignity. Ah, but he was superb! About him was a great shining, like a naked sword tempered in beauty and strength. Beneath his coat of rippling silk one sensed the soul of rhythm, and courage like white fire . . . Nor that last hour shall I forget. Even as I caught his low whinney I knew the wings of Pegasus had touched his shoulders. There amid the rumble of guns, Death had beckoned. But there, too, was something greater than death, shining down through the long long trailing centuries of Time . . . Beyond the cannon-mist I thought I saw him again, imperishable as all true beauty, one with the wind and sun, one with the glory of life—aye, and the glory of death."

"Remember him.
Somewhere in God's Own Space
There must be some sweet pastured Place
Where creeks sing on and tall trees grow,
Some Paradise where horses go,
For by the love that guides my pen
I know great horses live again."

But if ever there were horse heros deserving plaudits never bestowed, they were the ones which pulled settlers' wagons and homesteaders' plows and spent their flesh to help win a prospering nation. In the maze of sudden mechanization the pioneers' horses could be forgotten too quickly. It was proper that the warhorses be remembered but there would be injustice if the horses which played immeasurable parts in early farming were ignored.

One may try to imagine what the Canadian frontier would have been without horses—without the ones hauling passengers and mail and supplies, without saddle stock for the Mounted Police who brought order to a lawless area, without cow ponies, without the school ponies entrusted with the transportation of boys and girls, horses for work in grain fields, teams to haul wheat to elevators and even horses for the fun of a race.

The agricultural community produced no winged Pegasus such as was fashioned from dripping blood by Neptune and captured with golden bridle by Bellerophon. But let there be no mistake; the new soil had its equine heroes—like the celebrated Clydesdale stallion, Balgreggan Hero; the Cinderella Standardbred named Battleax; the stout-hearted Thoroughbred, Joey; the explosive bucking horse, Midnight and numerous other horses, like numerous people whose fame was purely local but none the less deserved.

Every rural resident in the heyday of farm horses could name some individual animal which because of personality or intelligence or faithful service, commanded special admiration and affection. Such a horse was Jack, unglamorous white gelding which hauled successive generations of children to a rural Manitoba school. He knew the route, knew how fast to jog, knew about stopping when a child fell out of the buggy. After delivering his charges within the school grounds at nine o'clock in the morning he would bring the empty buggy back to the farm, alone, and at thirty minutes before the time of school dismissal in the afternoon, Jack would be hitched and started, without driver, on the route he knew so well. Regardless of what small novice took up the reins, Jack's buggy in the course of twenty years never hit a gatepost and no child entrusted

4

to him was ever injured. Honorary degrees have been conferred upon candidates with less to show in the cause of education.

There was Shorty, another of the innumerable school ponies to earn gratitude and recognition. It was western Saskatchewan and a December storm blew in without warning. Temperature dropped suddenly as driving snow came in on the gale. The teacher at a rural school became worried and decided to dismiss her pupils early so they might be on their way home while there was daylight. But as the blizzard became worse she wondered if she should allow the children to start. Ten-year-old David had three miles to go but he always rode his horse, Shorty, and was determined to be on his way.

As David rode with face to the storm he soon became blinded by the freezing shafts of snow and numbed by cold. Unable to see, there was nothing for it but to drop the reins on Shorty's withers, give the brute his head and hope for the best.

As Shorty plunged on through the fresh drifts, David's parents became alarmed but realized that a search in such blizzard would be futile. They gazed anxiously into the driving snow and finally saw a dark shadow pass the house and move toward the barn. The father rushed out and pulled his chilled boy from the horse, intending to whisk him to the warm farm kitchen. But the lad, with admirable appreciation, was not ready to go—not until Shorty was given his feed of oats and hay. Asked if he were frightened, the boy replied: "Not very. I thought Shorty would bring me home."

Many pioneers in the West knew what it was to be caught in a blizzard as they rode or drove toward home. And many owed their lives to the horses which took them through.

Often, however, there was absence of human gratitude and tired old horses, after lifetimes of service, were shot or sold for what their emanciated bodies were worth in furnishing fox-feed. It didn't seem right that there was no better reward. But there were exceptions, owners with strong feelings for their animal slaves who ordered ease and good feed for the last years. Alex MacEwan, planning retirement for himself after almost fifty years of farming, declared that his horses would have the same release from hard work.

He sold his Saskatchewan farm and arranged for the customary dispersal of livestock and equipment. Those attending the auction expected to see the good draught horses, sons and daughters of Flash Baron, being offered along with pure bred cattle and machinery. But the horses were not being offered; by agreement, the neighbor who bought the farm would keep the horses in comfort for the balance of their natural lives. It was an expression of devotion to horses which served through the years when plowing was heavy and trails were rough. The horses never left that farm.

Gratitude did appear in unexpected places, as in an eastern city where, for a number of years, a Christmas party was held annually for the old horses which pulled the coal and junk wagons. Guests of honor received carrots, sugar and new blankets And at the annual Rangemen's Dinner at Calgary, July, 1955, the principal toast was to the Cowboy's Horse and two hundred ranchers and pioneers stood to pay their solemn respects.

It remains for somebody to raise a tangible memorial to the pioneer farm horses, as monuments have been raised to cavalry horses. To be appropriate, this image would not portray a prancing show horse with high head and swan-like neck and rounded body; rather, it would depict a dejected specimen with head held low, feet in the mud, ribs protruding pitifully and raw collar-sores on its scarred shoulders. It will not be an inspiring sight but it will be a reminder of what the Pioneer's Horses did in building a nation.

The fortunes of the horse have changed greatly. Mechanization displaced it on city streets and farm fields and led to a spectacular drop in draught horse numbers. Only in carrying stock saddles was the old role unchanged. But in keeping with a long record of ups and downs, horses found a new popularity with assurance of a lasting place in Canadian life—not as farm slaves but as pleasure horses for adults needing a change from mechanization and children needing the warm influence of animal pets.

A visitor from United Kingdom remarked with evident conviction: "You Canadians will never quit the horses. You seem to use them less and love them more." The visitor was right; Canadian sentiment for God's most graceful animals promises to be perpetual.

CHAPTER 2

Up From the Swamps

With a family history extending over many millions of years on this soil, what a story the horse might tell! From runt-sized Eohippus or Dawn Horse browsing in ancient North American forests to Starlight Koncarness winning her 50th Percheron grand championship in 1961, is a development ranking among the most fascinating in the whole realm of biology.

Clearly, the horse's association with these parts exceeds in point of time that of any other domestic animal. In the barnyard fraternity, only the turkey shares the distinction of a North American origin. Cow, sheep, pig and hen were brought to the Western Hemisphere since Columbus made his notable discovery. Even the dog, which was here in advance of the white man and long in the possession of North American Indians and Eskimos, was not indigenous but brought, no doubt, from Asia by primitive man when he entered this continent over the Bering Strait route.

While the cow's near relations have been on North American soil for a few hundred years and the dog's for a few thousands, the horse's ancestors made it their home for many millions of years and kept company with strange animal forms, some of them now extinct.

The horse family (Equidae) is a section of the biological order of hoofed-animals, Ungulata, embracing also the elephant, rhinoceros, ox, sheep, deer and pig families. Toe numbers vary within the group; the tapir, for example, has four toes on each front foot and three on each hind one; the rhinoceros has three toes on each foot, both front and back; the ox has two toes on each foot, and the horse is unique in having single-toed or monodactyle feet. But the horse was not always a one-toed creature—not by any means. Today's true horse may represent a union of several wild types but if those primitive forms had a common origin, it was probably North American. The earliest known ancestors—Eohippus—left their remains in both Europe and North America but only on this continent have all the succeeding genera and types been found to give the horse family an unbroken line of ascent. Darwin believed that all horses sprang from a common stock although he did not dismiss other possibilities.

The romance and tragedy of early horse fortunes in the Western World—told rather vividly by the fossilized pages of the rocks—must fire the imagination of every true student. Alongside a modern representative, the local horse of forty to sixty million years ago would appear as one of Nature's errors. That Dawn Horse was little if any bigger than an English Terrier dog. Although active, it was incapable of great speed. Refinement of legs was lacking and hind legs appeared longer than those in front. Its back was roached and in general outline the little fellow possessed none of the shapeliness and gracefulness so much in evidence in the modern counterpart. Teeth were short but adequate for the soft forest and swampland feed upon which it depended.

Keeping in mind the singular hoof development of today's horse, nothing about the miniature Eohippus holds more of interest than its feet. Each front foot had four toes—all in use—and each hind foot had three toes. The vestiges from other toes—first and fifth in the case of each hind—would still be in evidence. And for a forest and swamp dweller indulging in pawing soft earth, the toes would be handy.

In leg construction the radius and ulna of the forearm or upper front leg were distinct and separate, as were, also, the tibia and fibula in the hind leg above the hock.

Those who study the rise of the horse are entitled to speculate about the nature of the Dawn Horse's diet. It has been assumed that horses have always been vegetarian, as they are today. But what was a strictly herbivorous feeder doing with canine teeth which have persisted in the males? Would not such teeth, along with comparatively small stomach and multi-toed feet suggest that Eohippus may have strayed from a strictly vegetable diet and indulged to some extent in omnivorous feeding?

Before leaving the Dawn Horse one may enquire about its ancestors. Who were they? The skeletons of still earlier ancestral stock may yet be discovered. If and when they are found in the ancient rocks they can be expected to show five toes on each foot.

As time passed—a few million years—Eohippus moved a few steps upward on the evolutionary ladder and became Mesohippus, the horse of the Oligocene. Here was something bigger—about the size of a big dog instead of a small one—with three toes on each foot and all of them touching the ground.

The dank American forests of thirty million years ago suited these animals and they multiplied. Indeed, this may have been the only part of the world to have horses at that particular geological epoch; there is no convincing evidence of the presence of Mesohippus in either Europe or Asia. Only on this continent is there an unbroken record of the biological steps leading to the horses we know today.

Time passes. Horses of the next geological epoch (Miocene) are easier to recognize; in other words, they are more horse-like and the main branch of the family (Merrychippus) was showing an interest in the firm prairie country beyond the forests. At this point in the long series of changes, about twenty million years ago, the animals were bigger—more like small ponies of the present day. There were still three toes on each foot but the outside toes had drawn away to become useless to their owners. Only the enlarging central toe on each foot was bearing on the ground. The bones of the forearm, radius and ulna, were undergoing fusion, the union at this time being complete in older horses but still incomplete in foals. And corresponding changes were occurring in the bones of the hind leg, tibia or thigh bone becoming larger and fibula disappearing. Legs were becoming longer and stronger, ever so much better for speed which would be necessary if horses were to outrun their predator enemies in open country.

During this epoch, it seems, North American horses made migratory excursions into Asia. And somewhere along the route, they probably passed Asiatic elephants coming this way to establish their kind here—intercontinental free trade, as it were.

More complete retirement of lateral toes continued through more millions of years. Gradually the horse was abandoning the kind of feet which had served well during the millenniums of forest residence. Simultaneously teeth were changing from the kind suited to browsing succulent feeds to those with grinding surfaces and more useful in masticating upland vegetation.

The next geological epoch (Pliocene) probably corresponds with the appearance of man in some parts of the Old World. The horse of chief importance at the time has been given the name Pliohippus and the fossils show something as big as a donkey. Foot structure had altered until the superfluous side toes were scarcely noticeable. And now the horse was finding its greatly increased speed and using it to outdistance enemies in open country.

The following step in geological time (Pleistocene) witnessed the Ice Age and the appearance of true horses (Equus caballus). The animals may have reached their peak in numbers on this continent. Ten or more species existed and size varied to familiar extremes. William Ridgeway in his classical treatise, *The Origin and Influence of the Thoroughbred Horse*, (1905), says: "The Lower Pleistocene of America exhibits a great variety of races, ranging in size from horses far more diminutive than the smallest Shetland to those exceeding the very largest modern draught breeds."

And while size was increasing, brain capacity was enlarging and feet and legs were achieving the characteristics found in modern kinds, with well formed hoofs and no very conspicuous sign of rudimentary toes.

To fully appreciate the changes taking place, students should recall that each front foot of the modern horse corresponds to the middle finger of the human hand and each hind foot to the middle toe of human. Toes one and five were the first to become non-functional and disappear then the second and fourth went the same way. But those last two digits did not disappear altogether; they reappear in complete form in the embryo and survive as vestigal fingers or splint bones in adults.

Hence, the splint bones, about which horsemen frequently talk and worry needlessly, are not totally abnormal. Only when a splint involves the knee and becomes a threat to free and easy locomotion need it be seen in a serious light—and that is not often.

To carry the analogy another step: the horse's knee (carpus) is comparable to the human wrist and the hock (tarsus) pairs with human heel. If a horseman were to walk or stand like his horse, he'd be obliged to carry his weight entirely on the tips of his third fingers and third toes. A single trial will convince any experimentalist that the horse has come a long distance.

Before leaving the amazing evolutionary changes in equine feet and legs there should be at least a reference to those horny growths on the legs, commonly called callosities. In addition to the ones looking like weather-beaten warts on the insides of the legs, there are the small round ones occurring at the back of fetlocks in most horses and known as ergots. Why are they there and what, if any, use did they ever have? The questions have been asked many times.

Some observers will at once think of callosities in relation to displaced toes but some more appropriate association must be found. Nobody is sure of the answer but some biologists believe they see the chestnuts on the upper legs as degenerated wrist pads and the ergots as the remains of central sole pads such as are seen on a dog's feet.

Today's only surviving specimens are Prejvalsky's Horses described by Poliakoff in 1881. Contrary to what one may hear, the North American mustang was not a truly wild horse; as a strain springing from domesticated stock and adopting the wild state, it should be described as feral rather than wild.

Prejvalsky's Wild Horses, at home in the Gobi Desert of Central Asia, are commonly dun or mouse colored, with light shades above the nostrils and on the flanks. The mane is short and erect and there is no forelock. These sole surviving wild horses have convex foreheads, low withers, straight shoulder and loud voices. Their height is commonly between thirteen and fourteen hands.

But why didn't any truly wild horses survive on this continent where the race flourished for untold millions of years and where, even at the beginning of the Ice Age, their kind had advanced in numbers, size, speed and form to give them claim to one of the best of all biological success stories? The fact is that one of the great biological success stories ended in local disaster. Had some of their numbers not wandered to other parts of the world, horses would have suffered the same fate as the dinosaurs—extinction.

CHAPTER 3

Extinction on Native Soil

A nyone with sentiment for horses will likely seek a
mental glimpse of the wild bands in their native North
American settings of thirty thousand to fifty thousand
years ago—about the time the first man-creatures were
penetrating to inland parts of this continent. The soil had
already supported horse stock for millions of years—since
long before human kind in the Old World learned to stand
erect. Very early in their development horse ancestors may
have come face to face with the last survivors of North
American dinosaurs, although those small-brained mon-
sters were going into fatal decline before the era of
mammals.

When primitive man saw them for the first time, those
North American horses were among Nature's most successful adaptations for prairie living. No longer were they the
runty things impeded by needless toes and trying fearfully
to find hiding in the tangled forest. Many were the size of
modern horses; some in the area now marked by the State
of Texas stood at twenty hands. Already millions of years
up the evolutionary ladder, they were gaining refinement
and spirit, displaying flashes of speed for the sheer joy of
streaking across the plains faster than their enemies.

As instruments of Natural Selection, stallions fought for
the position of boss in the herds and the victors, with heads
held boastingly, pranced in circles to keep unwilling
harems together. Horse bands dominated the plains much
like prairie buffalo at a later time. They migrated northward in the spring, southward in the fall and mingled their

shrill neighs with the grunts, bellows and barks from strange neighbors like camels, elephants and mastadons. But soon thereafter the horse tribe fell upon bad times. It was the Ice Age although there is no proof that ice had anything directly to do with the decline. Whatever the reason, horses disappeared completely in the Western Hemisphere. Had it not been for horse stock which was by this time established on other continents, horses would be extinct today—as totally non-existent as the dinosaurs.

Living is never easy for wild creatures; destruction can strike without warning and without mercy. But what happened in the case of horses? What was the force bringing destruction on the very soil where they flourished and progressed for ages? Why did the western continents become graveyards for several of those large animal kinds of that period?

Horses definitely kept company with native camels. And, incidently, the camel's biological rise on this continent practically parallels that of horse. Fossil forms found in the Upper Eocene when the horse was no bigger than a small dog show camel ancestors of similar size. At that stage the camel had four toes on each foot, with lateral digits shorter than the two central ones. As in horses, retirement of unwanted toes was occurring more quickly in hind feet than in front.

Like horses, too, primitive camels remained on this continent until disaster in some form overtook them, about the time of the Ice Age. But before their disappearance in the West, members of genus Camelus wandered into Asia and from there into Africa. Perhaps the changes accompanying ice sheets were responsible for extinction but such is by no means certain because—even though ice sheets were three thousand feet deep in northeastern parts—the land area of the Americas would easily allow camels and other species to live a long distance from the actual face of glaciers. However that may be, related stock which went south gave rise to the South American llamas without leaving more than a fossil record behind in the North.

The rhinoceroses which moved from Asia were here through the early stages of horse development. And elephants adopted the continent when horses were still at the three-toe stage. The elephant's cousins, mastadons, were here too, and a little later, mammoths, biggest elephants of all time, twelve or thirteen feet in height and equipped with upturned tusks measuring up to thirteen feet. Specimens preserved in Siberian ice have shown them with long, reddish hair. But neither size nor red hair could save them and for reasons unknown, mastadons and mammoths went down to complete defeat while camels and horses disappeared in the New World but survived in the Old.

Presumably the native horses outlived the rhinoceroses, most of the camels and some branches of the elephant family. That they were still here when primitive man arrived thirty thousand or more years ago is shown by bones of horses and humans found together in some ancient deposits, also the discovery together in New Mexico and elsewhere of arrowheads and horse bones. Bones of camels, elephants, ground sloths and horses were reported with obsidian implements of human manufacture in regions about Fossil and Silver Lakes in Oregon in 1879. These and other discoveries seemed to confirm that the earliest humans on the continent saw horses and hunted them for food.

It may be assumed that the destructive forces—whatever they may have been—were at work twenty thousand or forty thousand years ago. But their form and what exactly caused the horse's luck to change are nonetheless puzzling. The environment must have suited the early strains for geological ages, just as it did the Spanish horses gaining freedom to produce the Mustang breed in comparatively recent times.

It will not be overlooked that the impact of a new creature, man, may have disturbed a biological balance which was delicate at the best of times.

Man's arrival may have coincided with the waning of the Wisconsin Ice Sheet. Whatever significance is attached thereto, it seems reasonable that climatic changes accompanying advance and retreat of ice would have bigger influences upon existing fauna, directly or indirectly, than the actual appearance of man. Biological adjustments must follow any change in climate. But in considering climate as the possible villain in the horse's downfall, it should be remembered that animals of the race were widely distributed on the two American continents with land masses extending all the way from Arctic to Antarctic, and whatever the death-dealing force, there was no escape from it.

How could a change of climate have altered things for the horse? One can only postulate. Lower temperatures could result in reduced feed and poorer quality, hence, possibly, nutritional failures. Another thought: when climate was cool, carnivorous animals would find prey like musk-ox in greater abundance; with the retreat of glaciers, musk-ox and caribou and other kinds normally at home in the North, would move back again, possibly leaving horse stock exposed more than ever to the predators and their sharp fangs.

In line with such reasoning, Canadian stockmen discovered that when rabbits were abundant, coyotes left farm sheep and poultry alone; but when rabbits went into one of their periodic declines, the domestic flocks again became the objects of coyote attack.

Speed was the horse's best and almost only means of protection from enemies and it is conceivable that security continued only as long as predators were unable to run as fast. But when it is remembered that North American buffalo resisted the carnivorous pursuers quite successfully, it becomes doubtful if the horse's speed ever failed to the point of making the race an easy mark for the carnivores. Lions in Africa prey upon zebras but have never constituted a serious threat to survival in the species.

On this point, R. Lydekker (*The Horse and Its Relatives*, 1912) offers some evidence concerning possible extermination by predators. "In most parts of America, the feral horses appear to have no special difficulty in defending themselves from the attacks of predatory carnivora, such as jaguars, pumas, lynxes, wolves, coyotes and bears. The case is, however, different in certain parts of Patagonia where pumas are so numerous that wild horses seem unable to exist."

The puma, commonly called panther or cougar, is an exceedingly active cat and at one time or another has been widely distributed on both North and South America. Even domestic herds of sheep, cattle and horses have been known to suffer loss from these killers and their kind may have been especially numerous in times past.

There are other possibilities—disease and parasites for example. Something like equine sleeping sickness carried by insects might have been the killer. Such a malady has occurred in epidemic form in recent years, bringing death to pastures and alarm to horsemen. Tick-borne diseases—some of them quite severe—are common in many parts of the world.

None of these suggestions, however, seems capable of explaining the horse's doom although any of them is likely to get as much support as the other generalization about man on his appearance having upset the state of equilibrium between horses and their enemies, real and potential.

The fact is that horses, camels, tapirs and elephants of their several types disappeared while American buffalo, deer and some other big animal species we know were able to come through.

Happily, horse stock at some time or times passed westward over Bering land bridge connecting Asia and North America. It was the route by which the first humans entered the continent from the parts of older settlement. Had no such "bridge" existed we can consider the possibility of horses being known today by fossils only because horses about the Oligocene had become extinct in the Old World. But those emigrant horses which went from the Alaskan Peninsula, as a lifeline for the race, fanned out across the Asiatic vastness to restock one continent and then another in the Eastern Hemisphere. Consequently, extinction on the Americas did not mean extinction such as overtook passenger pigeons and dodos. Horses were to flourish in far parts of the world, enliven the pages of history and return to reseed their kind on native North American soil. But for a few thousand years the American continents were horseless—completely horseless. It was a spell broken only by the re-introduction of horses by the Spaniards who followed Columbus to the New World. Exactly how long that state of horselessness lasted on these continents, nobody can say but it was long enough that American Indians had lost all recollections or knowledge of such animals. Not even in tribal legends had the horse survived. Indians seeing the Spanish horses were overcome by awe.

But before returning to re-establish their species on the soil of their forbears, members of the horse family were to encircle the earth, help mankind along the road to progress and stamp a vivid impression upon the cultures of many lands. As world travellers, no animals would surpass the records made by horses and dogs.

CHAPTER 4

In Fields Afar

Having acquired feet and legs for speed and graceful movement horses became world travellers. While still in the wild state they made their way into every habitable section of the Northern Hemisphere and later, as domestic animals, accompanied man into every part of the civilized world.

Although temporarily lost to the Americas where they made their most triumphant stand, their journeys in Asia and Europe enabled them to aid the cause of civilization almost from its birth. One of enlightened man's earliest lessons was that horses could serve him in various ways. Nothing changed the lives of primitive people more than the acquisition of horses to pull their chariots or carry them mounted. Little wonder that the gods were seen as having a special claim upon these creatures of grace and goodness.

At some point in the process of time, the world centre of horse propagation shifted to Asia—probably to what is now Siberia. Not far from there the only truly wild horses still survive, the Tarpan-type animals with big heads and short legs and known as Prejvalsky's Wild Horses. It's easy to imagine all horse stock later occupying Europe as well as Asia as having fanned out from that region, taking with them the typically north-country instinct to paw snow in order to feed on buried grass.

To meat-hungry men of the Stone Age, horses answered nearly every food need. Not only did early men consume the flesh but they cracked the long bones and fractured the skulls to get the tender morsels of marrow and brains. The extent of slaughter may be judged by bone deposits discovered at a Paleolithic campsite at Solutre, north of Lyons, in France. There was a cave big enough to shelter several families and presumably occupied a few thousand years before the Christian era. In two walls protecting the entrance were the bones of an estimated forty thousand horses, nearly all from young animals and foals, indicating a preference for tender meat even at that time. The bones for the most part belonged to horses which would be thirteen to thirteen and one-half hands and the Stone Age tools used in the hunt were left with them.

But it was with the domestication of horses that mankind's destiny took one of its most important turns. No invention, discovery or secret weapon left a more vivid imprint. The horse wasn't the first animal to be domesticated, the dog and ass being ahead of it. Where and when the act took place are not clear but writers tend to set the time as about five thousand years ago and the place either Mesopotamia where some of the first seeds of agriculture were planted, or China where the Mongolian Tarpan ponies were at home.

How did it happen? It's anybody's privilege to attempt a mental picture of the first bold steps: nomadic tribes living close to the bands of wild horses, crippled mares being taken alive and their foals reared in captivity. Then, to break the monotony of the Asiatic countryside, some daring young heathen delights his fellow-savages by staging the first race against time. Seated on a side of rawhide tied to the frantic horse's tail, he is transported across the country at a speed far greater than man had ever before travelled. An idea is born and the trick repeated. Better ways are found to control the animals—bone bits and reins—and then the adoption of wheels to produce chariots.

It is generally agreed that early man hitched horses to chariots or chariot-like vehicles long before taking to riding in either peace or war. Perhaps the small size of the Asiatic strains would make hitching more practical than riding; perhaps it took less courage to ride behind an untamed horse than to climb on top.

At any rate, by 2000 B.C., the Greeks were driving horses in harness and about the same time, some partly civilized tribes in Asia were mounted. Moreover, the first true horses were known to be in Africa about this time. Wild asses and zebras had established themselves on the Dark Continent at a relatively early geological age, probably getting there over a land-bridge from Europe.

There is no Biblical reference to horses in the time of Abraham but Joseph, when in Egypt about 1706 B.C., founded the noble art of horse trading, exchanging corn for horses. The author of the Book of Job, writing about 1520 B.C., knew enough about horses to be inspired by them but apparently did not see any of them on Job's own ranch. Job was a big operator—seven thousand sheep, three thousand camels, five hundred yokes of oxen and five hundred she asses—but evidently he had no horses.

When the Children of Israel were retreating from bondage in Egypt, they were pursued by Egyptian warriors, "even all Pharaoh's horses, his chariots and his horsemen." Nearby Arabia, significantly enough, was backward in adopting horses by Egypt played a leading part in distribution.

There is reason to believe that the first horses in Arabia were obtained from the Libyan tribes of Northwestern Africa. But from where did the Libyan horses come? It would simplify matters if it could be said that Libyan horses were brought from Asia but nobody is sure.

This much is clear: Libyans were mounted on fleet horses by 1000 B.C. and in the view of the oft-quoted Ridgeway: "from this North African stock all the best horses of the world have sprung." Resourceful horsemen, the Libyans are credited with inventing the four-wheel chariot and winning the admiration of their Mediterranean neighbors. In time their horses came to be regarded as the fastest in the Roman circus. And Pegasus, winged horse of mythology, was supposed to have been foaled in Libya.

According to Homer, horses were bred in Greece from the time of the Iron Age. Figures on the Frieze of the Parthenon and those on bas-reliefs of the period show strong resemblance to the wild stock of Asia but the Greeks are known to have come under Libyan influence, having imported improved Libyan stock and imitated the Libyans in riding and using four-horse chariots. A result was the inclusion of racing contests with four-horse chariots at the Olympic Games in 680 B.C., and the first competitions for mounted horsemen in 648 B.C. Men of Greece, recognizing the need for cavalry, continued to look to Libya for faster and better breeding stock.

When Xerxes I, King of Persia, attacked Greece and met with defeat in 480 B.C., he had a big army, a mighty fleet and the greatest array of horses ever assembled for war. In addition to an army of a million men, he had horse-drawn and ass-drawn chariots from India, horse-powered chariots from Libya and camel-riders from Arabia.

History of that period tells, also, that Alexander the Great, extending his conquests into India, was met by armies from the Punjab with four thousand cavalry, three hundred chariots and two hundred elephants.

The Romans were riding about 400 B.C. and had cavalry at least as early as 218 B.C. Bay and grey horses were Roman favorites, whites and duns the least favored.

Libyan horses—whatever their origin—were taken to Spain and northward as far as the Rhine. Germans of the time of Julius Caesar were mounted and although they used their horses in war, their battle technique was to dismount and fight on foot. In any case horses were bringing a new glamor to war, a new effectiveness to man's weapons.

Even on the British Islands horses were in use at least two thousand years ago. When Caesar invaded in 55 B.C., mainly to prevent help being sent to his enemies on the mainland, tribes meeting him in the Southeast had cavalry and chariots. Farther north only chariots were in use and the horses were smaller, probably of Celtic type.

Caesar was impressed by the horsemanship he saw on the Island. Charioteers would drive madly about the field of battle while warriors hurled darts. When enemy ranks were sufficiently disorganized, the fighting men would leap from the chariots and fight on foot while the vehicles and drivers withdrew, ready to return if rescue became necessary. Caesar watched in amazement when native horsemen performed acrobatics, galloped down steep embankments and walked along chariot poles to stand on neckyokes as horses sped forward.

During the Roman occupation of nearly four centuries, roads were improved and heavier cattle and superior horses were introduced. But the races of ponies running wild—Celtic in origin—survived to give rise to several British breeds, New Forest, Exmoor, Dartmoor, Welsh and others.

Following the Roman occupation, there came the Angles and Saxons, landing on the east coast, pushing the natives back and introducing cattle and horses from what was later the Northwest of Germany. Later came the Norsemen, at first to plunder and then to settle and they brought horses. But horse breeding was conducted indifferently on those British Islands until the Norman invaders introduced their chunky horses with height of about fourteen hands.

For five or six centuries after the Norman conquest, metal armor was standard equipment for mounted warriors. The adoption of chain metal and, later iron plate armor, called for powerful mounts and horse improvement became the special concern of the English kings. Knighthood was in bloom and a knight wearing his best and heaviest iron clothing—altogether, four hundred or four hundred-fifty pounds when he was in it—needed a big horse and draught type received its first impetus.

In the reign of King John (1199–1216) a hundred stallions "of large stature" were imported from the low countries and Edward III (1327–1377) brought similar stock to England. Henry VII was responsible for legislation prohibiting the export of horses and mares having a value of six shillings, eight pence, or more and went so far as to include Scotland among the countries to which good English horses could not be exported.

It was King Henry VIII, with an eye for a horse as well as a woman, who enacted the most sweeping legislation in connection with horse breeding. Anxious to increase the size, he maintained his own horse breeding establishments. And decrying the indiscriminant breeding of "horses and nags of small stature and value," it was provided in an act of 1535: "that all Owners or Farmers of parks and enlarged grounds of the extent of one mile in compass shall keep two mares, being not spayed, apt and able to bear foals of the altitude or height of thirteen handfuls at least, upon pain of forty shillings." Henry's legislation stipulated further that any such Lords or owners of lands would be fined forty shillings if they "shall willingly suffer any of the said mares to be covered or kept with any stoned horse under the stature of fourteen handfuls."

And still more of Henry's logic: all nobles whose wives wore French hoods, velvet bonnets or other expensive millinery, would not be permitted to use any except superior stallions. If a man could keep his wife in fine hats, he could do something for horses.

By an act of 1541, Henry provided that within certain named parts of the kingdom, none but stallions fifteen hands and over could be turned out in public pastures. Thus was the English Great Horse or Shire created. But the Great Horse lost its military importance following Cromwell's time and it was transferred to a less glamorous but safer position in agriculture. In the meantime, as England and Scotland were becoming the studfarms of the world, the mainstream of British interest turned to Thoroughbreds.

CHAPTER 5

A Breed Is Born

Some people would believe there was a special creation for horsemen and some horsemen seem ready to accept the theory of a similar beginning for Arabian horses. Chances are the famous breed's origin will never be explained to everybody's satisfaction but whether Arabian pedigrees run through King Solomon's mares to stock owned by Noah's family, or to less romantic introductions of horse stock at a much later date—perhaps during the life of Prophet Mohammed—really doesn't make any practical difference. One fact remains: the Arabian is the world's oldest improved breed of livestock and just as certainly the fount through which refinement and quality flowed to make and improve most other horse breeds.

As an ancient breed the Arabian has enveloped itself with fable and fiction. Sentiment comes easy to horsemen at any time and in the case of Arabians, it has grown to prodigious proportions. Mohammed, with obvious affection for a good horse, added to the emotional feeling. Remarks attributed to him indicate his attachment: "Every grain of barley given to a horse is entered by God in the Registry of Good Works;" and, addressing a horse, he said: "Thou shalt be for man a source of happiness and wealth; thy back shall be a seat of honor and thy belly of riches; every grain of barley given to thee shall purchase indulgence for the sinner."

But what were the opposing views about the time horses arrived in Arabia? Lady Wentworth saw the Arabian breed as being older than the horse stock of Libya and the Barbary

States. Barb horses came from Arabians, she argued, rather than Arabians from Barbs. Horses of her favorite breed were distinguishing themselves as race horses long before the time of Christ, she was sure. According to legend which brings Solomon's mares into the story, the King became so absorbed with his fine animals that he forgot his prayers. Then, filled with repentance, he turned all his horses loose to shift for themselves and the five mares to survive became the five pillars of the Arabian breed. But the evidence of a much later beginning is more convincing. The Peninsula of Arabia, with land area about one-third larger than the province of Saskatchewan, had no wild horses. Horses in the wild state would have found it a most inhospitable region. Its interior is desert, second only to the Sahara in size and except in coastal areas where rainfall is favorable and in the scattered oases, vegetation is meagre. Wild asses and camels lived in that hot, dry and poorly watered interior, but no native horses.

Not only were early horses strangers on the Arabian sand but the weight of evidence suggests no horse breeding by the people until early in the Christian era or until a time when the Arabs inherited a foundation of superior horse stock. One writer, (Lydekker) in ascribing Arab success to the good fortune of securing an advanced beginning more than to any special skill, says the people lacked even an elementary knowledge of animal breeding. He would place the starting point as late as the first part of the sixth century, A.D.

On this point Ridgeway had strong views: "Arab tradition," he said, "points to Egypt as the region from whence the best horses were obtained in the time of Mohammed and because Egypt's horses came largely from Libya, it is easy to think of the Arabian ancestry as tracing to North Africa."

And while opinions will differ about the probable origin of those North African lines, students will agree that men of the deserts who produced the two breeds or strains must have had something better with which to begin than the pluggy Tarpan types of Asia, such as reached the Valley of the Euphrates about 2000 b.c. and Palestine a short time later. And up to the years of Mohammed, born at Mecca in 570, the Arab people used camels.

Be that as it may, the best Arabian horses have been produced by nomadic tribes, the Bedouins of the Interior, notably in the province of Nejd, which is a central plateau with more than an average number of oases. It was long accepted that the best horses belonged to one or another of the strains called Al Khamseh, meaning "The Five." According to one legendary explanation, they were the five mares on which Mohammed and four followers made an escape from Mecca and upon which the prophet conferred a special blessing.

A more common explanation is that the Five Families in Al Khamseh trace to five daughters of the "Mare of the Old Woman." A warrior, it seems, was in flight. While making a brief halt to refresh himself, the mare he had been riding foaled. This was no time for either delay or sentiment and the foal was promptly abandoned as the rider continued on his way. But at the next stop, many miles across the desert, the filly foal caught up and was at its mother's side. Surely this was no ordinary foal but it was given to an old woman and in time became the mother of the famous "Five" and thus the mother of the breed.

There are still other stories about the origin. The five originals, according to another telling, were five mares owned by Sheik Salaman of the seventh century, the only ones to answer the trumpet calling them back to battle when a great herd of horses was drinking at a river.

Whatever the correct explanation of origin, the five noted strains, Keheilan, Seglawi, Hamdani, Abeyan and Hadban, were highly prized. The stallion Darley Arabian, a cornerstone of the English Thoroughbred, belonged to the Keheilan, most prized of the five lines.

The fact of the Arabs having horses had much to do with the extension of the Moslem religion. At the midpoint of the seventh century, A.D., the Arabs were conquering westward. Egypt fell to them, then Libya, Algeria and Morocco. Arabs and Moors mingled and in 710 the Moslem forces invaded Spain and then continued northward in search of fresh victories. But the Franks who were also good horsemen and had already conquered Gaul, proved too much for the invaders. After over-running Southern France, the men from beyond the Mediterranean were soundly defeated between Tours and Poitiers. Left behind were the best of the North African and Arabian horses and these prizes of war, distributed among French troops, were the means of bringing fresh blood and new quality to local horses—just as the imported stock had already done in Spain. No doubt even the Percheron breed which emerged in France owed much of its quality to the desert horses.

The breed was extending its influence in all directions. Arabian horses became the envy of people in many lands and despite a desire on the part of Arab people to retain a monopolistic control of the pure breds, stock found its way by one means or another—fair and foul—to India, Persia, Turkey, England, America and elsewhere, to be bred in the pure state and employed in crossing on native types. The Turkoman horse of Turkestan was the result of crossing Arabians on the Tarpan-like native stock; the Russian Orloff owes much to Arabian influence. And the greatest Arabian triumph of all was the English Thoroughbred.

When the first horses of the desert breed came to England is not known but monarchs and noblemen who rallied to the Crusades, returned with horses possessing special worth. Men of England were quick to recognize their value in racing and producing race horses.

When James I came to the throne of England in 1603, horse racing was just becoming popular and the king demonstrated more interest in light horses than in the formerly-popular heavy war horses. At Newmarket where the noted race course was founded during his reign the monarch built a residence in order to be close to his favorite sport. One of his purchases was an Arabian called Markham Arabian, secured from a Mr. Markham at one hundred and fifty-four pounds—no doubt seen as a reckless expenditure at that time.

Successive English sovereigns followed the example. Except for a short period during the Commonwealth when Cromwell forbade racing, breeding progress was steady. King Charles II not only entered his horses in the races at Newmarket and attended to see them perform, but he acknowledged a responsibility in the matter of improvement and sent his Master of the Horse, Sir John Fenwick, abroad to buy breeding stock. The forty mares imported, Barb, Turk and Arabian, became known as the Royal Mares—also as the King's Mares—and these represented a starting point for the Thoroughbred breed.

Three stallions with familiar names followed soon after and became breed cornerstones. The first was Byerly Turk imported to England in 1689; the second was Darley Arabian, a pure bred Arabian purchased in 1702 and the third, Godolphin Barb, bought in Paris where the animal was discovered hauling a water cart, about 1724. The latter was presented to Lord Godolphin and lived to be twenty-nine. All three horses—as names suggest—were of the North African and Arabian strains.

A new breed, destined to become the darling of the sporting world was in the making. The combination of substance and strength from native English mares and the speed and quality and courage of the Arabian and its relatives produced the English Thoroughbred, fastest horse in history. And perpetuating the Arabian tradition, the Thoroughbred in turn contributed to the making of other breeds in Britain and elsewhere, light and heavy.

The General Stud Book of England, makings its appearance in 1808, was the first published pedigree record for any breed, a landmark in horse history.

And while the ancient Arabian was being woven into the fabric of the Thoroughbred, it was being perpetuated as a pure breed and making its way to distant parts of the world. A stallion called Ranger was brought to Connecticut in 1765 and a son was ridden by George Washington during the Revolution. Importations of consequence followed from time to time, one of the most important consisting of twenty-seven stallions and mares of "the purest desert strain," made in 1906 by Homer Davenport, friend of Theodore Roosevelt and celebrated cartoonist with a New York newspaper. His difficulty in registering with the Jockey Club led to formation of the Arabian Horse Club of America in 1908.

But the world's most ancient breed was slow in capturing the North American fancy. For years it was almost unknown in Canada and making only indifferent progress in the United States. Then, suddenly, people re-discovered the grace and style and courage and romance of the Arabian and popularity soared. At once there was new admiration for the distinctive bearing of these chestnut or bay or grey horses, the bold stride, short coupling, sharp and dished facial features, level rump, fine hard bone and inherent stamina. Being small made them no less lovely.

But the stallion, Ranger, imported to Connecticut two hundred years ago wasn't the first horse to bring Arabian blood to North American soil. There was that pioneer introduction of horses from Spain, the stuff from which the Mustang and Indian horse sprang.

CHAPTER 6

The Blood of a Mustang

J ust about every frontiersman who saw the West before the years of settlement would tell in glowing terms of some particular Mustang, one with an air of mystery about him. In most cases the subject was a stud—buckskin, grey or black—that periodically enlivened the plains or graced the rimrock or haunted the riverbrake.

"There he was," one pioneer recalled, "standing like a marble statue on a rise of ground, perfect proportion, neck out like a crane and his silky coat glistening in the evening sun. Catch him? Sure we tried, often, but he was the swiftest thing I ever saw."

How was the Mustang bred? He and his strain lived in the wild state for an unknown number of generations but he was no scrub. Perchance he was a descendant of selected Spanish stock, superior horses, the first to gain freedom on the American continents after a few hundred or few thousand years of complete horselessness.

In returning to the Americas with Spanish adventurers who followed Columbus, horses breathed familiar air and pawed the ground on which ancestors roamed and triumphed for millions of years. But these were not like primitive stock; rather, they were refined, domestic horses, the pride of Spain and rich in the blood of good Arabian and North African strains. Thus, while one branch from the Arabian trunk was bearing the English Thoroughbred, another was reaching across the Atlantic to drop the seeds from which Mustang, South American Criollo and Indian horse strains would sprout.

Spain, whence these horses came in the 16th century, was enjoying its peak of greatness. Colonies almost encompassed the globe and until the epic defeat of the mighty Armada, Spain was Mistress of the Seas. But being a world power didn't lessen the Spanish interest in horses and horse breeding. Stock from North Africa and Arabia brought by invading Moors improved the foundation and, given national support, Spanish horses became faster and better. When men of Cordova province claimed the shapeliest specimens in the world, nobody disputed. Moreover, the Spanish horse stock of that period was no less distinctive in assortment of colors.

When the Spanish Armada was destroyed in 1588, horses rescued by the victors were used to improve the speed and general excellence of English strains and some, it is told, were sent directly to Newmarket.

Spanish royalty for generations encouraged horse breeding. Queen Isabella (1451–1504) who backed Columbus on his notable voyage of discovery, was a devoted admirer of good horses, with special fondness for those with gold colored and light sorrel coats and flaxen manes and tails. And in that age of chivalry, the rank of a Spanish Don was often judged by the quality of the horses he rode; at that, it would be at least as good an indication of social position as the composition of a wife's bonnet would be.

Such was Spain—a nation of horsemen—when Christoforo Colombo sailed westward on August 3, 1492, hoping, among other things, to prove a revolutionary theory that the earth was round. He carried no horses but after discovering land and returning as a hero with gold and captured Indians, he was again sailing westward, late in 1493. This time he was taking one thousand five hundred men and probably some horses for a settlement on the Island of Haiti which he called Esponola. Santo Domingo in what is now the Dominican Republic—seen today as the oldest settlement in the western hemisphere—was for many years the seat of Spanish authority in the New World. It was the base from which various horse-equipped expeditions were launched to Mexico, Florida and South America. It knew Cortez the conqueror of Mexico, Pizarro who won the Inca

Empire of Peru for Spain, Balboa who discovered the Pacific in 1513, Ponce de Leon who in his search for "perpetual youth" discovered Florida, and de Soto the discoverer of the Mississippi.

Certainly, it was at Santo Domingo that the first horses from Spain were landed, and from there that the first horses to reach the mainland—sixteen head—were taken by Cortez on his expedition of 1519. Hernando Cortez had achieved success in a campaign in Cuba and was instructed to take a fleet to the mainland with the object of collecting gold. One of his comrades, Bernal Diaz del Castillo, left a record of the sixteen horses—eleven stallions and five mares—taken on that journey to Mexico. The descriptions and colors are worth noting. Three were described as chestnuts, three light chestnuts, three dark chestnuts, three silver greys, one brown sorrel, one dun, one cream and one "dark."

A chestnut stallion with three white feet was described as "no good," but generally the writer's comment was complimentary. Several were described as good for racing. And as for the cream colored stallion, it can be assumed that he was the first Palomino on the continent. The gelding of horses was not generally practiced and the noble Spanish officers chose stallions ahead of mares for their riding enjoyment.

Cortez landed on the coast of the Gulf of Mexico early in the year and after laying the foundation for the Town of Vera Cruz, he marched toward Tenochtitlan, Aztec capital where Mexico City stands today. There he was courteously received by the native chief, Montezuma, and there he found an advanced civilization. The native ruler and his people were intrigued by the horses, delighted by their beauty and dumbfounded by their speed. They'd have given half the gold in Mexico to get them. But Cortez was determined to gain the gold without payment and in the violence which followed, Montezuma was killed and Cortez, with the white man's typical greed, succeeded in gathering the treasure.

More horses were landed for the same and later campaigns but some were killed, some lost and, perchance, some stolen.

An undertaking of special interest for horsemen was that of Coronado who early in 1540 was starting northward into unknown territory, hoping to find the "Seven Cities of Cibola" or "Seven Cities of Gold." The expedition—one to strike pride to Spanish heart and terror to native—included one thousand horses as well as cattle and sheep. Coronado's men discovered the Canyon on the Colorado river and reached a point somewhere in the present state of Kansas. They were the first whites to see the Central American plains but after two years of searching for the Cities of Gold, they returned admitting failure. The great would-be raider of native treasure had nothing for his king except a letter of regret.

But what of Coronado's horses? Many of them were lost. Some died; some were abandoned and a few disappeared "mysteriously." In an area which was not foreign to their natures and habits, no doubt those winning release survived and bred on the plains.

And Fernando de Soto, discoverer of the Mississippi, lost one hundred and fifty horses as he penetrated inland and crossed the great river in 1541. Again some of those Spanish horses died but others were abandoned or lost when they escaped. It is not too much to suppose that those gaining freedom had a part in founding the Mustang strain which was ultimately quite widespread on the western half of the continent.

Adaptation to the wild came quickly and completely. Stallions fought to lead the bands. Mares hid their foals until they could run. Instinctively they all avoided the muskegs in which there was danger. At once they regained the native ability to dash across rough ground without stumbling or injuring legs in badger holes. And when they ultimately felt lariats tighten on their proud necks, they could fight like demons— and did. Such were the Mustangs, horses of the white man's early West, now extinct.

But while the Mustang was propagating on the north continent, its counterpart, the Criollo, was doing the same in South America. Spanish horses had been taken there in 1532 and after. When the ruthless and cruel Pizarro, said to have been suckled by a sow on the streets of Trixillo in Spain, set out from Panama to see and explore the empire of the Incas in Peru—year of 1532—he had good horses. The natives, of course, had never seen anything like them and their conclusion was that mounted man and horse were one and the same creature. It suited the Spanish leader to perpetuate the myth. But when, in the course of attack, a Spaniard fell off his horse, this apparent coming apart of a strange new creature so surprised the natives that they relaxed in the struggle, giving the attackers an opportunity to escape.

Pizarro's horses, incidentally, were probably the only ones in all time to travel a warpath on silver shoes. When feet became sore, the need for shoeing was apparent. There being no iron, Pizarro ordered horseshoes made from the only metal available, silver.

Of the early introduction of Spanish horse stock to South America, the one of 1535 was most important to the Criollo or "Mustang of the Pampas." Don Pedro de Mendoza who founded Buenos Aires in that year, landed five mares and seven stallions. But the plan to build the town was almost immediately abandoned and the Spaniards deserted the place and left the twelve horses behind. Apparently the animals lost no time in establishing themselves and when Buenos Aires was refounded forty-five years later, wild horses were said to be quite numerous. Until 1596 it was assumed that these wild ones belonged to the King but in that year they were declared the property of anybody who could catch them.

South American people recognized special merit in these semi-wild horses, used them for crossing and bred to keep the strain alive. The well-publicized journey of nine thousand six hundred miles from Buenos Aires to Washington, D.C., made with two Criollo horses—Gato and Mancha—was one of the best possible demonstrations of endurance and adaptability. Bred in Patagonia, they were selected for A. F. Tschiffely who made the trip. Both horses were seventeen years old when the journey commenced. They started in April, 1925, and reached destination nine hundred days later. The route took the travellers to altitudes of 16,625 feet in Peru and 18,000 feet in Bolivia. But in spite of mountains, swamps and deserts, the horses completed the journey in fine condition. Both were alive at the age of twenty-eight years.

The Criollos, like the Mustangs, were sturdy and agile and made excellent stock horses. There was one obvious difference, however—colors; dun of one shade or another was common in the southern strain. And to the credit of the South American horsemen, studbooks for typical Criollo individuals were opened. Recording began in Chile in 1893 and in Argentina in 1917.

North American people, on the other hand, neglected such steps to preserve the breed that adopted the wild state, loved it and became as completely native as remote ancestors which had never seen a human figure.

It was unfortunate. Circumstances dealt harshly and that symbol of the early West disappeared. But the Mustang was not forgotten. Having displayed what seemed like inherited Arabian courage and fitted into the environment so readily, it became an inviting subject for stories and legends. If a certain white stallion known in the Milk River badlands had wings, he'd have outclassed the Pegasus of mythology as a candidate for immortality. And boys who were never inspired by the thought of piloting a space ship or winning the boxing championship from John L. Sulivan dreamed of catching a real, live, fighting Mustang.

CHAPTER 7

Indian Horses

There was no doubt about it; the white man's finest contribution to North American Indian life was the horse, partly offsetting the evil gifts of disease and alcohol.

After overcoming the first fears engendered by these new wonder-animals, the native people wanted horses, eagerly and urgently. To nomadic tribesmen battling for food and survival, horses seemed to meet their biggest needs, exactly. By their adoption as quickly as they could be captured, stolen or acquired in any way, horses changed the lives of the Indians as dramatically as tractors changed farming and electricity changed household management. As the first Indians saw them, horses were "big dogs" sent this way by a benevolent Manitou.

With the advent of horses into tribal life, Indians became instantly more effective in the chase, more powerful in war and more romantic in love. The areas over which they could roam were multiplied. The new way of life was wonderful. A mounted Indian was at once transported to a better world.

Not only did these big domestic animals extend the Indian's hunting and fighting ground but as a source of food in time of emergency, they increased security beyond anything previously experienced. An Indian had no wish to eat his horse any more than a modern swain would willingly part with his convertible; but hunger changes many things and horse meat saved Indians from starvation just as sleigh-dogs spared the lives of starving explorers in polar regions. Injured, aged and very inferior animals called "squaw horses" were killed for food without much hesitation but the better horses, an Indian's most prized possessions, were sacrificed only when starvation threatened. Once acquired there was just no substitute for horses and Indians felt rich or poor depending upon the size of their bands.

At first the few horses on the mainland were for Spaniards only and the white invaders tried to prevent their animals from falling into Indian hands. But southern tribesmen, quick to recognize the added killing power of mounted warriors, were inspired to steal. Considering possible reward, the risk of a thief being caught and killed seemed small. But the Spanish guards were vigilant and stealing on a one-horse scale was less than satisfactory. Indians waited impatiently to see Spanish horses being abandoned or breaking tethers. Coronado, it is known, lost horses; De Soto horses gained freedom and other Spanish conquistadors saw horses gallop out across the plains to return no more. But recovering abandoned horses after they adopted the wild state was not a simple matter for pedestrian Indians and even though Mustangs numbered 50,000 in the states of Texas, Colorado, Nebraska and Kansas by 1875, it seems fair to suppose that the Indians got their horses mainly from white men by theft or barter—preferably the former.

The Plains Indians had the greatest need for horses and became the best tribal horsemen. They were eager pupils and in remarkably short time became expert equestrians with a growing dislike for walking. The horse's back—with or without saddle—held a magic fascination for young and old.

As would be expected, some of the first tribes to acquire horses became the best horsemen. The Comanches, because of their geographic position on the southern plains, were among the first to see Spanish horses and were well mounted by the year 1715. Kiowa and Missouri Indians were riding almost as soon and then the Crows, Snakes and Mandans followed as quickly as they could get horses. Colonel Dodge pronounced the Comanches and Cheyennes as the best horsemen encountered during his years on the

United States frontier. Anyone said to "ride like a Comanche," was being paid a high compliment. Mounted Comanche warriors instilled fear in their enemies, being cruel as they were skillful. One of the Comanche warpath achievements consisted of hanging at the side of a galloping horse and shooting arrows from the under side of the speeding animal's neck or over its back, all the while using the horse to protect his own body against arrows or bullets. The same tribesmen had a strong passion for racing and ultimately owned many of the fastest horses. Racing, however, became popular with all the tribes and through it an urge to gamble found expression.

Not only were the Comanches good horsemen but they were among the most expert horse thieves. Their chief rivals for stealing distinction would be the Cheyennes and Kiowas. Horse stealing, however, was not restricted to the South; it became both necessity and pastime and whether the objects of thieving raids belonged to white men or Indians of other tribes didn't matter in the least. Custom was to take horses when and where they were found. Thus, domesticated horses moved northward and into British North American territory. With hostile tribes in possession of horses, it became an absolute necessity for neighboring tribes to secure them.

According to the late Prof. A. S. Morton of Saskatchewan, the first domestic horses seen in what is now western Canada, were along the Bow river about 1730. They were in possession of Snake Indians whose hunting ground extended from the Missouri River to the South Saskatchewan. Those mounted Snakes were too much for the pedestrian Blackfoot and Piegan braves. All that saved these latter were some of the white man's guns in the hands of the Crees and Assiniboines who came to help.

Having witnessed a demonstration of the value of horses, Indians of the Blackfoot Confederacy set out to get them by any means. Somewhere along the Missouri river, the

Blackfoot marauders located horses and after gathering them without opposition from the Snake owners, it was discovered that the Indian village had been stricken with small pox and left defenceless. Anyway, the Blackfoot now had horses and in the course of time Blackfoot horses were stolen by Crees and Cree horses stolen by Assiniboines.

Actually the first horses seen in the country of the Assiniboines—the eastern prairies—were two brought back by Pierre la Verendrye in 1741 following a visit to the Mandan Indians. The fate of these two pioneer horses is not known; presumably, they lived out their years around Fort la Reine—near the present city of Portage la Prairie—the base from which the la Verendrye expedition started.

Notwithstanding the early arrival of the two horses in what is now Manitoba, the Assiniboine Indians had to obtain their horse stock, as other tribesmen, by the delightful act of stealing. And no tribesmen became more proficient in creeping into an enemy encampment under cover of night and cutting the leash that tied a horse to the wrist of its sleeping owner, than the Assiniboines. The Blackfoot, most ferocious of the prairie Indians, became a better horseman and gave horses better care but he could not surpass the Assiniboine in thieving.

But to all prairie Indians, horse stealing became the most profitable and most glorious of all occupations—more fascinating even than collecting enemy scalps. An aged Indian Chief confessed that his two sons, because of their cultivated skill in stealing horses, were bringing their father great satisfaction and happiness in his old age. Every parent, of course, is entitled to take pleasure from the successes of progeny.

Horse stealing by Indians reached its peak in western Canada soon after homesteading began. Superintendent L. N. F. Crozier of the N.W.M.P., reporting from Wood Mountain in the year 1880, saw horse stealing prevailing "to a fearful extent." There were at one time, he noted, Sioux, Crees, Bloods, Blackfoot, Saulteaux and occasional war parties from the American tribes, all camping nearby, all stealing horses from the others. "I very much feared a serious collision between the tribes," he wrote.

Inter-tribe raiding to get horses continued for years. In October, 1885, the editor of the Macleod Gazette estimated three hundred stolen horses on the Blood Reservation alone, with the number being increased steadily. Most of these, he explained, were from Indian camps in Montana. Now and then, of course, the Montana tribesmen retaliated and the Calgary Tribune of May 23, 1888, told of thirty-one horses being stolen from the Blood Indians on a recent day; "the horses were stolen by Gros Ventre Indians. A party from the Blood Reserve has gone in pursuit and there will be gore if the marauding party is overtaken."

The Medicine Hat area suffered some of the biggest losses from horse thieves and at one time settlers were said to be carrying arms and sleeping in their stables to protect horses. A night herder who went to sleep holding his horse by a lariat awakened to find the rope slashed and the horse gone. Medicine Hat people became indignant over continuing horse losses due to Indian depredations and threatened to place the matter in the hands of a vigilante committee, Montana style. The Lethbridge News (April 27, 1887) commented: "Should the people of Medicine Hat find it necessary to take the law into their own hands, they will have the sympathy of the whole Northwest."

In selecting and in stealing horses, the prairie natives cared nothing for the white man's type ideals. Their horses had to be hardy; they wanted speed and they fancied bright colors. It was quite simple. Only one present-day breed—the Appaloosa—grew out of the Indian horse stock although the tribesmen were largely responsible for perpetuating certain coat colors and patterns ultimately enjoying popularity— Palomino, buckskin, and Pinto as well as Appaloosa.

Training counted for something in buffalo-runners but by the time the Medicine Hat people were having troubles created by rustlers, buffalo were a thing of the past. With the war-horse, the main prerequisites were speed and sure feet, and a good buffalo-runner was usually a good war-horse. For their purposes, the Indians had the best possible horses, close relatives of the Mustang and known ultimately as Indian ponies. American cavalry officers pursuing rebellious Indians in the '70s of last century, admitted their only hope of effecting capture was to do it in the first day of the chase; otherwise, the superior endurance of the Indian stock would place the tribesmen beyond reach of soldiers on more refined mounts.

The same small but hardy and indigenous horses provided the power needed by the earliest settlers in the Northwest. They were the first horses in the Red River Settlement after the colonists arrived and it was many years before the improved breeds were introduced. Horses at Red River in 1822, ten years after the settlement was started, numbered seventy-eight and all, one may be sure, were from the Indian stock. They were better suited to hunting than to agriculture but they carried men of Fort Garry community on the annual buffalo hunts, conveyed travellers and pulled the first plows through the gumbo sod beside the Red river. They were all-purpose horses, serving many needs before the new breeds appeared.

At least one early editor saw fit to pay a proper tribute. In the Regina Leader of October 8, 1885, he wrote: "The cayuse has done a good day's work in this country. His wants were few and his services many and various. If speed, courage and sure footedness were required he filled the bill as a buffalo hunter; if strength and endurance were required he was the freighter's standby. But though the days of buffalo hunting are past and the days of freighting are numbered, let us not forget the old friends of our need."

CHAPTER 8

Blue Blood in the West

Fireaway was a pure bred stallion, the first pedigreed horse of any breed in the Northwest. The particular breed he represented didn't matter much—more important that he was an aristocrat from England and his prestige across the buffalo country was like that enjoyed by Man o' War and Whirlaway a hundred years later. Had there been popularity contests to elect the Horse of the Year and Horse of the Generation, he would have won both.

The honor must have been merited because forty years after his departure, men still raved about his beauty and boasted about his progeny. The fact was that in crossing with native stock and bringing a measure of crossbred vigor to the offspring, Fireaway marked a new chapter in western horse history.

The first cultivation at Red River was done by hand. But garden spades and hoes were hopelessly inadequate in such a land of vastness and settlers with British ideals about farming wanted horses. Rather grudgingly they accepted the only ones available, the small Indian horses. These semi-native animals were reasonably appropriate, even though not fully appreciated. Alexander Ross, the Red River historian, described them well: "Their appearance is not prepossessing but they are better than they look. Few horses could be better adapted for the cart and saddle and none so good for the climate."

The Selkirk people continued to talk about improving the strain with breeding stock from England or Scotland and Governor George Simpson, in giving support to the idea, noted that settlers needed horses for farming; everybody needed horses for the annual buffalo hunt and the Hudson's Bay Company needed them for its brigades. If further reason were required to justify official encouragement, Simpson saw the possibility of horse breeding becoming a profitable source of revenue for the settlers.

Acting promptly, Simpson wrote: "Some plan must be fallen upon to increase our stock and improve our breed of horses as they are becoming very scarce and of such small growth as to be quite unfit for our work. Until late years we could get as many from the Indians . . . as we required, but now the Indians have few or none for themselves and, instead of providing us as heretofore, steal those we rear from our very doors although they are guarded by armed keepers." (This and following extracts from the Hudson's Bay Company journals are published with permission of the governor and committee of the Hudson's Bay Company.)

Simpson's plea led to a completely new policy and the importation of Fireaway. Great preparations were made; some heavy mares were brought from the south and the best mares in company service were selected for breeding—twenty-five head at Fort Carlton and twenty-five at far-away Athabasca river.

But the governor ruled against bringing the chosen mares together before the stallion arrived. He had three reasons: in the first place, if the good mares were in one band they might be wiped out in a bad winter; in the second place, a big group of good horses would attract the evil attention of horse thieves and, finally, many things could happen to a stallion being transported from England by sailing vessel and canoe.

Company officials in London did their part in pursuit of the plan and under date of February 23, 1831, a message went to Simpson: "We shall send out a stallion of proper breed by the ship to York Factory. We should think the experimental farm at Red river the best place to commence raising horses for the service."

Delivery would be a major undertaking, to be sure. The ocean journey by sailing ship could last for months and after it terminated at York Factory there would be the difficult expedition against river currents and windblown lakes by freight canoes. But at midsummer in 1831 the great horse was landed on the shore of the Bay and immediately transferred to one of the oar-propelled York boats which carried the freight between York Factory and Fort Garry. This, the last part of the journey, was by far the more difficult and the stud, trying to balance himself as the small boat rode the current, didn't like the experience any better than the men who squatted at his unpredictable feet. Once the horse fell overboard but swam to shore and was recovered and reloaded.

By canoe it was seven hundred miles and many portages from York Factory to Fort Garry and, finally, the horse was stabled at his destination without mishap. George Simpson could report delivery in perfect condition. "He will give us a better breed of horse," the governor wrote, adding: "He is looked upon as one of the wonders of the world by the natives, many of whom have travelled great distances with no other object than to see him."

Company officials, recognizing that Fireaway would fill the best horse thieves in the country with ideas, ordered a heavy guard, just as though the stable beside the river was sheltering the Crown Jewels.

There has been endless speculation about the horse's breeding, size and color. Some writers described him as a Thoroughbred, some suggested Arabian and others said Norfolk Trotter or Hackney. The evidence points strongly to Hackney. In the first place the name, Fireaway, has been common in Hackney breed history; actually dozens of horses have been recorded with the name. What should set all arguments at rest is a short statement in the diary of Robert Campbell, observant Scot who went to the settlement one year before, expressly to become sub-manager of the experimental farm.

Here is Campbell's description of Fireaway: "He was a splendid bright bay, standing sixteen hands and very solidly built, with a faultless shape. He was warranted to trot fifteen miles an hour and could do much better. His equal for improving native stock has never been imported into this country."

Fireaway's superiority was one point upon which nearly everybody in Rupert's Land agreed. And his offspring lived up to expectations, maturing into the best buffalo-runners and most useful road horses in the country. Indians and whites specializing in horse stealing went out of their way to snatch a son or daughter.

But what ultimately became of the great horse? On that point there is nothing but hearsay. One story had him sold to go to the United States; according to another he was stolen and whisked across the border, and still another story had him sent back to England after his outstanding breeding worth became known.

In any case, Fireaway disappeared but his reputation lived on—became almost a legend. When Rev. John McDougall travelled from Fort Edmonton to Fort Garry to buy supplies for his mission in 1864, he couldn't resist the chance to buy a young horse described as a descendant of Fireaway. And near Portage la Prairie, Farmer John Macdonald had a descendant which was so fast and good that Louis Riel's followers at the time of the Red River Insurrection were supposed to have taken time from their main purpose of building the New Nation to try getting the animal by theft. It was the same mare which Macdonald, at a later date, took from the plow and drove to Portage la Prairie to answer a challenge from a barnstorming stranger with a fast road horse.

On this occasion the honor of Portage Plains was at stake and the two horses participated in a 24th of May race on the town street. And in keeping with the Fireaway tradition, the plow horse pulling a democrat and hilarious Highlander raced to a convincing victory over the highly rated roadster from St. Paul.

Encouraged by success at the first venture in horse breeding, Hudson's Bay Company officials in 1848 decided to repeat the project, bring in another stallion. With precisely the same purpose—improvement of the native horse stock—this one called Melbourne was also bought in England and imported by way of Hudson's Bay. But this time the stallion didn't come alone.

Again there has been controversy about the breed but there is good reason for accepting Melbourne as a Thoroughbred. Those who argued that the horse might be a Hackney took the term "thoroughbred" as being the equivalent of "pure bred." This is unlikely because the General Stud Book for Thoroughbred horses—first record book for any breed—was published as early as 1808 and the English breed of running horses was known as Thoroughbred for many years before Melbourne's importation. Moreover, the name, Melbourne, occurs several times in Thoroughbred pedigrees.

Authority to purchase the horse was set down in company minutes dated May 10, 1848: "Ordered that Captain Pelly be authorized to purchase one thoroughbred stallion, Melbourne, at the price of two hundred and ten pounds." Then, on June 3, just a few weeks later, advice went out from London to George Simpson as follows: "The Prince Rupert also takes out a thoroughbred stallion, a brood mare, a bull of superior breed and two Ayrshire cows. Thomas Howsom Axe, a skillful groom, also goes out in charge of the stock. He is engaged on a contract for three years at thirty pounds per annum, with a gratuity of five pounds, provided he delivers his charge safe and uninjured at York Factory."

The two Thoroughbreds and three Ayrshires reached the mouth of Hayes river in safety and Horseman Axe qualified for his bonus. But his troubles were not over. Ahead was the most difficult part, hundreds of miles of wild water on rivers and lakes leading to Fort Garry. Furnished with ropes, sicles and oilcloth blankets for the horses, Axe loaded his livestock charges on the little boat and departed southward on August 28, 1848. After weeks of rowing and portaging during daylight hours and worrying about tether ropes and mosquitoes at night, the canoe brigade with its valuable cargo arrived at Fort Garry without mishap except for damage caused by sharp hooves on the bottoms of the boats.

There was correspondence about where Melbourne should be kept, the final decision being to hold him at Red River for the winter and bring twenty of the best mares from Fort Pelly in the spring. Mated to native mares and Fireaway offspring, Melbourne gave a fairly good account of himself. Most colts were bright bays like their sire and generally of good quality. But there were reverses; the grey Thoroughbred mare dropped a foal in the spring following arrival but before the summer ended both mare and foal were dead. Some time later, Melbourne kicked the groom and broke the man's arm. Obviously discouraged, Eden Colville, acting governor of Rupert's Land, wrote to George Simpson, admitting that the pure bred animal would prove to be a poor investment. He advised sending the stallion to St. Louis to be sold "for what he will fetch." But the advice to sell Melbourne was not taken and after a few years he was sent to Fort Pelly and used extensively at that place which had become the company's chief horse breeding station.

But the total horse need of western Canada was still small. The census figures for Red River Settlement showed two thousand and ninety-seven oxen and two thousand and eighty-five horses in the year 1862. At Fort Edmonton where the company maintained its biggest band of work stock, there were seven hundred head. For what was required in that pre-homestead period, horse numbers were adequate. But the situation was about to change. When the land rush started following passage of the Homestead Act, the need for horses soared like a sky-rocket. Before the homesteaders embarked upon their rush, however, there was the matter of establishing law and order, a task for brave men and good horses.

CHAPTER 9

The Mountie's Horse

In taming the Wild West, the North West Mounted Police horses were indispensable working partners with the men in uniform. Throughout the early years, a Mountie without a horse was like a woodsman without an axe or a soldier without a gun. Distances in the unsettled country west of Red River were great and in the pursuit of criminals, speed was of the utmost importance. There was simply nothing to take the place of horses and Colonel Robertson Ross who recommended a mounted constabulary for law enforcement following a reconnaissance of the West in 1872, recognized the fact.

But for horses it was a hard life and in spite of the best care possible under frontier circumstances, losses ran high. It was that way from the very day the new force left Fort Dufferin, south of Winnipeg, to make its way to an undetermined fort-site near the Rocky Mountains.

An act of Parliament in 1873 provided for the North West Mounted Police and Colonel G. A. French became the first commissioner. Men had to be recruited and horses selected. Almost at once, responsibility for the horses was assigned to one of the commissioner's former pupils in the Gunnery School of the Royal Military College at Kingston, James Walker, a man who was to become a prominent figure in the life of southern Alberta. Finding stock possessing acceptable saddle type was not easy there in the East where the heavy Clydesdale was almost everybody's breed.

But on June 6, 1874, three divisions comprising two hundred and seventeen officers and men with two hundred and forty-four horses left Toronto for service in the far West.

The two special trains carrying the untried force travelled by way of Chicago to Fargo, North Dakota, from where men and horses took the one hundred and fifty-mile trail to Fort Dufferin, just inside Manitoba.

Walker was still in charge of horses and, before the great westward trek began, had a chance to demonstrate a horseman's fibre and determination. Two hundred and forty-two horses were being held in a rope corral when a violent midnight storm broke over the camp. With flashes of lightning, claps of thunder and the spooky flapping of canvas covers on transport wagons, the horses became frantic and broke from their corral. Wrecking a score of police tents, the mad animals dashed blindly to the South. A few men were injured.

In momentary flashes of light, Walker saw what was happening. To halt the stampede was obviously impossible. But with presence of mind and a horseman's skill he caught the halter of one animal as it tried to dash away. Saddling this one at once, he rode away through the darkness broken only by shafts of lightning. On and on the stampede continued, across the International Boundary and deep into North Dakota. But the tenacious Walker was still close in pursuit and by sunrise he had gained control of the exhausted police horses.

In the meantime the men at Dufferin were completely horseless and completely helpless. But after using five different mounts and riding an estimated one hundred and twenty miles, Walker arrived back at the camp with all the horses except one which was never found.

At Dufferin the recruits from the East were joined by a smaller group from Fort Garry and plans drawn for the great adventure across a thousand miles of unmapped Prairie to establish order in an area rapidly becoming notorious for the ruthlessness of its whisky traders and ferocity of Blackfoot Indians.

On July 8 the ordeal began. No spectators were present to enjoy the sight, no reporters to record it, no cameras to capture it in picture. But what a spectacle the long cavalcade must have presented! Moving in an orderly way were one hundred and fourteen Red River carts, seventy-three wagons loaded with supplies, one hundred and forty-two work oxen, ninety-three other cattle and three hundred and ten horses. As far as possible everything moved with military precision, even though nobody except an occasional Indian could be impressed. After the first day on the trail men of the force didn't see a single human habitation.

But Commissioner French, with a soldier's eye for order, had overlooked nothing; even the horses were grouped for color. Proudly, he reported: "The column presented a fine appearance. First came A Division with splendid dark bays and thirteen wagons. Then B with dark browns. Next C with bright chestnuts, drawing the guns and ammunition. Next D with the greys, then E with black horses, the rear being brought up by F with their light bays . . . To a stranger it would have appeared an astonishing cavalcade; armed men and guns looked as if fighting was to be done. What could ploughs, harrows, mowing machines, cows, calves, etc., be for? But the little force had a double duty to perform, to fight if necessary, but in any case to establish posts in the far West."

At the outset the expedition seemed glamorous indeed. But as the days went by the toilsome aspects became plain—especially for the horses. Before departing, Commissioner French heard a Winnipeg man say: "If you're lucky you may be back by Christmas—with forty percent of your horses."

The police didn't exactly leave a trail of dead horses but losses were high enough to prove the extremes of hardship—high enough to make the story unpleasant to horse lovers. At best, the frontier was a hard master. Oxen demonstrated how they could work on rations of grass without grain. Horses lacked the physiological capacity to derive sufficient nourishment from roughage alone and the hope of maintaining sufficient supplies of oats or other grain for them proved impossible to carry through.

During the first sixteen days of travel, three horses died and three more became weakened to the point where they had to be abandoned. And as time went on the situation grew worse rather than better. The Commissioner reported on the fact of "horses and oxen failing and dying for want of food . . ." And by September, one of the men making the journey could record in his diary: "Horses starving . . . Horses dying daily."

On a side trip to Fort Benton, Montana, Commissioner French and Assistant Commissioner James Macleod bought more horses and hired the incomparable Métis guide, Jerry Potts. Then, after more weeks of gruelling effort, the Force of '74 halted beside the Old Man River to build Fort Macleod. The surviving horses were pathetically thin and weak and with no stable accommodation there seemed slight chance of them living through the winter. On Jerry Pott's advice, Colonel Macleod decided to send as many as could be spared to winter at Sun River, more than two hundred miles to the South. With Inspector Walsh in charge and Jerry Potts as guide, a group of police left Fort Macleod on October 30, taking seventy-seven of the thin horses and some oxen and cattle to the more sheltered winter grazing in the South. Even that proved a misadventure for the horses; near Milk River there came up a November blizzard and some of the weakest horses never managed to get through the new drifts. But after two weeks on the trail, the remaining horses and cattle were turned over to a rancher at Sun River and Constable McKernan was left to maintain a watch for the balance of the winter. Walsh and the other men returned amid such luxury as the police wagon and four-horse team would afford. But at mid-December, Walsh was again going south, this time with another band of horses considered unlikely to live through the winter in the North.

As the demands of patrol work became known, the police commissioners knew one of their problems would be in securing replacement horse stock. Locally there was nothing except bronchos and the young easterners in uniform were reluctant to attempt the dangerous work of domestication. But what else could be done?

Anticipating the police trade, Jim Christie drove a big band of above-average broncho horses from Idaho and young policemen helping Charles Rivers—better known as Buckskin

Charlie—received their lessons in roughhouse breaking methods. Charlie knowing no fear, would drop from a bar across gateposts to land on the back of a surprised broncho and cling there until the fatigued brute gave up. Story had it that in running buffalo he had on occasions leaped from his horse to the back of a galloping bull and ridden the wild critter until it collapsed. It wasn't the way eastern officers wanted their horses broken but there was no alternative.

The trouble of keeping horse numbers up to strength continued. In 1878 the need was estimated at four hundred and fifty head but only three hundred and fifty were in service and two hundred ready for heavy work. In the next year, the horse account showed twenty horses discarded, twenty-seven having died, one stolen and eighty-four bought for replacements.

At first the officers wanted eastern horses but gradually their ideas changed. A few ranchers began breeding specifically to meet police needs. The Stewart Ranch at Pincher Creek was the first to furnish the kind wanted—horses with height of fifteen hands, short backs, stout bodies and good feet. After buying forty-two horses at Fort Macleod and one hundred and thirteen at Calgary in 1886, Superintendent Herchmer was ready to pronounce the western horses as better than their eastern counterparts for police work, hardier, more certain in footing, less susceptible to disease and better able to work without grain. As far as he was concerned, there'd be no more eastern horses, especially when the Ontario stock cost two hundred dollars per head while the native horses could be bought at one hundred and twenty-five dollars.

By 1888, Herchmer, the commissioner, could report that all horses in use were western bred. None but the hardiest could stand up to patrol work. "No comparison can be made between the work done by our horses and those of any other force," he wrote in his report (Dec. 31, 1888). "Not only have our horses frequently to travel in pursuit of horse thieves and other criminals over fifty miles a day for some days but when merely patrolling in the southern country, want of water frequently compels parties to exceed this distance for several

days. A detachment of G Division in September on one march
. . . had to go seventy miles with loaded teams in twenty-four
hours. To this must be added the extreme cold winters and the
absolute necessity, when duty calls, of taking horses from stables to camp on the bleak Prairie for days at a time . . . As a
rule, however, our men take great pride in and care of their
horses and I have frequently known men to take their own
blankets for their horses during storms."

If more needed to be said about the work of police mounts, the
one hundred and forty-one horses kept at Fort Macleod travelled a total of 295,222 horse-miles on patrol in a single year.
They had to be good horses but Commissioner Herschmer by
this time knew where to find the best ones. Reporting for 1889
and recounting the one hundred and twenty-five replacements
bought during the year, he said the best breeding animals from
which to get police horses were on the North West Cattle
Company Ranch west of High River, Michael Oxarart's ranch
in Cypress Hills and the Quorn, west of Okotoks. The North
West Cattle Company, later known as Bar U, was at this time
trying a Standard Bred cross while the other two were using
high class Thoroughbred stallions on native mares. Selected
three-year-olds from these ranches in 1890 cost an average of
one hundred and twenty-five dollars but six years later, when
depression hit the horse business, most of the police needs
were being met by sons and daughters of the famous Quorn
Ranch Thoroughbred stallion, Eagle Plume, at sixty dollars
each.

It was a hard life for horses but so was homestead toil or
railroad construction. Society's debt to the police horses—as to
other work stock of the period—was great and it is reassuring
to know the debt was not overlooked. Superintendent Deane,
reporting from Lethbridge for 1889, wrote: "We have a couple
of very old police horses which have done good work in their
day and these I propose to send to herd permanently where
they can end their days in peace. An evening handful of oats
will not cost much."

CHAPTER 10

Mounts for Marathon

W hen the mail or dispatches had to go through with haste in pre-rail and pre-telegraph years, it took a man on a good horse to do it.

Communication was important in peace time, doubly so in time of war. During the North West Rebellion there were many calls for hardy volunteers to deliver important messages, in each instance to press horse or succession of horses to the limit of endurance and face danger at every bend in the trail. Again, the semi-native horses selected for those exhausting runs proved their unusual resources of stamina.

As Indian hostilities mounted out of sympathy for the Métis cause, there was anxiety for the safety of settlers. Home Guards were organized, demanding the most efficient communications possible under the primitive circumstances. The "pony express" organization operating at that time on the one hundred-mile trail between Calgary and Fort Macleod was considered to be one of the best. Superintendent Cotton of the North West Mounted Police was in charge and the riders were mostly seasoned cowboys—like Dan Riley, later Senator Riley, of High River.

The average time for delivery of a packet of dispatches— either northward or southward—was twelve and one-half hours. With two men in readiness at the Leavings—on the Oxley Ranch northwest of Fort Macleod—two at Mosquito Creek, two at High River and two at Sheep Creek, a message could be carried in five laps of the relay, each of approximately twenty miles.

The editor of the *Fort Macleod Gazette* boasted about Superintendent Cotton's dispatch system being "well nigh perfect" and added that the average delivery time was likely to be reduced to ten hours. Such would mean an average trail speed of ten miles per hour for the hundred miles. It would also mean nothing less than a cantering pace for much of the two hours or so each stout-hearted horse or pony was under saddle at a time.

During the same trying period in prairie history there were emergency runs like the one made by Big Tom Hourie, well deserving of a horseman's plaudits. Unfortunately, only a little is known about Big Tom's horse, as much a hero as its rider.

General Middleton, in command of eastern forces, was on his way to put down Louis Riel's Métis uprising near Duck Lake. Having left the new Canadian Pacific Railway at Troy—later Qu'Appelle—and marched as far as Humboldt, it was deemed imperative that certain instructions be delivered to Colonel Irvine at Prince Albert in the shortest possible time. Of course, the assignment would be both difficult and dangerous, partly because of distance and partly because the route would lead through the Métis community where insurgents were already in possession of the ferries and crossings on the South Saskatchewan.

"Is there anybody at Humboldt who could carry this to Prince Albert by tomorrow noon?" Middleton asked. "It leaves only twenty-four hours, you know, and it's a hundred miles but whoever undertakes to do it can take any horse in the unit."

Old Peter Hourie, with the blood of two races coursing through his veins, had been appointed interpreter to General Middleton. Having heard the question, he answered: "You get my boy Tom. He can do it."

The young man—six feet, five inches tall and broad in build—was called and asked if he would make the trip. The offer of "any horse in the unit" was repeated. Big Tom agreed to go. Quickly he looked over the well-bred and well-groomed eastern horses from which he could make his choice. They were bigger than local stock and much more handsome. But intuition told Tom Hourie they would not have the endurance needed for this test and he announced conclusively: "I take my own horse; I know what he can do." Tom's horse was a buckskin, considerably smaller than the cavalry stock from the East, of unknown breeding and by no means handsome. Brush or curry comb had never touched its hide. For its size, the gelding was strong, however—had to be to carry the big plainsman. Some years earlier, the animal was used to run buffalo and buckskin and man now understood each other perfectly.

The afternoon sun was still high when Tom Hourie packed some food for himself and slung a bushel of army issue oats tied in two sacks across the back of his saddle. Man, saddle and supplies weighed at least three hundred pounds—burden enough on even a short journey for a thousand-pound cayuse.

With Middleton's message pinned in the pocket of his shirt, Tom Hourie mounted and rode away with no more display than if he were about to call on a neighbor to borrow buckshot. As on other long trips, he held the buckskin to two gaits, walk and lope. That way, he knew, he'd obtain the most miles without overtaxing the horse's resources.

As the sun went down on that April day, 1885, Big Tom was on foot, walking to spare his horse between spells at the lope. It was cool and, with clouds blotting out all stars, any ordinary rider might have lost his sense of direction. But as a native of the Northwest, this man's judgment about direction was almost instinctive and even his horse, when set on a certain course, seemed to hold it as though guided by a built-in compass.

There was an early night stop—a brief one—while the buckskin ate a ration of oats. A few hours later, there was another. It being springtime, there was no lack of water for horse or man. While the horse was consuming oats, Big Tom munched on bread and meat from his saddlebag and then both pressed on through wooded areas where some of winter's snow remained, around sloughs and across prairie meadows. The night was long and with every passing hour Tom knew he was nearer to South Saskatchewan where Riel's men would look with angry suspicion upon anybody travelling that way.

Sure enough, soon after sun-up, as Tom and buckskin were close to the river, they were intercepted by Riel's scouts carrying carbines in their hands and hate in their hearts. But Hourie's story sounded reasonable; he was anxious to visit some relatives, he explained, and learn if they were safe. He was allowed to go on after refusing their invitation to join them in their fight to end the white man's rule in the West.

About the moment Tom reached the river, the Riel scouts received the message that this man on the buckskin horse was working for the soldiers and must be captured. As they were taking up the chase in hope of catching him, Tom was turning his noble little horse loose and trying to determine how to cross the river, still being churned by ice from the recent break-up.

Removing the shirt in which Middleton's message was pinned, he tied it about his head to improve the chance of the letter being kept dry in the event of mishap while crossing. That done, he jumped on a big piece of ice, then on another and another and was progressing well until the one on which he was standing capsized and he was plunged into icy water. From that point he had to swim—there was no choice—but he was able to do it and finally emerged on the other side about the time Riel's men reached the east bank and announced their bitterness by firing a few shots in his general direction.

After riding eighty miles, almost non-stop, and swimming the river, Hourie was still twenty miles from Prince Albert but he struck out on foot and at mid-day was placing the dispatch in Colonel Irvine's hands. The task was completed, on time, thanks in large part to a good horse. It is not known if Big Tom Hourie recovered the game little horse but most people will agree that the buckskin as well as man earned high military honors.

Actually, the mounted marathoners of those years worked in various ways and went by various names. The Pony Express which became a legend in the Western States was essentially a mail service, brainchild of a Kansas business man who saw possible fortune in a faster service over the near-two thousand-mile route between St. Joseph, Missouri, and Sacramento, California.

Delivery time by stage coach had been twenty-five days. With good horses and plenty of oats and strong riders, reasoned William H. Russell of a prominent Kansas freighting firm, the mail could be carried on that route in half the time and governments would be eager to provide contracts and subsidies.

Inaugurated in 1860, the Pony Express enterprise appeared to be meeting with success and total travelling time on the nineteen hundred and sixty-six miles of plains, forests and mountains was brought down to as low as seven days and seventeen hours. Letter-senders objected only mildly to a carrying rate of five dollars per letter at the start but saw the charge reduced to a dollar for half an ounce.

Volume of business seemed to be good and horses and riders were distinguishing themselves by completing their scheduled runs without delays. From a business standpoint, however, there was one serious defect; the cost of transporting a letter was actually several times the dollar or even five dollars paid in the form of postage and late in October, 1861—two days after a telegraph line to the West was completed—the famous Pony Express operations ended.

The Missouri-California Pony Express lasted less than two years but its story makes one of the romantic chapters in western history, marked by horses giving their best efforts and horsemen facing risks on every mile through unsettled Indian territory. In recognition, 1960 was formally declared Pony Express Centennial Year in the United States.

The longest organized mail route in the Canadian West prior to the coming of railroads was on the Saskatchewan Trail, almost one thousand miles of twisting wheel-ruts cut between Fort Garry and Fort Edmonton. For many years the freight on this life-line moved by Red River carts travelling in what were called "cart trains." But a regular mail service at intervals of three weeks was established in July, 1876, and thereafter Her Majesty's Mail went by cart, saddle horse or dog team, depending upon season and weather conditions. Mounted mail carriers going through in twenty-two days without change of horses were averaging about forty-five miles per day. A cart train loaded with freight took two months to go all the way from Winnipeg, through Portage la Prairie, Shoal Lake, Humboldt, Batoche, Carlton House and Fort Pitt to Edmonton.

Long rides were really rather commonplace in those years when travellers had no reasonable alternative. Even John Palliser who conducted Western Canada's first comprehensive survey of resources and prospects qualified as a marathon rider after leaving Fort Carlton on October 11, 1857, to make his way to Fort Garry and Montreal. It was at the end of his first season on the plains. He was at Touchwood Hills on the fourth day of the journey, Fort Pelly on the seventh, Fort Ellice on the twelfth and Fort Garry on November 1, exactly three weeks after leaving Fort Carlton.

Palliser's horse was one of those acquired at Fort Garry some months before and carried qualities transmitted from Fireaway on one side and Indian stock on the other.

CHAPTER 11

On Stage Coach Trails

With the pleasant sound of approaching hoof-beats, rattling wheels and a whistling driver, the stage coach and four or six-horse team rolled into the lives of frontier people, then just as quickly rolled away, the music growing fainter and becoming lost on Prairie trails.

Here were horses in an essential role. In hauling Red River carts and heavy freight wagons, oxen did very well but horses had the stage coaches all to themselves and performed with galloping splendor. The best horses for stage coaching, according to a veteran driver, were blacks and bays weighing between one thousand and two hundred and one thousand and three hundred pounds, of broncho breeding and with some mysterious feeling of sympathy for a slightly inebriated man with the reins. The BX Company, long in stage coach business on British Columbia's Cariboo Road, scoured Mexico, United States and Alberta to find suitable horses and finally maintained its own breeding ranch near Vernon.

Foremost among the stage coach routes of Canada was that Caribou Road built to accommodate the gold rush traffic. The first coaches, property of Francis Jones Barnard, ran between Lillooet and Soda Creek in 1863 on a ten-day schedule. Two years later, as roads permitted, the service was extended from Yale right through to fabulous Barkerville—a four-day journey. On return trips the coaches carried all manner of express—gold, corpses, criminals and mail as well as ordinary passengers. Now and then there was a highway hold-up.

East of the mountains stage coaches appeared on various runs—Calgary to Edmonton, Fort Macleod to Lethbridge and Calgary, Qu'Appelle to Prince Albert, Saskatoon to Battleford and so on. Generally an owner started modestly with double-seated democrat capable of seating four or six people, depending upon their proportions, then advanced to Concord coaches hauled by four or six horses and offering the finest luxury in long-distance travel.

Manufactured by Abbott and Downing of Concord, New Hampshire, the coaches were equipped with leather springs to mercifully reduce the bone-bruising jolts on all trails. But a sideways motion made many passengers seasick. Sitting with touching snugness like lovers, six passengers could be accommodated on the inside while one might sit with the driver and a few more on the rather precarious top. A Concord rumbling into Calgary from the South on one occasion carried thirty people in and on it.

The Concords made their Prairie appearance on the well-rutted lifeline between Calgary and Edmonton in 1883, offering a weekly service each way. One coach drawn by four-horse team left Calgary and the other outfit left Edmonton at exactly the same time each Monday morning. They'd pass at Red Deer Crossing and arrive at their respective destinations at about the same time late on Friday, after four days on the two hundred-mile trail. The fare was $25 dollars per person, each way, and baggage up to one hundred pounds was allowed. And adding further to similarity in northward and southward service, the two regular drivers had exactly the same names; both were Pete Campbell. For convenience, one became known as "Little Pete," and the other, "Big Pete."

Often they were on time but nobody was surprised when they were late. Delays could result from bad roads, stormy weather and broken wheels. Once, just north of Calgary, there was highway robbery with driver and passengers being set afoot. Delay because of horse trouble, strange to say, was almost unknown.

Horses, of course, were well conditioned, hardy and spirited. When they lost all the marks of inherent wildness, they lost much of interest for those blithesome fellows who drove them. Hitching lively horses presented problems but there was an accepted order in procedure. Passengers were notified to take their places before the teams were brought from stables and then the driver mounted to his seat. The coach thus being ready to receive horses, the wheel team was driven into position, reins handed to the driver while hitching went forward. At this point the lead horses were brought to their places and the second pair of reins was handed to the driver. Finally, all being ready, the driver released the hand brake and shouted to the prancing horses to be off. As team galloped and coach lumbered over rough trail, passengers had reason to hold their breath. But after a run of quarter of a mile, the team settled down to a sensible walk or trot.

Horses were changed at twenty or twenty-five miles. On level ground they trotted most of the time but proud reinsmen always ensured a reserve of energy for a spectacular spurt as an outfit approached a destination or stopping place. Every driver chose to leave town at a gallop and arrive with the same kind of dash and dust.

Coach drivers, like "bullwhackers" displayed pronounced individualism. Often they were noisy; generally they had unlimited resources of tall tales; sometimes they sang or whistled as they drove; frequently they could drink liquor without becoming impaired; always they were hardy fellows with pride in their resistance to extremes of heat and cold. Like train conductors and ship pilots they were responsible for their outfits and insisted that their authority be recognized. On the trail, a driver expected to be accorded the right-of-way without argument and at stopping place, without waiting for invitation, he sat at the head of the table.

When Prairie pioneers talk about stage coaches and coach horses, somebody will mention Frank Pollinger who, sober or otherwise, was the greatest driver of them all. Often he frightened his passengers to the point where they were ready to scream but always he delivered them and was never known to lose a bag of mail. More than once he faced hold-up men but for such contingencies he carried an extra mail bag filled with straw and carefully sealed. At the moment of a hold-up, this bag was thrown to the desperados and while they were prying into it, Pollinger was cracking his whip over the buttocks of his four or six horses and gaining a good lead on anyone who might pursue.

Polly, as he was known to everybody on the Prairies between Winnipeg and Rockies—and as far north as Frenchman's Butte where he took part in suppressing the "Rebellion" of '85—came originally from Oklahoma and grew up with horses and cattle. After riding the Montana range he took to stage coaches on the trail between Fort Benton and Fort Macleod—a three weeks round trip.

Sometimes he drove four horses, sometimes six, carrying mail and passengers on routes radiating in various directions from Fort Macleod. For a time he made weekly trips to Calgary and, later, three trips per week to Lethbridge.

Polly succeeded, intentionally or otherwise, in leaving vivid memories with about everybody who rode with him. A. M. Pinkham, son of Bishop Pinkham, writing in the *Calgary Herald*, July 12, 1924, recounted a typical experience when travelling as a passenger from Fort Macleod to Lethbridge. Never one to advance the cause of temperance, Polly was in his usual fine fettle and the Fort Macleod departure raised a customary cloud of dust. At Kipp where the river had to be forded, water was especially high and horses were obliged to swim. But the climax to a memorable journey was at the approaches to Lethbridge. On the grade leading down to the ferry, Colonel Steele of the North West Mounted Police came from behind with team and buggy and unnoticed by Polly, passed the stage without even a greeting.

The celebrated stage driver was incensed that anyone— even a high officer of the N.W.M.P.—would have the nerve to pass Her Majesty's mail. Instantly his famous whip cracked and the four horses responded with readiness to run. Taking a shorter hold on the reins, Polly turned the team off the trail to take an untested shortcut over the hill and down a steep slope to the ferry. "Hold on boys," he shouted to the passengers, "you'll be all right."

The team responded. The coach creaked and rattled to the top of the hill, hit more stones and started down the other side, swaying dangerously from side to side. Horrified passengers took firm grips, shut their eyes and uttered silent prayers. But in a moment the outfit was on the river-bottom, coach taking the curve on two wheels and coming to an abrupt stop on the ferry. The river craft started across and just as it was too far from shore to warrant returning for late arrivals, the vehicle carrying Colonel Steele appeared, but had to wait for the next crossing while Polly gazed back with satisfaction he was totally unable to hide.

The recollections of Corporal R. G. Mathews (2012) of the N.W.M.P. were typical. Writing in the *Third Annual of Scarlet and Gold*, he commented: "His reputation was almost international; and as a driver he was a marvel. Six-horse teams take a little handling at any time. When they are composed largely of half-broken bronks they take a very great deal of handling and that was the usual composition of Polly's teams. I made a good many trips with Pollinger . . . but I never once knew him to be sober; as a matter of fact, the less sober he was the better he handled his horses . . . It was nearly dark when we rattled down the rocky main street of Fort Macleod with Polly's whip popping like a shot-gun and the horses stretched on the dead run. This, it appears, was his invariable custom as it was to pull up with a sudden jar in front of the Macleod Hotel, his team scientifically set back on its haunches."

Every driver encountered accidents and Polly did not escape. But he never turned back on a trail. After upsetting when fording the Old Man on a wintry day, he righted the vehicle and drove on for the next two hours in frozen clothes. And with newspaper men, Polly was ever the hero. The *Lethbridge News* of March 10, 1901, reported: "The weather yesterday afternoon was decidedly unpleasant. The storm was even worse in the west than at Lethbridge. About ten o'clock the old veteran stage driver, Polly, started out from Macleod with the coach well filled with eight passengers. It was raining at the time but when he got on the big hill the storm of wind and snow struck the party, overturning the coach and lifting Pollinger out of the seat. 'But you bet your life I held on to the strings,' he remarked when describing the adventure. The coach was again righted and the driver . . . managed to reach the house of Mr. A. J. Whitney where they were put up for the night, reaching Lethbridge about ten this morning. Considerable anxiety was felt in town for the safety of the party but it was thought that if any man in the country could bring them through safely, that man was Pollinger. The police, however, started out this morning in search but had only gone a short distance from town when they saw the broad smiling face of Pollinger, bobbing up serenely in his place on the old stage coach."

But it was on the Montana side of the line in 1896 that Polly had his narrowest escape. It was early winter and in a sudden and violent blizzard, he lost the trail and drove aimlessly until the horses gave out. He was driving alone on this occasion. Setting out on foot in hope of finding refuge, he was finally overcome by exposure and hunger and collapsed in the snow. But an Indian found him, partly buried in a drift—"more dead than alive"—and carried him to an Indian Agency hospital where amputation of both legs was thought necessary. With the return of consciousness, however, Polly insisted that a horseman needed legs and his would recover. Determination saved him to drive for more years before he retired and died at Medicine Hat.

CHAPTER 12

Horses for Homesteads

Then came that period in western history when the horse was king, when Clydesdales and Percherons were prime topics of conversation and a few horsehairs on a man's coat gave no reason for apology.

Homesteaders required power, required it urgently. The earliest settlers in both East and West had no reason to consider either steam or gasoline as a solution; their choice was between oxen and horses. Without exception the preference was horses but some settled reluctantly for oxen, promising themselves they'd sell the "bulls" or quarter them for winter beef as soon as a change could be made. But many a settler's shack heard the earnest prayer: "Please Lord, spare my oxen—until I can get horses."

Those bovine brutes held advantage in being able to "live off the land"—in other words, work on rations of grass, while horses needed grain as well. But oxen were slow, sulky, totally uninspiring. When hitched to a sweep or "horse power" for the purpose of generating belt power, they became hopelessly dizzy. Their companionship did nothing to relieve homestead loneliness, while their attitude toward work and gad flies did a great deal to change the hitherto respectability of many Bruce County vocabularies.

Horses, however, were not easy to acquire. The cost exceeded that of oxen and supply fell far short of demand in that period when homesteaders were flocking to western soil. The settlers saw two—possibly three—sources of supply: the East offering reliable work stock at high prices, the range country with its cheaper stock of uncertain temperament and, perchance, the few bands of unbranded and unclaimed wild horses. The most promising wild prizes were in British Columbia and some Prairie people organized wild horse round-ups in mountain country and returned with hostile nags of doubtful value.

A few wild bands on the Prairies attracted the gaze of power-poor homesteaders. One such herd—about twenty animals headed by a black stallion—ran between Tramping Lake and Sounding Lake in Saskatchewan. This group, it was supposed, traced to horses abandoned by a notorious rustler who had been driven from his Canadian headquarters close to Heart's Hill in the present Saskatchewan.

Among the ox-driving homesteaders looking covetously upon those wild horses was a young Scotsman, Jack Vallance, who later represented the constituency of South Battleford in the House of Commons. After a lot of talk about how these wild creatures could be captured, he and his neighbors resolved to try. They knew the difficulties. The wild horses had speed and stamina, perhaps too much for the heavier horses available for the pursuit. But the chance of gaining more farm power seemed to justify any effort.

The wild band would never be corralled, the homesteaders agreed. The alternative was an organized drive with relays of fresh mounts to simply exhaust the wild ones. If the hunted horses could be kept on a course, the homesteaders would be ready to enter the chase with fresh mounts every six or eight miles.

The wild things lacked nothing in heart and courage and in the first day of the operation only one was captured. But the plan was continued and other members of the band were taken. Obviously, the best horses would be the last to be roped and homesteaders saw the black stallion, always in the leading position, as the top prize. And, strange as it seemed, a little bay mare was constantly at the stallion's side. When a drive was started, the stallion would whinny and the mare would come to him, touch her muzzle to his flank and run with him.

After several days of hard and exhausting riding, only the stallion and bay mare remained uncaptured but they were being worn down and they too were finally roped. Men and horses alike were weary but there was shock in store for the homesteaders—discovery that the bay mare was totally blind. At once it was clear why she ran with her head at the stallion's flank; his eyes served both and tears came to human eyes witnessing the climax. Some of the men were for releasing stallion and mare to be re-united in their wild but devoted ways.

But homestead needs were greater than sentiment and the captured horses were led away to be enslaved in harness. Years passed and the wild horse drive was almost forgotten. Then, as Jack Vallance drove on a country road he noticed a dejected black gelding drawing five school children in a buggy. There was something familiar about the animal and he stopped to enquire. Sure enough, it was the noble equine male which headed the wild band and defied capture by the homesteaders for so long.

But unclaimed wild horses, being few in numbers, provided no practical solution to the problem of need and, hence, homesteaders, when in position to buy horses, had to decide between eastern animals with hairy legs, bog spavins and expressions of resignation, on one hand, and branded broncho stock with rebellion showing in their eyes, on the other. The eastern horses had collar scars from years of service on Ontario farms. Facing frontier toil at a time when retirement would have been appropriate, they were more willing than able. Having eaten timothy all their lives, they didn't readily take to slough hay. Glauber salts in alkali water irritated their sensitive intestines and drinking from stagnant ponds resulted in swamp fever. Many of those eastern Clydes passed peacefully away before they were in the country for a full year.

The broncho horses, on the other hand, came with halters—often the only leatherware to which they had ever been exposed. Some were reputed to be broken to harness but homesteaders hitching them for the first time had reason to doubt. Hatred of harness and humans burned in their wild hearts and they had no compunctions about protesting with their feet.

At the slightest provocation the broncho horses were ready for a run-away; a gust of wind, a rolling tumbleweed or the sudden rattle of trace-chains was sufficient to start a run and when one horse in an outfit bolted, others were ready to follow. Being of light construction, a buggy could suffer complete destruction in a run-away. Where a wagon was involved, the harness was likely to break before the gear. The worst runaway of all was the one in which four or six-horse team participated, taking seed drill or harrows on a mad and destructive run.

On the Bell Farm at Indian Head where everything was done on a grand scale, ten four-horse drill teams dashed away when the horses in one outfit took fright at a whirl of dust. Pandemonium reigned as forty frantic horses tried to run and kick their way free of those implements with screaming discs.

Run-aways made rather commonplace scenes on town streets, so common in early Calgary that the newspapers stopped reporting them unless some person was killed or seriously injured.

The worst possible combination was when inexperienced immigrants undertook to drive half-broken broncho horses. Barr Colonist Englishmen about to start over the two hundred-mile trail to the district later known as Lloydminster, in 1903, bought all the horses offered at Saskatoon, including broncs with only a superficial acquaintance with harness.

Whenever possible those "green" newcomers bought their horses with the harness on them in order to avoid the conundrums they know must accompany harnessing. In leaving Saskatoon, they had expert assistance in hitching but from there on every driver had to depend upon his own resources. There were eight run-aways in the first hour and settlers' effects were strewn along the trail as far as Warman. At the end of the first day of travel, the landseekers faced another test, that of unhitching and unharnessing. The task of unhitching was accomplished with fair success but before unharnessing for the first time, the wary Colonists considered the possible difficulties in getting the harness back on the horses in proper manner next morning. The odds seemed against success and some of the drivers decided to leave the harness on their horses all night. A few others, according to C. E. Thomas who was with them, took even more novel precautions; as Thomas walked through the camp on that first night on the trail, he saw horses bearing conspicuous chalk marks, horizontal marks and vertical marks on the hides. What could be the explanation? It was simple enough. Colonists facing the worry of getting complicated harness gear back where it belonged next morning, had chalked the exact places for bellybands, collars, tugs, backbands, bridles and so on. This way there'd be something resembling a diagram to guide bewildered strangers through the great ordeal of fixing the harness where it belonged.

But after exasperating their homestead owners, running away unnumbered times and kicking some farm implements to bits, those bronco horses settled down to perform much of the heavy pioneer work in converting fibre-tough sodland to improved farms.

Regardless of the source of the settlers' first horses, replacement stock became necessary and as farming expanded, the need for horses was multiplied. Horse breeding became a leading industry and a new specialist appeared—the importer and dealer in pure bred draught stallions. Homestead communities provided the markets. For several decades all towns and cities had sales barns but Brandon emerged as the Horse Capital of western Canada. As early as 1886 the place had twenty-three livery stables and a prospective buyer could find stallions for sale at all of them.

Train loads of stallions—chiefly Clydesdales, Percherons and Belgians—were brought in, to be sold and distributed across the West.

Salesmanship became quite professional and farmers, in some instances, discovered to their sorrow that spavins, curbs and broken wind came with stallions they bought at high figures. Brandon horsemen told about the young man who turned his back upon a proposal to enter the ministry in order to sell horses and then reported the decision to his father. Said the old man: "Son, if you've decided to sell stallions, you'll probably bring more men to repentance than you'd ever do from a pulpit."

Every established farmer aimed to breed his own replacements and the extent of local interest may be judged from surviving records. Colquhoun and Beattie with five stallions standing at the Baubier Stable on Eighth Street in Brandon, bred six hundred and seven mares in a single season without taking a stallion out of the barn. Beecham Trotter of the firm of Trotter and Trotter could tell of paying over $3,000,000 for horses bought from the East to be sold from Brandon headquarters.

The trade in all its fancy forms was basically an expression of homestead and farm needs. Every farmer was a horseman and every farm boy aspired to be a horseman. A youth's practical education began, it seemed, with grooming and harnessing but he knew that to command farm country respect he had to master the arts of breaking colts, rolling manes, tying tails and driving tandem teams with four or six reins. They were the Golden Years in horse husbandry. When Canada's horse population reached 3,610,000 in 1921, the average western farm had about ten head. Horses on farms were as essential as oars in a rowboat. A farm without them was unthinkable.

CHAPTER 13

The Livery Stable

I f horsemen of the Gay Nineties had a fraternal headquarters, it was the town livery stable, musty smelling institution
with as much local importance as the shopping centre of a later
period. It was where town and country met, the best possible
place to measure the pulse-beat of the community. Officially,
its dual purpose was to furnish stable accommodation and
feed for farm horses driven to town for part of a day and rent
vehicles with horses to travellers who had the affluence to pay
fifty cents an hour for country driving.

But there was still another function—unscheduled but no
less important; it was in providing a meeting place for people of all walks of life. If a man couldn't be located at his
village home or in the poolroom, the most likely place to find
him was in the warm and stuffy waitingroom-office combination at the livery stable through which urban and rural
people moved constantly. And men with private business—
be it drinking, fighting or trading horses—saw the stable as
the place to go. If the waitingroom was too open for the business at hand, there were the darkened stalls.

Ostensibly at least, the livery stable was for horses and
farmers were the chief customers. A few parsimonious Sons
of the Soil blanketed their teams and tied to the stockyards
fence rather than pay at the rate of twenty-five or thirty cents
per horse for the shelter of the stable and a feed of oat
sheaves. But most farmers drove directly to the stable, lured
by the human associations of the place about as much as the
comforts for horses. On any winter day, enough horses were
present under the frost-encrusted roof to offer a thorough

75

study in types and breeds and on Saturday afternoons, every stall was occupied.

Most horses were stabled there for a mere two or three hours while farm women bought groceries and men priced new seed drills and stocked up with sweatpads. It was worth quite a lot for the horse owner to know that whether he was in town for an hour or the duration of a three-day "bender," his team or saddle pony was assured of feed and water and shelter.

To accommodate irregular calls for hired livery outfits, the stable operator was obliged to keep a group of reliable road horses and collection of buggies, democrats and cutters. Most requests came from medical doctors, preachers, bill collectors and landseekers. Now and then a young fellow wanted a horse and well polished buggy or phaeton with which to take his best girl for a Sunday drive. Experienced horsemen were trusted to drive themselves and could get a horse and buggy for fifty cents an hour or three dollars a day. Those travellers who required a driver to accompany them on country calls paid dearly for their inexperience—a dollar an hour for team and teamster.

As a group, the collectors were the best horsemen and members of the clergy the poorest. Every liveryman kept an ancient horse considered almost foolproof for his ministerial customers making country visitations and even then the reverend gentlemen could get into serious trouble in their driving. A liveryman in northern Saskatchewan could tell of renting a slow horse and buggy to a parson and his wife for calls upon rural members of the flock. The liveryman's last words to the minister were to assure him that the horse was entirely reliable—"as long as the rein doesn't get under his tail." Hours later, while a gentle summer drizzle fell to barely moisten the ground, the old horse was seen plodding back to the stable, the parson still giving the most diligent attention to his driving while his wife, following his instructions, held an umbrella over the horse's rear end. The churchman was taking no chance on rain getting under the horse's tail.

Now and then those who rented livery horses encountered serious trouble. Occasionally a horse would run away, with damage to the buggy and injury to the customer. Sometimes a careless renter neglected to properly tie his rented charge and horse—still hitched to the vehicle—returned to the stable without a driver. Hours later, an embarrassed customer would arrive on foot, trying unconvincingly to explain how it was one of those unavoidable accidents, something which might happen to the most expert horseman.

Then there were times when neither horse, buggy nor customer returned. Suspecting theft, the liveryman then notified the Mounted Police and a search was instituted. With a horse and buggy, a thief couldn't get out of the country very rapidly but in the majority of cases, police found evidence of horse and vehicle being sold and culprit, with money in his pocket, taking flight by train. Sometimes the thief sold only the vehicle and made his departure as rapidly as possible on horseback.

When the livery trade was big enough, the operator tried to have a horse or team to fit the particular requirement of every need. He'd have a pair of quiet old blacks whose experience had imparted an appropriate feeling for funerals. A pair of high-lifed bays might be kept for weddings and gay occasions; and for the needs of young lovers, a horse's appearance was more important than speed. One liveryman, with the wants of the Lothario in mind, kept a beautiful dappled grey which would prance for the first quarter of a mile away from the stable and then settle down to a slow and lazy gait on country trail. The old horse understood the circumstances of courtship. Parking on country roads would never do at all but there was no moral law against using an exceedingly slow horse which would faithfully hold the trail while the knotted reins hung loosely over the dashboard.

All things considered, the hiring of horses was the least attractive part of livery stable operation, hard on the animals and always risky because of unreliability of some strangers who were entrusted with outfits. Too often the horse which was fresh when taken from the barn, returned scratched, whip-marked and exhausted.

But in a real sense, the village or town livery stable catered to the needs of men as well as horses. Women had reservations about going beyond the waitingroom and mothers instructed their children not to loiter there. But for mature males, the stable seemed to meet about every need. Wayward fellows who spent all their money and were wary about going home late at night, bedded down in the straw of a vacant stall and, in the morning, volunteered to work with a five-tined fork as an expression of gratitude for the bed.

Commonly, the livery stable became a headquarters for the local veterinarian. Operations like filing horses' teeth and firing spavins—always top entertainment for the idlers who occupied the softest chairs close to the stove—were performed right in the stalls. The veterinarians of that time were essentially horse doctors, experts in treating colic and emasculating colts. Although most "vets" welcomed admiring audiences, all resisted repeated livery stable conspiracies to obtain free advice about treating sick animals back on the farms. The veterinarian who was always ready to tell a story or share some local gossip, became as silent as the grass when professional secrets were sought.

The stable operator, never a man to reject a profitable sideline, generally had one or two stallions on the premises. There for public service or for sale, stallions were always a proper topic for public discussion. To the debates about breeds, there was no end. Men who could never be accused of intolerance with respect to matters of human color, race or creed, were bitterly prejudiced about breeds of draught horses and the livery stable arguments concerning the merits of Clydesdales, Percherons and Belgians never ended.

Naturally, the man who had a horse to sell or trade, went to the livery stable and it was a dull day when at least one transaction wasn't concluded there on the plank floor behind the rows of stalls. A few individuals seemed to spend most of their time trading horses, buggies, herd bulls or anything likely to be needed, provided they were paid a difference in cash. They were the men who, by reputation, always had a "roaring" good horse or "rattling" good buggy for sale or trade.

Community-wise, one of the livery stable's finest contributions was as a meeting place—sort of social centre of gravity for the district. Its doors were never locked and, in winter, the big-bellied heater in the waitingroom was never cold. Customers would come and go, halting long enough to hear a story or listen to some gossip, but the non-paying guests generally outnumbered all others, and the competition for the best chairs close to the stove was as keen as that of two robins after the same worm. Politicians had the good judgment to pay frequent calls because they knew this place to be the hangout of kingmakers.

Long before it was time for nominations, the men who sat close to the livery stable stove decided who would make the best member of Parliament and who should be elected to sit on the school board. Nothing in the community escaped the notice of those who congregated at the stable; and when the editor of the local weekly faced the dilemma of insufficient news for his columns, he repaired to the odoriforous atmosphere of the stable and came away with more stories than he could use—and some he dared not print.

Many of the citizens who made the livery stable their hangout were men who farmed in some capacity during the summers and relaxed in the winters. Some were just community characters, reluctant to work at anything beyond the point of necessity. Every stable appeared to be the home base of at least one n'er-do-well who might rate somewhere between a tramp and a handyman. He could witch wells, pour babbit, stick pigs and tell exactly what the next month's weather would be like, but he never worked more than necessary to ensure food needs.

Sometimes he was allowed to keep his coffee pot on the stable heater and sleep in a cot behind a horseblanket curtain in the waitingroom, in return for morning help in cleaning the livery stable. But he was a cheerful fellow, ready to help at anything, as long as there was no danger of it leading to steady work. Through the winter he was making the acquaintance of all the horsemen in the country and all summer he was away visiting them and enjoying their hospitality. With the first cold days in the fall, he would be back at his winter base, a re-activated member of the livery stable fraternity.

But the glory of the livery stable, where the pungent odor of sweating horses mingled with the distilled essence of frontier character, departed. Gone is the sound of shod feet on the unsteady plank floors; gone is the lantern throwing a dim light to aid a late traveller to find his own horse; gone is that linchpin which held town and country people in the closest possible state of understanding. Nothing has been found to take the place of the old livery stable—or provide as much warmth, enlightenment and horse feed for thirty cents.

CHAPTER 14

Horses of Iron

For a few dramatic pioneer decades, draught horse supremacy in farm fields was unchallenged—like the stock saddle at a rodeo or beef stew in chuckwagon fare. The only visible disagreement concerned breed superiority and on that point men argued as bitterly about the merits of Clydesdales and Percherons as they did about the virtues of Liberal and Conservative parties.

With no difficulty, horses overcame the competition created by oxen and there was every reason to expect a similar triumph over the bicycle. Horsemen at the beginning of the twentieth century laughed at the idea of their draughters being displaced by anything as artificial and unreliable as automobile or other self-propelled mechanism.

"The horse," said the editor in the second issue of the Farm and Ranch Review, dated March, 1903, "has successfully survived the bicycle craze and now, when he promises to contest the field against the automobile with every prospect of winning out, western breeders had better cease worrying about the horseless age—which will only precede the manless age by a short time—and be on the lookout for the best stallions their means can afford for the coming season."

But the challenge from mechanical power was not something to be treated lightly. Harnessed steam was the first to be tested in farm operations. Portable steam engines made most acceptable substitutes for horsepowered sweeps used to drive threshing machines and grain crushers—and performed without the boiler explosions which the sceptics had anticipated.

Then there came the earth-shaking steam tractors. Not only were these heavy, bridge-wrecking things able to propel themselves but they had drawbar power to pull ten, twelve or fourteen plows through virgin earth. Such mechanical leviathans travelled at a snail's pace—even slower than the homesteader's undernourished oxen—but some farmers were sufficiently impressed to mortgage their farms and place orders.

As buyers discovered, however, the iron giants were expensive to operate, even though their principal consumption was wood and water or straw and water. They were cumbersome to move and their boiler flues reacted badly to alkali water, often the only water available in western districts. Too often the purchase of a steamer marked a farmer's first step on the road to financial ruin.

The gasoline tractor was next. Big ones breaking rural quietness with their explosive pulsations led the way. Horses hated the cannonading from their single cylinders and tried to run away. Like the steam traction engines, they were constructed for heavy drawbar loads at low rates of speed. On soft ground they bogged down, became helpless like bull teams in a bog. Their future, according to loyal horsemen, was gravely in doubt.

Until the years of the First World War, neither steam nor gasoline power was making any serious inroads upon the position of the universally popular horses. Then, suddenly, these new mechanical wonders were winning public attention and a place in day-to-day discussions. It reached the point where the two most over-worked topics in debating society circles across the West were: "Farm vs. City Life," and "Horses vs. Tractors For Farm Power."

In the debate on power, tractor supporters made points about reduced labor requirements and economies effected by the fact of no consumption of feed or fuel when not working. Those upholding the other side, with confidence in their cause, talked about the horse's ability to furnish replacements by natural reproduction, the fertilizing value of manure, lower operating costs and higher quality of work performed—and usually won the judges' decision.

One of the most convincing bits of evidence submitted by the horse supporters in the course of those repetitious debates came from one of the bonanza wheat farms in Alberta, the Noble Foundation, where power of three types had been employed side by side. With horses it had been shown to cost forty-two cents an acre to do plowing; with steam tractors the cost was sixty cents an acre and with gasoline tractors, seventy cents an acre.

That seemed like conclusive proof of the everlasting superiority of horses. But it was 1916 proof and had little or no application twenty or forty years later, after gasoline tractors had been transformed, not only in shape and size, but in efficiency and versatility.

Meantime there was growing competition between the two forms of tractor power—steam and gasoline—and nobody was very sure which would emerge as the victor. Showring rivalry in horse classes was at its keenest point about 1908 when the Winnipeg Industrial Exhibition introduced its famous Motor Competition. Horsemen sneered at the proposal and wondered what crazy invention would be foisted next upon a gullible farm society.

But in spite of sarcasm from horse barns at the Winnipeg Exhibition, the Motor Competition created unprecedented interest. Open to the world, it was for tractors weighing up to 14,000 pounds. Manufacturers were invited to display their models in action before competent judges, just like a class of draught stallions presented in the showring. The judges in the first year were William Cross of the CPR and A. R. Greig, later Professor Greig of Saskatchewan University.

Score cards were popular among horsemen at that time and a score card was prepared to guide the judges in determining degrees of tractor suitability for farm work. Points were allowed for power, economy in use of fuel and water, distance travelled without replenishing, turning ability, protection of working parts from dust and mud, accessibility of parts, speeds, ease of manipulation, clearance of working parts from the ground and, finally, price, F.O.B. Winnipeg. Nine makes took to the contest field in that first year. But the performance of those primitive tractors left much to be desired. Two broke down but returned to the competition after receiving major repairs. A third one broke down and was unable to return. Delays because of minor mechanical troubles were common but the spectators were forgiving—all except the horsemen. When rain fell on the third day, heavy drive wheels ground their way into the Winnipeg gumbo and became helpless.

The judges made their decisions, awarding first prize and gold medal to the Kinneard-Haines entry, a thirty-horsepower gasoline model weighing 13,530 pounds and pulling six plows. It was one of the first major triumphs for gasoline over steam, creating both glee and disappointment such as a Percheron win over Clydesdales in the six-horse team class might be expected to produce.

Thereafter for some years the Winnipeg Motor Competition was an annual event attracting international attention. Representatives came from the United States Department of Agriculture and some from across the ocean. Ignoring modesty, Winnipegers elected to call it the Farm Motor Competition of the World. By 1913, with twenty-five tractors competing, only two were steamers, a J. I. Case and Sawyer Massey. The steam engine, still the favorite for threshing, was in decline for other field operations but not giving up without a struggle. And gasoline fueled tractors were being reshaped to improve their suitability for the needs of medium size farms. Horsemen could no longer shut their eyes to the threat as manufacturers prepared for a major advance upon farm fields.

At war's end an entirely new type of tractor came from Ford assembly lines, Fordson they called it. Its four-cylinder-motor and startling road speed of eight miles per hour made strange contrast with the sluggish big things with heavy flywheels. This low-priced, light-weight innovation was designed to accomplish just about anything a four or six-horse team would do. It was at once popular and ushered in a new day for both tractors and horses, a day of phenomenal expansion in tractor use and a day of dramatic decline for farm horses.

In 1921, Saskatchewan alone had well over a million horses and only one farm in ten had a tractor. Forty years later there were as many farm tractors as farms and only one horse per farm on the average. The same province in 1925 had one thousand two hundred and seventy-four stallions enrolled for public service; in 1957, only one hundred and fourteen.

They called it progress but it wasn't all beneficial. At least some blame for soil pulverization and related deterioration could be laid at the door of mechanization and high speed tractors. Conservationists pointed out that tractors can be used to spread soil-renewing manure but they cannot make it.

There was another debit—loss of markets for the products of the soil. The committee which conducted a country-wide study for United States President Herbert Hoover observed that reduction in the use of horses and mules and the simultaneous release of crop land previously growing feed for work stock was a big factor contributing to the surplus of farm products so embarrassing and costly in the '30s and later.

Dean Curtis of Iowa State College warned American farmers in 1926 of new marketing difficulties if they substituted "mechanical power produced by gasoline for horse power produced by farm feeds." He said that if they continued to replace corn with gasoline, they would, in the long run, pay more for gasoline and take less for corn.

The period of transition from horse farming to tractor farming produced the most severe horse depression the country had seen. Farmhorses became suddenly unemployed and of little sale value. The inferior ones moved to processing plants and there seemed no other market for many of the good ones. With thousands of unsalable animals eating western grass the Co-operative Horse Marketing Association was formed in Saskatchewan in 1944 for the specific purpose of liquidating part or all of the surplus. Abattoirs were operated at Swift Current and Edmonton and nearly a quarter of a million western horses—many possessing the best of breeding and quality—were slaughtered, processed and sold as pickled or canned meat to Belgium and the United Nations Relief Organization. Nineteen million dollars worth of products went from those plants and the meat helped to relieve post-war hunger in Europe.

But it was an uninspiring chapter in western horse history, inevitable though the adjustment might be. Unfortunately, the reduction in horse numbers proceeded with no thought to possible needs in the future. Draught horse breeding almost ceased, it being forgotten that at least a small number of the best heavy horses should be given opportunity to reproduce their kind.

It was difficult for the older horsemen to accept the reversal of fortunes. But the old order had changed; the draught horse's former place of eminence was gone and the pride of its loyal admirers suffered injury But there were horse lovers who saw good in the change and welcomed an order in which faithful slaves were released from the former burdens of toil. The tractor was the winner in the new agriculture but the horse wasn't altogether the loser, having been freed from various degrees of fatigue, collar sores, cruel drivers and emaciation due to overwork. In that there was reason for satisfaction, just as there was rejoicing when horses were honorably discharged from warfare on man's futile battlefields.

Yes, draught horses were relegated to a minor role but not to disappear. The years of adjustment were frustrating but they passed and all the old breeds along with a rich stream of story and sentiment were assured of survival.

CHAPTER 15

The Bonnie Clydes

In the drawn-out battle for draught breed supremacy, the Clydesdale, with stylish white markings, high quality and gay action, found its biggest advantage in being first on the Canadian scene. Acceptance was general before breeds like Percheron and Belgian had opportunity to challenge. Early adoption was explained by the intense loyalty of Scottish settlers for their breed. Brooking no compromise in ideas, they placed quality of feet and legs above all else and their feeling for Clydesdales was equalled only by devotion to heather, oatmeal porridge and the poetry of Burns.

Flames of sentiment for their breed blazed as high on the Prairies as in Lanarkshire. It might be silent sentiment and undemonstrative but it was no less real—as with C. A. Weaver of Lloydminster whose stallion, Wee Donald, won the Clydesdale grand championship at Chicago International on three occasions. There was a banquet in the exhibitor's honor at Lloydminster, to which Miriam Green Ellis, well known figure in agricultural journalism, journeyed. Her comment: "The Weavers, father and son, were quiet men. They were a bit difficult to interview and finally, in desperation, I said: 'I guess you like Wee Donald pretty well.' To which the elder Weaver replied, slowly, thoughtfully: 'Yes, many is the pipeful of tobacco I've smoked, just sitting in the stall and admiring Donald.'"

Cradled in the Valley of the Clyde River, breed progress followed a succession of great sires. Prince of Wales, foaled in 1866 and Darnley in 1872, inspired the Scottish horsemen and these stallions founded two notable lines carrying their names far across the western world. Nothing brought more pride to a Clydesdale owner than to tell that his horse was a son of Craigie Beau Ideal by Craigie McQuaid, by Bonnie Buchlyvie, by Baron of Buchlyvie, by Baron's Pride, by Sir Everard, by Top Gallant, by Darnley.

Under the tutelage of more than a hundred years of Glasgow Stallion Shows—with the sponsoring Agricultural Society exercising a right of first choice to hire any stallion or stallions brought forward—the breed developed with iron-like bone, refinement of hocks, obliquity of pasterns, prominence of hoof heads and excellence in action. In weight the Clydesdale was surpassed by at least three breeds but in quality and flash by none. Scotland's horsemen had concluded that a horse was as good as its feet and legs and some judges on both sides of the ocean were facetiously accused of pulling their hats down on their eyes to such level that they could see nothing above a horse's legs.

In time the Clydesdales came in for severe criticism for lack of thickness and muscling but they continued to win the biggest share of inter-breed draught gelding and team classes. A two, four or six-horse hitch of dashing Clydesdales could not go unnoticed by anybody near the ringside.

The first to Canada was the stallion Cumberland, imported in 1840 but the principal Canadian foundation came with importations about the time Volume I of the Canadian Stud Book was published in 1886. Foremost among the "founding fathers" of the breed was McQueen, foaled in 1885 and imported as a two-year-old to win at the American Horse Show on the Lake Front in Chicago the same year. Throughout rural Ontario the name of McQueen became as well known as that of the editor of the Globe.

There were Clydesdales in Manitoba as early as 1881; stallions were taken to the foothills ranges in 1883 and at least one was delivered at Douglas Lake Ranch in British Columbia in 1887. The first stallion of note in the West was Charming Charlie, foaled in Scotland, 1883, and bought by

Alex Colquhoun of Colquhoun and Beattie of Brandon. The purchaser told of contracting to pay the Aberdeenshire owner a dollar a pound for the horse as a three-year-old and having to pay $2163, with the Aberdonian refusing to "knock off" the three dollars. But Charming Charlie was undefeated at Winnipeg and Brandon for five years.

When Alex Galbraith opened a sales stable in Brandon in 1891, Clydesdale stallions being sold from the numerous barns in that city far outnumbered those of all other breeds combined and that popularity was maintained for another twenty-five years. Brandon remained a Clydesdale stronghold. Where else could a spectator find forty-one two-year-old Clydesdale stallions in a single class as were seen there in March, 1912, with Dunure Sparkling Hope placed at the top?

West in the Territories, various notable breeding establishments were started in the '80s, one by W. H. "Scottie" Bryce of Arcola, one by A. and C. Mutch of Lumsden and one by Robert and John Turner at Calgary. These men were importers as well as breeders. Bryce who settled near Arcola shortly after coming to Canada, in 1882, imported such widely known horses as Perpetual Motion and Baron of Arcola—and one of Scotland's greatest sires, Bonnie Buchlyvie, almost came to western Canada on Bryce's order. When in Scotland in 1912, Bryce and James Kilpatrick inspected that stallion at Seaham Harbour and tried to buy him. Failing in this, Bryce instructed Kilpatrick to pay up to a certain high price for the horse at any time opportunity arose. At the Seaham Harbour sale in 1915, Kilpatrick bought the horse at five thousand guineas and immediately cabled Bryce but the message arrived the day of Scottie Bryce's funeral. Had the Laird of Doune Lodge been alive, Bonnie Buchlyvie would probably have come to Saskatchewan.

As the horse business flourished in the West, Clydesdales attracted numerous able and devoted breeders. But among importers, none would equal the record made by wee

Ben Finlayson, master showman of his time. One has only to recall that it was he who imported Dunure Norman, First Principal, Golden West, Johnny Walker, Sansovina, Edward Garnet, Arnprior Emigrant, Lochinvar and Riccarton Landmark. In that group were three winners of grand championships at the International Show at Chicago and four winners of the supreme honors at the Canadian Royal.

Ben Finlayson's work had much to do in making the West unique in showring performance. During the ten-year period beginning with 1920, Canadian-owned stallions won the Clydesdale championship at Chicago in every annual show—and most of the winners were from Saskatchewan. Wee Donald, owned by C. A. Weaver of Lloydminster won in 1920, '21 and '24; First Principal, owned by the Manitoba Department of Agriculture, was grand champion in 1922; Mainring for W. B. Cleland, Troy, Ontario, won in 1923; Green Meadow Footstep for University of Saskatchewan, won in 1925; Forest Favorite, owned by Haggerty and Black, Belle Plaine, in 1926; Sansovina, owned by John Sinclair, Congress, in 1927; Lochinvar, for John Falkoner, Govan, in 1928; and Sonny Boy for A. Johnstone, Yellowgrass, in 1929.

But circumstances brought Clydesdale breeding interest to a climax at the University of Saskatchewan at Saskatoon, where W. J. Rutherford was Dean of Agriculture and A. M. Shaw was Professor of Animal Husbandry. The program bringing together many of the most aristocratic Clydesdales outside of Scotland started with a request from the Saskatchewan Horse Breeders' Association to the Saskatchewan government for assistance in horse improvement. The government agreed to buy a stallion of outstanding quality in Scotland and place him at the provincial university. A purchasing committee was appointed and members proceeded at once to Scotland. But reluctance on the part of Scottish horsemen to part with their best sires prompted the committee to buy two young and untried horses instead of one reputation sire.

Purchased were the yearlings, Craigie Enchanter and Bonnie Fyvie, both foaled in 1919, both with distinguished showring winnings. But there was trouble ahead. First the Percheron breeders objected to the "official prejudice" in favor of Clydesdales. Then, two months after arrival, Craigie Enchanter died from strangulation of the intestine resulting from a tumor. Next, Bonnie Fyvie developed stringhalt and was destroyed in 1926. To compensate in part, Craigie Fyvie, known as the Gift Horse, was presented to the university by the Scottish horsemen.

But bigger things were in store for the university farm. The purchase of the Cluett stud in Massachusetts was acknowledged as the most important event in Canadian Clydesdale history. William Graham of Ontario had been commissioned in 1918 to buy the best Clydes procurable in Scotland for United States breeders, F. L. Ames and George A. Cluett. The mares assembled and shipped were described by a Scottish correspondent as the best to leave Scotland at any time.

Included in the first shipment for Ames was the yearling stallion, Kinleith Footprint, bought at $6000. But Mr. Cluett was anxious to have this son of Dunure Footprint and took him at $10,000. And when Cluett Clydes—thirteen of them—were acquired by the Prairie university in 1923, Kinleith Footprint came with them.

The mares included such aristocrats as the Cawdor Cup winner, Rosalind by Dunure Footprint, Craigie Sylvia by Apukwa, Langwater Jessica by Fairholme Footprint, Eva Footprint by Dunure Footprint and Fyvie Queen by Kismet. Rosalind had been Cawdor Cup winner in 1916 and was imported at a figure reported as $15,000. Her filly foal Rosabel, was grand champion at Chicago International in 1921 and purchased by Captain Montgomery to be shipped to Scotland. Craigie Sylvia, big and thick, had a fine show record before importation in 1919 and was grand champion at Chicago later that year. Eva Footprint's price was $10,000. And Langwater Jessica, for whom Mr. Cluett paid $3000 as a yearling was American bred, out of Jess of Craigwillie, once owned in Alberta.

Any way one saw these Clydesdale immigrants to Saskatchewan, they made a notable group. And their coming was at a total cost to the university of less than had been paid initially for certain individuals among them.

How did it happen? Sentiment undoubtedly played a big part. Dean Rutherford had judged at the International and was widely known and widely respected by United States horsemen. George Cluett, when faced with the necessity of selling, thought of Rutherford and wrote to him: "If I could feel that the best of them would be kept for breeding purposes at your university, I would be willing to sell the entire lot to you for $10,000, which, as you will realize, is only a small fraction of their value."

The Cluett horses were brought to Saskatchewan and some of them went on to win distinction while some did not. A stallion foal with Langwater Jessica made fame by winning the grand championship at both the Canadian Royal Winter Fair and the Chicago International in 1925. And as a brood mare, American-bred Langwater Jessica pretty well outshone her pure Scottish stable-mates. Her finest performance was in 1930. On March 22 she gave birth to a filly foal later named Julia. On the same day, Craigie Sylvia died in foaling but left a healthy orphan filly which was named Sylvia. Langwater Jessica was persuaded, with some difficulty, to adopt the orphan along with her own foal. The mare was a good feeder and milked like an Ayrshire. Her performance may be judged by the fact that both foals were chosen to be exhibited at the Canadian Royal Winter Fair that fall. And, in a large class, Julia stood second and Sylvia, third, speaking well for the aging mare's summer activities.

It was a glorious chapter in Canadian horse history but it ended abruptly. Clydesdales became comparatively unimportant. Nobody seemed to care that highly-regarded strains were being allowed to become extinct—and the box stalls once graced by Kinleith Footprint and Langwater Jessica and the others were being allocated to cattle.

CHAPTER 16

Percherons "To Beat the Clydes"

In the hey-day of draught horses, every farmer was
expected to declare allegiance to one breed or another—
just as he would support reciprocity or Canada Preference.
Either he was a "Clyde man" or "Percheron man." Nobody
could be neutral.

The Scottish breed had a substantial head start in the race
for popular favor but the Percheron came in at a gallop,
determined to win. Two prime purposes inspired the
Canadian breeders, one to furnish useful draught animals for
farms and other purposes and, second, to "beat the Clydes."
In supplying utility horses possessing muscle and good temperament, the Percheron people succeeded eminently; and
while the supporters were unable to vanquish the
Clydesdales in team competitions, they did see their breed
surpass the other in numbers of Canadian registrations.

It seems impossible to say when the first Percherons
were brought to Canada. French horses of the diligence type,
with the medium weight, endurance and activity needed for
stage coach work, were taken to the new colonies on the
St. Lawrence river from time to time. One was sent as a gift to
the governor of New France in 1647 and was probably the first
French horse on the North American continent. Eight years
later the St. Lawrence settlers received twenty mares and two
stallions from the Royal Stable of Louis XIV. But who can say
that these were Percherons or of the strain which brought distinctiveness to the horses of La Perche district in Northwestern
France? One may presume a relationship between all French

strains and that the Canadian breed which evolved in the province of Quebec had the same ancestors as the true Percheron. Perchance, those various strains shared equally from the refining influences of Arab and Barb horses left behind when North African invaders were routed south of La Perche in the 8th century.

French horses came early but it wasn't until after 1876—when a Norman Horse Stud Book was published in the United States—that Canada had any pure representatives of the Percheron breed. Some were then bought from M. W. Dunham of Illinois, long a leading importer. Only in 1907 was the Canadian Percheron Association organized at a meeting in Calgary. W. B. Thorne of Aldersyde, Alberta, became the first president, serving until 1911. For twenty years the association was essentially western, with none but Alberta presidents.

Organization was George Lane's idea. The long, lean, like-able cowboy who came to Canada to work for the North West Cattle Company in 1884, wanted no office for himself. But throughout the early years, he was the great force behind the Association and the dominant personality in it. He was born in Iowa and riding the Montana range when Fred Stimson of the North West Cattle Company placed an order for the best cattleman available at $35 a month.

Having seen what Percheron stallions did to improve the range horses of Montana, Lane was determined to introduce the breed on this side of the line. In 1888 he drove two Percheron stallions and thirty non-pedigreed mares from Montana to the Canadian foothills. A few years later he bought the Flying E ranch in the Porcupine Hills and, then, in 1898, secured the entire stud of pure bred Percherons belonging to James Mauldin of Dillon, Montana—thirty-five head in all— and drove these along with one thousand two hundred grade horses to his foothills range. With a further purchase of Percheron horse stock from Riverside Ranch in North Dakota, George Lane was at once a large scale breeder of both pure bred and grade Percherons.

Nor did expansion stop there. About the beginning of the century, Lane, along with Gordon, Ironside and Fares, bought the Bar U Ranch for close to a quarter of a million dollars and proceeded to make it one of the leading Percheron breeding establishments in the world. The best sires were chosen and there were importations from France in 1907, '08 and '10. The importation of 1909 was of special importance—seventy-two mares and three stallions costing an average of $1000 per head in the native land.

When Louis Aveline from La Perche visited Alberta in 1915, he declared the Bar U Percherons as good as any in France. Moreover, for some years the Bar U had the world's biggest band of pure bred Percherons. At the time of George Lane's death there were seven hundred head of registered horses.

In Lane's opinion, the stallions, Paris, foaled in 1889, and Presbourge, foaled in 1900 and given the first entry in Volume I of the Canadian Stud Book were the best used in the early period. But, surveying all the years of operations, Halifax, bought from Colquhoun and Beattie of Brandon for $3000, would rate as best sire.

Foaled in France in 1907, Halifax was imported to the United States and then brought to Canada by the Brandon horsemen who exhibited him at Winnipeg Industrial Exhibition in 1909 to win the supreme draught horse championship, over all breeds. It was the first time a Percheron had won this distinction in competition with the Manitoba Clydes.

George Lane made more history, lots of it. His Bar U cattle increased to over 25,000 head; he was one of the Big Four Ranchers who backed the famous Calgary Stampede of 1912 and it was on his suggestion that Edward, then Prince of Wales, resolved to purchase the Beddingfield Ranch adjoining the Bar U, in 1919. Of genuine historic significance, too, was Lane's export shipment of Percherons to England—a reversal of the traditional westward movement of breeding stock on the Atlantic. In 1918 he export twenty-six pure bred Bar U mares and the stallion, Newport by Halifax. The reception in England was favorable and in the next year a bigger shipment followed, fifty-three head in all, giving the breed a foothold in the land where Shires and Clydesdales and Suffolk Punch draughters had long had things to themselves. George Lane might have been described as Canada's "Mr. Percheron." It was he more than any other who set the breed on its upward course and when he died in 1925, annual Percheron registrations were threateningly close to the Clydesdale totals. Breeders had consolidated their ideals, favoring stallions of one thousand eight hundred to two thousand pounds, standing sixteen to seventeen hands, with symmetrical bodies and long-wearing feet and legs. Actually, the Canadian breeders, more than their United States contemporaries, were emphasizing quality with strength in the underpins.

Moreover, there was a new generation of leaders in breeding and showing. New names appeared to claim Percheron championships, some of the best known in that period being Carl Robert's Monarch which won grand championship awards for stallions at the Canadian Royal in 1926, '27 and '29, Charlie Rear's grey mare, Blanche Kesako with a Cinderella story and two Royal Winter Fair championships, Rear's stallion, Dean, also with two grand championships at the Royal, and, a little later, Hardy Salter's black mare, Starlight Koncarness, whose record at twenty years of age stood at forty-nine grand championships at major Canadian shows, including the Royal Winter Fair.

Members of the Percheron fraternity could not forget Charlie Rear any more than the baseball fans would forget Babe Ruth. His role with Percherons was much like that of Ben Finlayson's with Clydesdales and his name is connected with scores of winners in the '20s and '30s. His business methods proved exasperating to people around him but his devotion to horses was of sterling quality, more than enough to compensate for eccentricities.

His acquisition of those two notable show animals, Dean and Blanche Kesako, were rather typical. Rear and a well known United States horseman were travelling by car in Iowa, both interested in buying stallions. They stopped at a farm place late on a morning and, while strolling through the stable, Rear casually opened the door of a box stall and reeled with delight at what he saw, a fine grey colt. The thrill of finding what he had been looking for mingled with alarm that any outward display of enthusiasm would make it more difficult for him to buy the young stallion and, quickly, he closed the door and walked away to divert attention.

The two visitors accepted the Iowa farmer's invitation to stay for dinner but the Canadian had no appetite for food; he was excited and, pretending to be feeling ill, he excused himself and walked back to the barn, alone.

Now he could take a long and studied look at the young stud. "Yes sir," he said to himself, "that's the horse to beat the Clydes in Canada." But instead of trying to buy the colt then and there, thus exposing his pent enthusiasm, he took an option on all the horses on the farm and drove away. When a safe distance from the farm, he telephoned back to say he was taking the grey colt called Dean.

As time was to show, the Rear choice was good. Undefeated for many years at western Canadian exhibitions, Dean was grand champion at the Canadian Royal in 1930 and '31, and a daughter, Crocadon Katisha, was grand champion for George Fraser of Tate, Saskatchewan, in 1936.

As for the great show mare, Blanche Kesako, Rear more or less "discovered" her on a country road in southern Saskatchewan. It was the district of Meyronne, not far from Vanguard and Kincaid where Rear began to deal in stallions in 1912. Foaled in 1918, the mare was eight years old when Rear saw her hitched to a load of grain. As he drew to one side of the road to pass the team and wagon, he noticed the grey mare and, intuitively, pressed hard on the brakes, sending his car to a jolting stop in the ditch. Understandably, his mind was on Percherons and only Percherons. Inspection confirmed the mare's great size and quality—wonderful flat bone and hard hocks. Scratching his face and trying to appear indifferent he offered to buy the mare then and there but the owner refused to sell.

A year passed and then the owner was having an auction sale. Rear's memory was good when horses were concerned—not so good otherwise—and he was present "just to see how the farm machinery would sell." But of course he bought the mare, bought her and her mate together for $410, then sold the mate for $200. When somebody enquired where he would ship the mare, Rear replied: "Toronto." Then what he had done weeks before became clear; determined that he'd own the mare and confident of her excellence, he had made entry for her at the Royal Winter Fair, in his own name.

And so, Blanche was sent by express to Toronto because the Saskatchewan exhibit was already on the way. But she was not fitted for Royal competition. Her feet were cracked and she reacted badly to her first train ride. She was homesick for Meyronne, refused to eat and didn't impress the Toronto judge. But the next week at Ottawa she was more like herself and gained the grand championship. It was then, returning to the West, that Rear reported receiving an Honorary Degree from the National Breweries; he was now Charles Rear, H.C. Asked what the letters stood for, he replied: "Horse Crazy." But Horse Crazy or not, he was one of the great horsemen of his generation.

In 1929, Blanche Kesako was reserve senior champion at the Royal and in both 1930 and '31, grand champion. She was then sold to Carl Roberts of Manitoba and in 1934, the great Cinderella mare was sold again, this time to go to Australia.

In 1929, too, a young horseman farming at Crossfield, Hardy Salter, became secretary of the Canadian Percheron Association, a post he was to retain for the next thirty-five years and more, giving leadership to breeders and clinging tenaciously to the conviction that Canadian agriculture still needed some Percherons, regardless of the degree of mechanization in the country.

CHAPTER 17

Muscle-men
of the Horse Family

B efore the advent of mechanization, a team of massive
Belgian geldings was the nearest equivalent to an earth-
moving bulldozer. Here was the ultimate in size and
muscling. It did seem inconsistent that Belgium, one of the
smallest countries in Europe, would be the home of the
biggest breed of horses. Pride of the native land, the strain
was there for many centuries. Caesar, it seems, had praise for
the horses he saw in that part of western Europe about two
thousand years ago and after the Gallic Wars, ordered some
of them taken to Rome. But however ancient the Belgian horse
strain may be, the breed's acceptance in Canada came late.

In 1908, a year after the first association was formed, the
best it could show was a paid-up membership of three in all
of Canada and new registrations for the year numbered
sixteen—one from Alberta, fourteen from Quebec and one
from the United States.

There were reasons for late acceptance. In contrast to the
widely favored Clydesdales, Belgian emphasis had been on
powerful draught middles with apparent disregard to legs.
Wherever Clydesdale feet and legs were seen as models, people didn't know what to make of this breed reflecting entirely
new draught horse ideals. The older horsemen were scorn-
ful—sometimes insulting. "Built like beef bulls," said one
critic with broad Scottish accent, "but not as good in the hocks
and pasterns."

The sarcasm was not entirely without point. Even though
the Belgian bodies showed magnificent thickness and

muscling, there was a certain shapelessness about the limbs which wasn't changed until the introduction of sires like Paramount Flashwood and Lefebure's Clarion shortly before and shortly after 1920. Like bashful lovers, Canadian horse users acted with fearful hesitation for a time, then embraced the breed. Ultimately, the annual Belgian registrations in Canada were outnumbering those of either Percheron or Clydesdale. The Belgian won its inter-breed battle, even though, like other draught breeds, it lost the war against tractor power.

The province of Quebec, still the breed stronghold in Canada, received the first pedigreed Belgians in this country. That was 1902, many years after the initial introductions of Clydesdales and Percherons. A stallion was brought to Brandon from United States in 1905 but it wasn't until 1910 that Belgians were more than novelties in western Canada. By that time, Vanstone and Rogers of Wawanesa, Manitoba, were importing, also W. W. Hunter, Olds, Alberta; Hector Delanoy of St. Amelia, Manitoba; the Belgian Horse Ranch at Calgary and the firm of Eugene Pootmans and Sons, Antwerp, Belgium, which opened a branch stable at Regina. Louis Nachtegaele of Saskatchewan made an important beginning in the next year.

At the onset of the First World War the breed had a foothold and was being seen at fairs and exhibitions. But progress was slow. The Old Country type with piggy legs lacked appeal for western people although farmers gazing for the first time at Belgians seen at the fairs said they'd like to have horses with such bodies and better underpinning.

Before very long there was something of a transformation and Belgians with better feet and legs appeared upon the western scene. The man who led the way in making the change was George Rupp, farmer and breeder at Lampman, Saskatchewan. Rupp, an Iowa man, came to Saskatchewan in 1907, bringing a conviction that Canadian farmers needed the weight, easy keeping qualities and good dispositions of Belgian horses. His first purchase was a stallion called Comet and this was followed by an importation of mare and an outstanding stallion, Paramount Wolver, first son of the celebrated Farceur to enter Canada.

In reforming the breed on this continent, giving it more appeal for farmers, a big measure of the credit must go to that sire, Farceur, foaled in Belgium in 1910 and imported as a two-year-old by William Crownover of Hudson, Iowa. The horse's first success was in the show-ring, a grand championship at the Chicago International in 1913. But more important was the excellence of his offspring and at the Crownover dispersion sale in 1917, Farceur was bought by C. G. Good, Ogden, Iowa, for the record sum of $47,500. At the head of the Ogden stud he remained, the breed's acknowledged king on this continent, until his death in 1921. Then, following a custom in the native country of the breed, Farceur's remains were buried below the stall he had occupied and the barn dedicated to his memory.

For some years, Farceur breeding was all the rage and sons and daughters were in the keenest demand. Most offspring were roans like the sire and they possessed flatter bone, sharper hocks and more definition of pasterns than most Belgians seen previously—without losing the characteristic symmetry, well sprung ribs, thickly fleshed loins, heavy croups and gaskins and extra weight. Farceur himself weighed two thousand, two hundred pounds and sons, Oakdale Farceur and Supreme Farceur, each weighed two thousand, four hundred pounds.

Saskatchewan's George Rupp was one of the first to recognize the potential of Farceur breeding in creating improvement and his Paramount Wolver, bought from William Crownover, confirmed the view. When this stallion was brought to Canada, Rupp's Pioneer Stock Farm had the biggest band of pedigreed mares in Canada. Paramount Wolver was shown to many grand championships at Western exhibitions and, ultimately, in 1920, was sold to go back to Iowa at $11,400.

In the meantime, the Belgian booster, George Rupp, acquired another and even better son of Farceur, this one, Paramount Flashwood, considered by many students as the greatest breed specimen western Canada has had at any time. Bought as a two-year-old in 1918, Paramount Flashwood was a full brother to the mare, Lista, many times a champion at state fairs and champion at the International Shows of 1916 and 1917. In the year in which Rupp bought him, the stallion was reserve grand champion at the International.

Flashwood was a massive colt, weighed two thousand and ninety pounds at the age of two years and six months, and two thousand, three hundred pounds when shown at Waterloo as a three-year-old. At maturity, his height was eighteen hands. He had unusually fine action as well as exceptionally good feet and legs. With all this there was no lack of muscling. No doubt it was his personality coupled with quality and exceptional action which inspired gossip to the effect that his mother was sired by an imported Coach Horse. But one is entitled to enquire how a one-quarter Coach Horse could have such commanding scale and weight.

Flashwood's showring career was climaxed at the National Belgian Show, Waterloo, Iowa, in September, 1919, where his Saskatchewan owner showed him to win the grand championship, while his stablemate, Paramount Wolver, stood next to the top in the class for four-year-olds.

After Waterloo, Paramount Flashwood was retired from the showring and used extensively in Rupp's Pioneer breeding stud. But a great breeding record was cut short by his death in December, 1922. In writing to the Nor'West Farmer following the horse's death, Rupp said: "I feel the loss very keenly, as Flashwood was not only a horse, but a part of the family. The loss is partly offset by a $25,000 insurance policy carried by the Hartford Insurance Company."

Isaac Beattie, horseman extraordinary who judged extensively, said Paramount Flashwood was the second best Belgian he had ever seen; the only better one, in his opinion, was Pioneer Masterpiece, bred by George Rupp on his

Saskatchewan farm, a horse which after winning many championships, was accorded the high honor of being borrowed for use on the C. G. Good farm at Ogden, Iowa, where the immortal Farceur spent his last years.

Another Farceur horse foaled the same year as Paramount Flashwood, came to Saskatchewan. He was Monseur, bought by Robert Thomas of Grandora in 1919 and used until the animal's death at Christmas time in 1939. Thomas, an Ontario man in the West from 1892, bought his first pure bred Belgians in 1912. And here again the prepotency of Farceur expressed itself, as evidence the domination of western showrings by Monseur get for many years. At the Royal Winter Fair in Toronto, the story was the same. Sons of Monseur were grand champions there four times, a grandson once and a granddaughter once.

Paragon Major, retained for use by Mr. Thomas, was considered Monseur's greatest son. In winning the grand championship at the Royal in 1923, '24 and '26, he did much to popularize the breed. But the worth of Monseur and his famous son can be appraised best by winnings in the get-of-sire classes at the Canadian Royal. The older horse, through his get, won the class on two occasions and the younger horse in four different years. It meant that Robert Thomas, with the offspring of Monseur and Paragon Major, had the distinction of winning the class at the Royal no fewer than six times in the course of the first eleven years of the show.

That record, while adding to the fame of the Farceur line, gave Robert Thomas a place of honor among the breed builders in the West, with men like George Rupp and Arthur Lombaert of Mariapolis, Manitoba and some others.

Pioneer horsemen recall with glee the new standard of Belgian quality brought to Alberta by the dark chestnut American-bred stallion, Lefebure's Clarion, imported by Layzell and Parr, later sold at $11,000; and then Carmen Dale of the Farceur line, imported by Charlie Rear and shown to win four grand championships at the Canadian Royal Winter Fair, for his eastern owners, Haas Brothers.

For a time the western centre of Belgian horse activity was quite clearly at Saskatoon where regular shows brought together horses from many of the country's best breeders—Robert Thomas, Grandora; Dr. H. E. Alexander, Saskatoon; Charlie Rear, Saskatoon; William Nesbitt, Kerrobert and others from farther afield were regularly in competition.

The Canadian Belgian Draught Horse Association was organized and incorporated under the Livestock Pedigree Act in 1907. But if the number of registration transactions be taken as an indication, it was anything but impressive. Later the name was changed to Canadian Belgian Horse Association and only in 1920 was volume 1 of the Stud Book published. Progress was more pronounced after that date.

No draught horse body has been able to really flourish during recent years in the face of all the attractions in modern tractors but members of the Canadian Belgian Horse Association have fared rather better than the others, thanks in large part to the breed's continuing popularity in Quebec. The 1960 registrations for Canada showed one hundred and eight new entries for the Clydesdale Stud Book, one hundred and forty-eight for Percherons and one hundred and ninety-nine for Belgians. Of that Belgian total, however, one hundred and eleven or fifty-five percent of the registrations were from the province of Quebec. And most of the others came from Ontario breeders.

The Clydesdale lovers were still not convinced that weight could in any way nullify the importance of quality but a large share of practical horse users who had their own ideas about utility and either hadn't heard of Baron's Pride or didn't care, indicated a strong fancy for the "muscle-men" of the horse family.

CHAPTER 18

The Pulling Contests of 1925

"Heavyweight Championship of the World Goes to Lumsden," a news writer proclaimed in August, 1925, and nobody in Saskatchewan and neighboring provinces was so ill-informed as to confuse the event behind the announcement with a prize fight. It was the match of the year, the highly-publicized climax to a series of horse pulling contests enjoying public attention in both United States and Canada at that time.

All the western exhibitions made features of pulling competitions in 1924 but it was at Regina in the next year that excitement reached fever pitch; in addition to coming at the end of an exhibition season, the contest concluded a spectacular rivalry between a team of Percherons which seemed to belong to Saskatoon and a team of Belgians adopted enthusiastically by Regina. The two proud Saskatchewan cities had witnessed conflict in many forms but nothing appearing more like a death struggle than the pulling tests—not even the battle for the provincial government's favor in locating the University of Saskatchewan.

Saskatchewan alone had a million horses at that period, enough to give every farmer ten head to feed, water, groom and harness before breakfast. A short time earlier, Brandon people could line up two hundred draught stallions for a parade marking the official opening of the Winter Fair. Horse pulling, then, was a new and exciting innovation for farming people who knew all about horse breeding and horse feeding and moved in a society where horses practically ruled men's hearts as well as their fortunes.

And so, it wasn't surprising that horse pulling as an indication of training and inherent strength, caught the public fancy, especially in western Canada.

There had been numerous private pulling contests in earlier years. When hundred-bushel loads of wheat had to be hauled from threshing machines over soft ground, it sometimes happened that every team working around the outfit was put to the test with nothing more tangible by way of prize than a plug of chewing tobacco. And as long as stable manure was piled high on stoneboats, the incentive to measure a team's capacity was ever present. But in 1924, the pulling competitions became public attractions.

It started south of the boundary where an Iowa State Experimental Station man invented a heavy machine on wheels by which a team's pulling power could be accurately measured—dynamometer, they called the monstrous thing. Saskatchewan's Professor A. E. Hardy travelled to Iowa to see and study it, then returned to Saskatoon to make a duplicate. In the summer of 1924, the Saskatchewan-made dynamometer—looking like an army truck—was shipped from one exhibition to another to remove all guess-work about which competition horses were the best pullers.

Conducted under the same rules as contests in the United States, the performance of Canadian horses began at once to astonish everybody. The best record made by a team in the United States up to that time was a pull of twenty-five hundred pounds on the dynamometer for the regulation distance of twenty-seven and one-half feet. But at Calgary Exhibition that summer, almost at the beginning of the fair season, a team of Clydesdales won the competition by pulling two thousand, six hundred and fifteen pounds, a new world record.

At Edmonton Exhibition in the week following, a team of Percherons pulled two thousand, six hundred pounds and at Saskatoon, after just one more week, all previous records fell with a resounding crash. There, in front of the Saskatoon Exhibition grandstand, Dan and Tag, Percheron geldings owned by R. B. McLeod of that city settled gradually and doggedly into their collars, giving all the effort they possessed, to register two thousand, nine hundred pounds for the full distance. The dynamometer dial made it official. It was a new world record with many pounds to spare.

But the excitement was only starting. Trains carrying exhibits and midway moved on to the next fair, at Regina, and the heavy dynamometer went too. There was the usual big entry of draught horses seeking opportunity to demonstrate their pulling power. Included was a team of Belgian geldings weighing three thousand, seven hundred and ninety pounds—Jumbo and Barney—owned by Gibbs Brothers, Lumsden. The massive Belgians had the muscling and the experience to be winners and, as things turned out, Regina people were soon ready to claim the team and annex the nearby town of Lumsden; the Gibbs team not only won the contest but set the third world record to be made by Canadian horses in the brief period of four weeks. The qualifying pull was three thousand, one hundred pounds, full distance. It was hard to believe, especially for the people from Saskatoon who saw their world championship being snatched from them so soon. And to be outpulled by a Regina team made the loss doubly unpalatable.

At once there was a long distance telephone conversation between the two well-known exhibition managers, Dan Elderkin of Regina and Sid Johns of Saskatoon. Neither would ever miss a chance to fill grandstand seats. Sid Johns, acting on behalf of his fellow citizen, Bob McLeod, issued a challenge to meet the Regina Champions in front of the Regina grandstand on the following afternoon—the Saskatoon champions to pull against the Regina champions—for a purse of $1000.

Things moved quickly. They had to because time was short. The horsemen concerned accepted the challenge. McLeod's Percherons were given some extra oats and shipped to Regina by express that night. The cost of the express would have bought a good pair of horses but it was no time to quibble about expense.

It was Friday afternoon and Dan Elderkin smiled as the turnstiles revolved faster than usual. Somehow, even in the absence of radios, word circulated about the battle of equine leviathans and every grandstand seat was occupied before the hour of the contest. A world championship was at stake, also the honor of two jealous cities and two rival breeds of draught horses.

The Belgian team pulled first, registering an even three thousand pounds for the twenty-seven and one-half feet. It wasn't as good as the pull of the previous day but it was still a good one and the South Country fans cheered with delight. Then the Saskatoon team pulled, making exactly the same number of pounds. The suspense was precisely as Dan Elderkin might have ordered and the crowd—mostly Regina supporters—roared for more.

The teams pulled again. The horses were willing and loyal and one owner or the other was going to win $1000. Both teams started the dynamometer at a traction pull of three thousand, one hundred pounds but neither managed to take it the full required distance. The McLeod Percherons, however, had the better distance—eighteen and one-half feet—and won the handsome cash award. The Saskatoon supporters, acting like city residents whose football team had just won a Grey Cup, rushed from the stands to give their affection to the big black geldings.

There was still something unsatisfactory about it; although the Saskatoon team had won the prize money, the Regina team retained the world record from its notable pull of three thousand, one hundred pounds for regulation distance on the previous day. But any way one looked at it, the Canadian horsemen had reason for prideful satisfaction and Wayne Dinsmore, secretary of the Horse Association of America, explained it as the equivalent of a team starting a load of twenty tons on granite block pavement.

But the show wasn't over. There'd be another year and the two big teams were taken home to feed up on the best of oats and hay in preparation for the contests which were sure to come in 1925, even though no formal plans had been announced or made. No horses or athletes in the country received better care during the ensuing winter, with just enough pulling to keep muscles hard and the animals in perfect fit. And all through that winter, Percheron and Belgian adherents across the Prairie country argued hopefully about which team would "do it" next time.

The big contest of 1925, the one about which men in livery stables and country elevators speculated, was again at Regina. Farmers planning their "day at the fair" made it coincide with the pulling competition. Dan Elderkin made sure that everybody in Saskatchewan knew about it.

Both teams were at the peak of condition and fit. Both were heavier now. Weight was important. It might be the deciding factor. The Gibbs team, tipping the scale beam at two tons, still had the weight advantage.

As Dan Elderkin anticipated, the grandstand seats were full, but this time, the Saskatoon Percherons as well as the Regina-Lumsden Belgians had cheering fans by the hundreds. Most of the home city supporters, it seemed, brought betting money with them and were laying it on even terms.

The Saskatoon team pulled first—three thousand, two hundred pounds and met all the distance requirements—to set a new world record. Sid Johns shook another ten dollar bill in the air but nobody was now ready to cover it. Sad as it was for the loyal Saskatoon crowd, however, the new world record was destined to stand for only a matter of minutes because the Gibbs horses, enjoying their two hundred pounds of weight advantage, pulled three thousand, three hundred pounds, a fresh and most convincing world record.

The Saskatoon team won in the previous year and qualified for the thousand dollars reward but now the Regina-Lumsden followers were taking sweet revenge and making the most of it. Then, having won the exhibition contest to the satisfaction of everybody in southern Saskatchewan, the Gibbs team pulled again to see if its amazing record might be bettered. And sure enough, its record was bettered—three thousand, three hundred and fifty pounds—another new world record for the third time in that day.

It wasn't a good day for the loyal Saskatoon citizens, being beaten by their rival city; and it wasn't a good day for Percherons, being outpulled by the Belgians. But nobody in the country felt anything but pride when reading what a United States writer had to say about Canadian draught horses. The article, appearing in the *Breeders' Gazette*, published in Chicago, carried the title: "Does Canada Have Better Draught Horses Than The United States?" The author then went on to give an opinion that Canada, on the strength of pulling contest records—made with a machine of United States invention—did have the best. Certainly nobody in the Canadian farming country disputed the conclusion.

The pulling contests had their heyday and then public interest fell away, just as horse numbers dwindled. Only at a few western places, like Millarville in the foothills, will one still see the noble draughters giving their last ounce of effort and being driven by men who haven't forgotten the old arts of horsemanship. Elsewhere in Canada there is still scattered interest, notably in the Maritime provinces where one will find enthusiasm for both horse pulling and ox pulling.

As for the old dynamometer, it almost went for scrap but its sentimental value was recognized in time and it found a good home in the Western Development Museum at Saskatoon.

CHAPTER 19

The Big Sixes
and Their Drivers

A six-horse tandem in polished harness and charged with
energy distilled from generous rations of oats, was long
the zenith in Canadian showrings. While draught horses
were still lugging the country's plows, it was every farm
boy's dream to drive a massive show team at summer or winter fair, enter the ring at a reckless gallop, manipulate half a
dozen reins in controlling the six tons of vibrant horseflesh,
listen to cheers from an admiring crowd of spectators and,
finally, come to a halt in the centre of the arena to be awarded
a red ribbon.

Not every horseman experienced the thrill of driving a
winning team but, at least, everybody had opportunity of
watching and enjoying those classes of six-horse hitches competing for the judge's attention. Happily, even after tractors
displaced horses in farm fields, the six-horse teams succeeded
in holding their places of distinction in Canadian showrings.
And why not? A class of "sixes" with superior type, good fit-
ting and proper training, and presented by skillful drivers, has
never been bettered as a regular part of exhibition programs.

Some critics argued that the showring tandems consisting of
three two-horse teams had no background in utility. It was
true that in the course of ordinary field practice, horses were
rarely hitched that way but farmers did drive tandem field
outfits consisting of three or four horses in a pole team and
another three or four in front. Occasionally, twelve horses
were hitched in three rows of four.

In hauling wheat over country trails, four-horse tandems—each consisting of pole team and lead team—were quite common and six-horse tandems were seen at times. But back of these tandem road teams in agriculture were the four, six, eight and even twelve-horse tandems used by early freighters.

The pioneer press made frequent reference; the *Edmonton Bulletin* of December 13, 1884, reported: "Two four-horse and two six-horse teams belonging to Ad. McPherson are expected to arrive shortly with loads of green apples, fresh oysters, whisky and other Christmas groceries." The same paper, on April 3, 1886, mentions that: "Messrs. Collins and Brazeau of Fort Saskatchewan arrived on Saturday from Calgary with freight for A. Macdonald and Co. The former drover an eight and the latter a four-horse team."

The freight-team pride of the South was an outfit belonging to Lavasseur and Stedman and driven by Murphy Sullivan who was regarded by Pincher Creek residents as the best in the business. On this point, the *Fort Macleod Gazette*, December 12, 1884, indulged in a little boasting: "The general comment is that the twelve-horse team belonging to Lavasseur and Stedman is a mighty fine one. And the way that Murphy Sullivan manipulates these twelve with four wagons, in and out of intricate alleys and narrow streets, by the aid of a single jerk line operated from the saddle horse on the near wheel, could put a city coachman with two horses to shame."

In the years that followed, every horseman aspired to be an expert driver and the six-horse team contests at Canadian shows came to be regarded as testing grounds for drivers as well as for horses.

Clydesdales with their fancy flexion of joints and snappy action won most of the four and six-horse team awards through the years but no breed had a monopoly on superior drivers. Members of a group of older horsemen sitting on bales of hay were asked to name the greatest showyard drivers in western Canadian horse history and, as might have been expected, various teamsters of renown were recalled—Alex Fleming who drove the George Lane Percherons, Scottish Andy Haxton who drove for Sheas of Winnipeg and then went to the United States, Bobbie Burns of Edmonton and, at a later period, the eminently successful Allan Leslie of Watrous.

Lawrence Rye of Edmonton, himself a top driver, said of Fleming: "I showed against him for six consecutive years after 1913. He always carried a long bullwhip and while holding all six lines in his left hand, he'd crack it over his horses' backs and then collect the reins in both hands. It was sort of rough in those days and he'd make me mad when that whip would crack alongside my horses and just scare the daylights out of them. But, say, Fleming was a driver, the best I can recall."

Alex Fleming was an Ontario man who came west as a North West Mounted Police recruit in 1881 and drove extensively while in the force. In 1908 he went with George Lane and in the next year travelled to France for the big importation of Percherons for the Bar U Ranch, seventy-two mares and three stallions, the best to be bought in the native land.

But drivers grew no less skillful, even though horse numbers declined and no record surpassed that of Allan Leslie whose driving career began with homestead oxen and ended with Clydesdale champions under the bright lights of the Canadian Royal Winter Fair. Born near Brandon in 1887, he was on his way to a homestead west of Watrous in the spring of 1905. Leaving the railroad at Strasbourg, he had sixty-five trail miles to drive with six oxen hitched abreast to the wagon, five horses tied behind, and all other possessions—plow, bags of seed, a tea kettle and porridge pot—on top.

Four of the six oxen had never been hitched until that day and the young homesteader's departure from Strasbourg was at a mad gallop. But the green oxen became tired and were soon ready to travel at their slowest gait. The same oxen did the breaking on the homestead but Leslie was cherishing some ideas about exhibiting draught horses. At the very first fair held at Watrous, in 1912, he was a contestant and from there he entered horses at Saskatoon and Regina and, finally and rather naturally, at the Canadian Royal Winter Fair. His appearance at the Royal was in 1924 and he won first prize in the light draught team class.

In 1931, Leslie won in the light draught six-horse team class at the Royal and back at Watrous the Board of Trade entertained at a community dinner to honor the Leslies. Even at that time, before the driving competitions were instituted at the Royal, Allan Leslie's masterly horsemanship was being recognized and J. G. Robertson, Live Stock Commissioner in Saskatchewan, pronounced him "the best driver in Canada."

At various times he won the four and six-horse team classes at the Canadian Royal. What he considered his best six-horse team consisted of Johnny, Sandy, Tommy, Bruce, Prince and Donald, all but Johnny having been sired by Clan McNee and raised by Leslie. But it was in the Royal driving competitions that the record was positively unique. For six consecutive years the driving class was offered and the man from Watrous won it on every occasion.

Toronto spectators were overwhelmed. As one eastern newspaper explained it: "When the Watrous farmer drove his six-horse team and wagon into the ring last night in competition with all other teams, the crowd forgot about the jumpers, saddle horses and ponies they had come to see and delivered round after round of thunderous applause. The big six circled the ring in perfect line, drew up in line as a single horse. When the red ribbon was pinned on Tommy, one of the leaders, the noise was simply deafening."

Another Torontonian wrote: "Allan Leslie, cool-headed horseman from Watrous, Saskatchewan, drove his well-matched Clydesdales into the most decisive win in the heavy six-horse team class and into the hearts of the public by his clever driving and giving the crowd an eyeful of masterful horsemanship."

Wherever he went with his well-mannered show team it was the same. At Vancouver in 1934, the Leslie driving was described as the finest display ever witnessed at the coast. On a circuit of exhibitions in the Western States in 1938, the reactions were the same and people asked: "What is the magic in this man's control over a six-horse team? What strange power does he have to make his horses respond to signals which are almost lost in the distracting din of an exhibition?"

To these questions, Leslie answered modestly: "We've worked together quite awhile—the horses and I—and we sort of understand each other."

There was ample proof of that understanding. After winning the driving competition at the Royal Winter Fair five times, Allan Leslie faced his sixth test. His friend and neighbor, Smith Steen, helped him hitch for the contest and everything seemed to be in order. With customary dash, the big outfit entered the arena but at the instant of entry, Leslie became conscious of a buckle on the rein of his off lead horse being caught in a ring on the swing team. To stop for the purpose of correcting the trouble after entering the judging arena and coming within the gaze of judges would almost certainly rob him of any chance of winning. The alternative was to attempt the performance, practically without the use of reins and at the risk of accident.

The decision was made quickly; it had to be made that way. He would take the chance, keep his dangerous predicament to himself and hope to escape more serious trouble. As always, success or failure would depend largely upon the lead team and this time he'd be driving it with signals and one rein. It was too much like a bird trying to fly on one wing to be in the least bit funny. With wagon rattling, the six big horses galloped on while Leslie tried to appear unruffled. To onlookers the horses were being driven and manoeuvred as usual, cutting the figure eight with speed and precision and with no outward evidence of danger—not even when the lead team brushed the arena railing on one turn. Once again, the red ribbon went to Driver Allan Leslie and his Prairie entry. But when streaks of tell-tale whitewash from the arena fence were seen on the collars of lead horses, Leslie knew how close he had been to trouble. For that sixth driving championship, he gave the horses full credit, explaining that he had just gone along for the ride.

Otherwise, there was the clearest evidence of skill in all Leslie driving, as an arena incident in one proud city demonstrated clearly. Throughout this show there had been less than reasonable co-operation on the part of the fair management. On this particular night, as the team was about to make its spectacular run into the brightly lighted arena to delight five thousand spectators, Leslie paused to ask the director in charge to have a certain hardwood table removed from the centre of the ring.

But nothing was done. Those responsible for the evening performance, quite evidently, knew very little about six-horse teams and even less about horsemen and the table remained in its menacing position. Although visibly annoyed, the driver did not repeat the request but simply whistled for the horses to make their dashing entry.

On the first turn, while horses were still at a gallop and the man with the reins was driving a little more intently than usual, the hub of the heavy wagon struck the corner of the offending table, dashing it into a thousand unoffending pieces. Then, the problem of the hardwood table having been solved to the horseman's satisfaction, the driving performance continued as though nothing unusual had happened.

Driving champion Allan Leslie and the magnificent Clydes in his big team which thrilled many thousands of Canadians at fairs and exhibitions, understood each other, beyond all doubt.

CHAPTER 20

Slim Moorehouse at the Reins

"A herd of horses in harness" was a fair and proper description of the long hitch driven by Slim Moorehouse on Calgary streets in 1925. The outfit, consisting of eighteen two-horse teams driven tandem, was long enough to rival the great string of oxen in a certain bull-train hauling freight on the Macleod Trail in the 1880s—so long, according to the salty bull-whacker who guided it, that "the two bulls in the rear were walking in manure up to their hocks all the way."

The Moorehouse performance was a feature attraction at each of two Calgary Exhibition and Stampede events and when spectators saw the block-long train of teams and loaded wagons being skinned around sharp corners in the down-town business section, they recognized the man with eight reins in his weather-beaten hands as a master in the art of driving.

One visitor remarked that if he were obliged to drive as long an outfit, he'd want a telephone connection with the lead team, a couple of hundred feet away from the driver. In making turns in the Calgary business section, the lead horses were at time completely out of the driver's view.

Slim Moorehouse was a modest farm hand who drifted into Southern Alberta when wheat farming was becoming big business and the Prairie town of Vulcan was, in point of grain delivery, already something of a metropolis. In 1923, year of bumper crops across the West, he was working for Jim Dew of the Bar O N Ranch back in the Buffalo Hills, about twenty-two miles from Vulcan.

Farmers obliged to haul grain that distance to elevators quite naturally looked for ways of reducing the time required. Instead of driving two horses on a wagon load of wheat, they hooked two or three wagons together and hauled the unit with four, six or eight horses. It took expert hands and fingers to control such an elongated tandem but it was a time when driving skills were highly developed in all farming communities. Moorehouse, as one of those Buffalo Hills horsemen with experience in handling four or more reins, wondered if still bigger team outfits—much bigger—might be possible and practical. With an inventive turn of mind, he was determined to find out.

On another farm, not far away, Joe Whittam was displaying some of the same curiosity about big teams and before the two men realized it, they were participants in an unplanned contest to decide who could drive the bigger road team. Moorehouse went over the trail with a wagon-train of wheat hauled by twelve horses in six two-horse teams. Next, Whittam drove out with sixteen horses and neighborhood interest mounted the way it would be expected to soar in an election for reeve. It was now Moorehouse's turn to do something and he replied with twenty horses in a single hitch and then had all winter to plan for a still bigger outfit, one to discourage all rivals and end the contest.

Trouble was that Moorehouse ran out of horses and wagons. But he borrowed from the neighbors—harness, wagons, horses, mules and a couple of cables for use in making a bigger hitch—and finally drove away with twenty horses and ten mules hauling eight wagons filled to the top with hard wheat. Twenty-two miles along the trail he drove the great wagon-train into a Vulcan elevator, unloading one wagon at a time until the last of one thousand one hundred forty-four bushels had been dumped. Then, he turned the thirty-horsepower outfit toward the Buffalo Hills and home.

That was November, 1923. Calgary Exhibition and Stampede officials heard about Slim Moorehouse and his unbelievably long drag of horses and mules and wagons and eagerly invited him to display the outfit on city streets during show week.

The invitation was duly accepted and Moorehouse, with some horses borrowed from Glen House of Gleichen, loaded eight wagons with twelve hundred bushels of wheat, hitched twenty-two horses and ten mules, and drove off in the direction of Calgary. After five or six uneventful days on the trail, the outfit was halted on Calgary's outskirts, there to make camp while the Exhibition and Stampede was in progress.

Calgary's big week opened with the traditional Monday morning street parade and Moorehouse with his horse herd in harness was there to take his place at the rear. Travelling on city streets would present new problems and dangers and all reasonable precautions were taken. Don Briar rode with Moorehouse, prepared to apply brakes to wagon wheels if necessary and four outriders accompanied in case of trouble somewhere between the pole team and the leaders.

Sharp at 11 A.M., Glen House gave Moorehouse the signal to start in the parade. Slim tossed away the remains of a homespun cigarette, gathered eight reins and issued a shrill whistle to the understanding lead team—Dan and Chubb which along with four other horses and the mules were Slim's personal property. The forward teams had to move first, taking up the slack in a long line of leather traces, like a train of freight cars responding to the starting pull of a locomotive. The honest horses and mules, though strange to city sights and sounds—and never before on pavement—settled into their collars as though accustomed to everything on the streets. Outriders, watchful for trouble, saw nothing demanding their attention and finally relaxed to enjoy the parade.

A major test came at the corner of 10th Street West and 7th Avenue where the parade route changed to an easterly direction. But displaying good training, horse and mule pairs did exactly what was necessary in order to make a perfect right turn; leaders Chubb and Dan rounded steadily, cautiously, understandingly, and the others did the same. Only one horse moved clumsily, stepped over a trace, but it wasn't serious.

Slim tightened his handful of reins and roared "Whoa." The outfit stopped; the tug was corrected and with only seconds delay the driver whistled the signal to be moving again.

The crowds cheered at this spectacle: one man sitting nonchalantly on the foremost of eight loaded wagons and in perfect control of a block-long outfit. Slim Moorehouse and his team seemed to make a sizable parade by themselves.

The parade ended, with Moorehouse as the undisputed hero of the day. Horses, mules and wagons returned to the temporary camp in the Manchester district but each day throughout the Stampede week, the thirty-two horse and mule outfit was driven across Mission Bridge and down 4th Street to stop on 1st Street West, between 7th and 8th Avenues. There was one difficulty: the city block wasn't long enough and the lead team stood around the corner on 7th.

At weeks' end, while exhibition visitors talked about the display of training, driving and horseflesh, Moorehouse and his charges took the trail toward Vulcan and Buffalo Hills, stopping only long enough at a city elevator to unload the twelve hundred bushels of wheat he had been hauling for ballast.

The interest created by the team seemed to grow rather than diminish and there was a demand for a return appearance at the Exhibition and Stampede of 1925, marking the 50th anniversary of Calgary's birth. But at this point, the Canadian Percheron Association assumed an important role. Professor W. L. Carlyle who had become secretary of the Percheron Association, recognized the very great promotional advantage which would result if Slim Moorehouse's return to the city were with an all-Percheron outfit. He had no trouble in convincing his Percheron colleagues and Rancher Chris Bartsch undertook to obtain the necessary horses from breeders in the Gleichen district. Slim Moorehouse was quite agreeable to the idea and found himself with a band of all-black Percherons, good ones, the lightest weighing sixteen-hundred pounds and many of them over eighteen hundred. They still had to be trained to work in a multiple tandem, however.

With ever bigger ideas, the Moorehouse plans now called for thirty-six horses in harness—eighteen two-horse teams—and ten wagons of wheat. That was the outfit which drove away toward Calgary about ten days before the show of 1925, with Ernie Richardson from the Exhibition and Stampede present to bring formality to the departure.

This time, both men and horses looked like professionals in the show business. Not only were the horses of superior quality but they carried polished harness and Slim Moorehouse wore a brightly colored shirt. Accompanying, too, was a well-provisioned chuckwagon hauled by four black Percherons. Even the outriders were well mounted on blacks and with a couple of spares there were, altogether, fifty color-matched horses in the party.

Driving the thirty-six horse unit, considerably longer than the one seen in the previous year, Slim Moorehouse again took part in the parade and spectator interest was in no way less. But this time, the great cargo of wheat carried on the wagons was not all in bulk. In the last of the ten wagons were six thousand miniature sacks of wheat to be given away as souvenirs, each little bag bearing the inscription: "World's best Marquis wheat grown at Gleichen, Alberta, hauled by world's largest team." The six thousand souvenirs were tossed out during the parade but the demand far exceeded the supply.

Again the Moorehouse horses performed with perfect co-ordination and precision, taking the sharp turns slowly, individual animals in turn stepping methodically over the heavy cable as it was drawn sideways by teams ahead. "It was beautiful to watch," said an admiring horseman.

The Percheron Association missed no opportunity to capitalize on the display of good and shiny black horses. Tractors had not yet taken over in farm fields and every farmer was a horseman, with or without breed prejudice. Toward the close of the exhibition, the lead team and one other from the Moorehouse string were entered in the dynamometer competitions, then at their peak of popularity and not only won their respective weight classes but made world pulling records for heavy and light agricultural teams.

And on Saturday night, in front of the grandstand, the thirty-six horses in harness made their last public appearance. There to extract the last bit of advertising out of the popular display, W. B. Thorne of Aldersyde, president of the Canadian Percheron Association, made a platform presentation to the owners of the black horses, a trophy carrying the inscription: "Presented by the Canadian Percheron Horse Association to the Gleichen Horse Breeding District in token of appreciation for the world's longest team, composed of Percheron horses driven by one man at the Calgary Jubilee Exhibition and Stampede, July, 1925."

As the team was driven away from the grandstand, a host of boys, men and women followed to further express their admiration for driver and horses. Among those who followed was a visitor from beyond the Atlantic, Captain Bertram Mills, manager of a three-weeks show and circus staged annually in London, England. He had come to Calgary expressly to see the team, he confessed, and he was still following as the sun was settling into the foothills and Slim Moorehouse was driving from the grounds, still mumbling about the horses being magnificent and the driving a masterpiece.

Thus ended the biggest "one-man parade" in the history of Canadian exhibitions.

CHAPTER 21

Milk Route Princess

In earlier years, horses making the largest number of city friends were the ones hauling milk wagons—big, easy going mares and geldings with about as much understanding of turns and stops on the routes as the white-coated drivers who accompanied them. Customers who couldn't call their delivery man by name, spoke in familiar terms of Chief or Clyde or—in the case of Calgary—the highly esteemed steel grey Princess of Union Milk stables.

Storybooks told about the country mouse that became a city inhabitant and the farm boy who adopted urban life and advanced to be president of the company. But it would be an omission if notice were not taken of the thousands of farm-raised horses bought for use in pulling drays, coal vans and milk wagons before street work was assigned to trucks. For many years, city buyers combed the country for horses suited to street purposes.

But working on pavement or gravel-encrusted roads was hard on horses and seven or eight years was about as long as most of them could stand it. Unless feet and legs were exceptionally good, the constant pounding on the hard surface led to crippling and the necessity of early retirement to an environment offering softer footing.

Rubber shoes were tried but the result was unsatisfactory. There had been a double reason for trying rubber; citizens complained when the clang of metal shoes striking pavement broke their slumbers at 4 A.M. The rubber shoes used experimentally gave relative silence but they were found to grip the street so completely that fetlocks and ankles began to swell more than ever and men in charge went back to iron horseshoes, notwithstanding the ire of light-sleeping householders.

Keeping street horses properly shod was a difficult and an unending task. Equine feet were not created for city streets and, on pavement, metal shoes lasted only three or four or five weeks. So big was the problem that companies like Union Milk, with a large number of horses, maintained a full-time blacksmith.

Saskatoon, in 1935, had more than fifty horses regularly employed in milk delivery; Calgary had a hundred. It was a time of transition, however. Horses were still regarded as more economical than motor trucks on milk routes where stops were numerous, but trucks were winning attention. The old delivery wagons were getting new wheels; solid rubber tires had replaced steel a few years earlier and by 1935, pneumatic tires were being adopted. At the same time, milk wagons were being converted from two-horse to single-horse units.

While the wagons were pulled by two-horse teams, the most popular animals were the light and active ones—about twelve or thirteen hundred pounds each—but with the adoption of one-horse vehicles, the animals had to be heavier and those weighing sixteen hundred and fifty to seventeen hundred pounds were immediately favored. The heavy horses were somewhat slower but their disposition suited the job and there was an evident decline in run-aways.

To be a good milk-route horse, breaking and training were extremely important. Mature draughters with reputations for reliability back on the farms where they were raised and worked were not always satisfactory on the streets. George Gauld who came from Stirlingshire, Scotland, in 1925 and took charge of Union Milk Company horses in Calgary—where as many as seventy-two, including spares, were kept at one time—preferred to get young and unbroken horses and thus have complete control of their education for street use. He would break at three years of age, concentrating on starting and stopping, then let them winter in the country and bring them back for steady street work at four years of age.

In breaking young horses, he abandoned the time-honored blinkers—used only open bridles—and observed fewer tendencies to run away.

Under his care were Clydesdale, Percheron, Belgian and crossbred horses and he became convinced that the Clydesdale-Percheron crossbreds, with phlegmatic temperaments from Percheron parents and added wearing qualities from the hard bone and "shock-absorber" pasterns of the Clydesdale, had the best street records.

In every string of horses, as in every group of men, there were those individuals gaining special notoriety. Two of the most famous draught horse personalities on the streets in George Gauld's time were grey mares, Princess and Blossom. The latter, with pronounced weakness for sugar, worked on the city centre route for years. Everybody frequenting the city's main streets knew her and many of them—too many—carried sugar lumps for her enjoyment. Milk company officials were pleased to find their horses making friends; one said that having horses on good terms with the public was about as important as having friendly drivers. But the indulgence in sugar could be carried too far. "Some horses got the idea that collecting sugar was more important than delivering milk," and certain of them became difficult when their titbit wasn't forthcoming. When one of those horses expecting sugar was given a pinch of snuff on a Calgary street, the practical joker received a bite on the upper arm, severe enough to draw blood and teach a lesson.

For Blossom, there was nearly always a lump or two of sugar in front of the Palliser Hotel and the only circumstances causing her to deviate from a straight course on Ninth Avenue was failure of her admiring friend to be there with the customary ration. A picture exists of the grey mare, still hitched to the wagon, standing on the front steps of the

Palliser, looking for the sugar she had come to expect as her right.

But notwithstanding unorthodox antics when in quest of sugar, Blossom was never involved in a run-away or wagon wreck. Her sagacity became something of a legend. At hitching time early in the morning she would walk from stable unattended, identify her particular wagon in a line of forty-two vehicles and back into position between the shafts. And on down town streets, when an operator parked his car immediately in front of her when the wagon was parked at a curb, she would respond to her driver's distant whistle—signal to come along—by backing a few paces, then pulling a safe distance to the left and moving forward without ever colliding or making contact with other vehicles.

Even better known in the city community was Princess, another grey mare, half Clydesdale, half Percheron. Bred at the E. P. Ranch in the foothills, she came to the city as a three-year-old in 1928. She was a massive mare, weighed eighteen hundred and fifty pounds at maturity and stood sixteen and one-half hands. Exhibited regularly in classes for singles and just as often in two, four and six horse teams, Princess was usually at or near the top when ribbons were distributed.

But the record made by the illustrious Princess was unusual in other ways. In the first place, she possessed unusual lasting ability and remained on the same eight-mile route in Calgary, seven days a week, until twenty years of age. It was noted that her deliveries of three hundred and fifty quarts of milk a day for almost seventeen years gave her a lifetime record of more than two million quarts or five million pounds, to say nothing of the tonnage in bottles, cases and wagon hauled regularly.

All residents on the street knew Princess and had words of greeting for her when they met. She was familiar with every stop she was expected to make and when a new man took over the route, Princess could practically show him where to go. When, at Christmas time and New Years, a driver received too many rations of cheer from hospitable customers and lost his sense of direction, Princess brought wagon and driver back to the stables in perfect safety.

And although appearance on the street—moving steadily or standing unattended while motor traffic raced past— made her seem like a paragon of placidity, once in the showring, she displayed the spirit of a chorus girl and pranced to attract the attention of the judge. In the heavy delivery and agricultural classes in which she was shown most commonly, style was desirable along with short backs, deep ribs, heavy muscling, straight action and quality of bone.

When retired at the age of twenty, they said she had never been in a run-away, never been responsible for breaking as much as a milk bottle. It was quite a record because run-aways, the bane of every distributor's life, occurred now and then in spite of precautions. With wagons carrying milk and glass bottles, the consequences could be serious indeed.

George Gauld recalled the day a team delivering milk on Calgary's south side ran away and wrecked a row of power poles, leaving Mount Royal district without electricity for an evening. On another occasion, a new team of sorrels being introduced to a route in the Sunnyside district was startled by a rabbit bounding across the street. Away at a mad gallop, the horses crossed a boulevard and ran through several back yards. The climax came when the hub of a wheel on the swaying wagon struck the corner of a house, taking a portion of the wall completely away and exposing a frightened housewife in the embarrassing act of getting out of bed.

Every city had its milk wagon accidents, leaving milk and broken glass on the streets. Somebody said he found it difficult to understand how milk route horses were on good behavior at any time when they had to go to work so early in the morning. Union Milk Company horses received their first feed of the day when George Gauld came into the barn at 1 A.M. At 3 A.M., they were harnessed and by 3.30 A.M., they were hitched to the wagons and moving toward their delivery routes. It was a one-shift day but by 9.30 A.M., it was time for each horse on the streets to receive a gallon and a quarter of oats in its nosebag. Back in their stalls by mid-afternoon, there was hay and an evening feed of boiled barley. A day's ration, on the average, consisted of twelve pounds of grain, a few ounces of bran and twenty-four pounds of hay.

That's about the way it was in every city, good horses, nicely painted wagons and each milk company striving to present the finest outfits on the streets. And every city had its Milk Wagon Princess, a reliable delivery animal to which men, women and children felt an attachment. The part she filled in the service of producers, distributors and consumers was very great.

But however much the public enjoyed those good horses paying daily visits, their disappearance was even more sudden than the displacement of draught stock in farm fields. Some dairies made the change from horse to truck delivery gradually; some did it at one full swoop. For the company employing the grey Princess, 1953 was the year of change. Horses were dispersed; forty-five white delivery wagons became surplus and the six-horse team show harness which had cost $2200 was donated to the Calgary Exhibition and Stampede. It was about the same with milk distributors in every big city and another romantic chapter of horse history was closed.

CHAPTER 22

The High Steppers

If Calgary had a right to be called the Hackney Centre of the Continent in the twenty-year period after 1890, the chief reason could be none other than the efforts of Rawlinson Brothers whose ranch was on the north side of the Bow River, eleven miles west of the city. What they did for Hackneys on the new western soil was like the J. D. McGregor contribution with Aberdeen-Angus cattle and A. P. Stevenson's work with fruit.

The Rawlinsons were educated Englishmen with inherited wealth, an unfailing love for horses and some conspicuous eccentricities. Rather than read local newspapers, they would await the arrival of the Old Country mail, even though it was a month old when delivered.

But Hackney history in the West began long before the time of the Rawlinsons. As mentioned in another chapter, the celebrated Fireaway, first horse of a recognized breed in Rupert's Land, was an English Hackney. Some people described him as a Norfolk Trotter but that did not necessarily distinguish him from the better known breed. Actually, the Hackney breed was constructed rather squarely upon a foundation of Norfolk Trotter, an ancient strain thought to trace to stock brought to England by Norse invaders.

When the Hudson's Bay Company brought Fireaway from England by way of Hudson's Bay to Fort Garry in 1831, the matter of breed was of slight consequence; what was sought by company men making the selection was simply a stallion capable of improving the semi-native horse stock of the country. And there is no doubt that Fireaway on the

131

Indian-raised mares of the plains produced the best buffalo runners known to the hunters. Hence, it is worth noting that Fireaway—Wonder Horse of his time—was the first Hackney in what is now western Canada; and the first Hackney was the first pure bred horse of any breed in the country.

Hon. M. H. Cochrane of Hillhurst, Quebec, imported Hackneys exactly fifty years after Fireaway's arrival but these did not leave the East and the Rawlinsons were no less the western pioneers in propagating pedigreed horses of their chosen breed.

The land of their choosing was not of the best quality for cultivation but it was excellent for horses and from it went Hackneys which won championships at the biggest horse shows in Canada and the United States. The Hackney, the Rawlinsons were convinced, was the all-purpose horse for the West, fine for crossing on broncho stock, suitable for saddle purposes, big enough to do farm work and stylish enough when hitched to carriage or dogcart to make everybody stop and gaze. It was just a matter of time, they reasoned, until everybody would want horses of this carriage or heavy harness breed and anyone with stock to sell would make a fortune.

The only discernible threat to the future of good Hackneys at the time was the growing popularity of bicycles, about which the *Moose Jaw Times*, June 7, 1895, carried a solemn warning: "How far the bicycle will supersede the horse is hard to say but there is no doubt that it is obtaining a hold in our West that is astonishing. Clergymen make their parish calls on the steed that tires not, neither does it consume oats; doctors make sick calls; creditors make the oft-repeated visit and young men and maidens tell the old, old story during the exhilarating spin in the gloaming on the whirling wheel. The West wants the bicycle. It was built for it. The only hindrance to its general adoption has been the first cost."

Yes, bicycles might have utility, the Rawlinsons and other horsemen conceded, but as a mark of luxury and lofty living, nothing would ever take the place of fine horses, especially high-stepping Hackneys hitched single, double or in tandem and driven by a coachman in an ill-fitting uniform. Prosperous businessmen in Toronto, Montreal and New York chose this means of transportation and were thus delivered at their offices at 9 A.M. At 5 P.M., the same Hackney-hauled carriages called to take the proud owners home. Who wouldn't be proud to ride back and forth behind the trappiest team on the Avenue and listen to the drum-beat rhythm of prancing feet?

Speed was not the aim; rather, it was that proud bearing, stylish carriage of head and neck and the extreme flexion of joints which only the Hackney possessed. The display of action, whether in the showring or on the Avenue, was partly an expression of inherited tendencies, partly training and weighting of shoes; but in any case, the performance was supreme and when a man of that period became suddenly wealthy, his first major luxury was a team of high-steppers and carriage.

When a resident of the frontier town of Lashburn in northwestern Saskatchewan, caught sight of an elegant coach and Hackney tandem being driven by an immaculately dressed coachman—a stylish outfit he recalled seeing at the Toronto Exhibition a few weeks before—he was momentarily surprised. But the explanation was easy enough to understand. James Morrison Bruce of that community had inherited a fortune and at once set out to buy the best Hackneys, Clydesdales, Shorthorns and Ayrshires for his Tighnduin Farm, four miles northeast of the town. Lashburn furnished fewer spectators and rougher streets but the Toronto Hackneys stepped as proudly as they had done previously on Yonge Street. And coming to Tighnduin at the same time were the imported Hackney stallion, Netherhall, and a carefully selected group of English mares.

There was no question about Hackney popularity. Visitors to all the early winter fairs witnessed strong competition in the breed classes and even some ranchers chose Hackney stallions for range breeding. But the undisputed leaders in the Canadian field were the Rawlinsons with all the requisites in ideals, patience and financial resources. They were more interested in breeding than in showing but they were regularly among the exhibitors at Calgary and horses purchased from their ranch became champions at numerous other shows in eastern Canada and United States. The stallion, Saxon, and mare, Pricilla, were bought from the Rawlinson Ranch as yearlings and then went on to win about everything in sight at the World's Fair at St. Louis, including the championships in both male and female divisions of the show. Saxon sold later for $5500. Nobody expected the continent's fanciest horses to come from the Bow River country, even before the provinces of Alberta and Saskatchewan were carved out of the old North West Territories.

The most famous Rawlinson stallion, however, was Robin Adair, a dark chestnut standing sixteen hands and possessing the personality of a gentleman. Foaled in 1890 he was one of many high class and highly priced Hackneys brought from England to accept foothills fare but he never lost his beauty and presence. After being used for breeding for ten years, he was sold to an eastern buyer, then exhibited at the Pan-American and New York Horse Show to win the stallion championships at both. Although the horse left the Rawlinson Ranch for a few hundred dollars, he sold later in the East for $11,000.

When it came time for the Rawlinsons to disperse their famous stud of horses, many of the best mares were daughters of Robin Adair. It was the horse sale of the decade—"Undoubtedly the greatest Hackney sale ever held in Canada, if not on the whole American continent," according to an editor of that day. Taking place at the ranch on July 25, 1907, it was twenty years after the brothers had come to the frontier and selected their ranch land, almost within the shadow of the Rockies.

The Rawlinsons were retiring, going to South America and the sale catalogue showed one hundred fifty-nine horses, most of them Hackneys of the best English strains. Of course the sale attracted the eyes of horsemen everywhere and they came from United States, eastern Canada, British Columbia and many Prairie points. The *Calgary Herald* reporter noted that: "Half a dozen automobiles, dozens of rigs and scores of horses conveyed the crowd to the sale which was in every way a remarkable one." The preparations left nothing undone. A grandstand was built for the comfort of the guests and a range steer was slaughtered to furnish beef for the noon lunch. In a big tent close to the sale ring, "unlimited other refreshments" were served. And Jordison Brothers of Calgary were auctioneers for the occasion.

It was the biggest event in the horsemens' calendar in 1907 because it was, with apologies to the editor, "a sale of the best stock in America if not in the world." The cash receipts for the day totalled about $50,000 and most of the good horses were bought to remain in Alberta.

A few of the animals would go back to England, some to eastern Canada and United States but the biggest single buyer was J. W. Reed of the Baxter, Reed and Company Ranch at Olds. Reed, formerly of Iowa, was already pioneering with pure bred Hereford cattle and Belgian horses, having brought some of the first pedigreed Hereford females to what is now Alberta in 1902. It should be noted also, that it was the purchase of one hundred twenty pure bred Herefords from Baxter, Reed and Company in 1912 which gave Frank Collicutt his significant start with the breed, leading to what was at one time the biggest herd of pedigreed white faces in the world.

Now J. W. Reed was ensuring that the best of the Rawlinson Hackneys would be retained in the West and he paid $20,000 to get the cream of the offering, including the imported stallions, Commodore and Flashlight.

"The Rawlinson bunch of Hackneys has been the best advertisement Calgary ever had," the *Calgary Herald* said editorially (July 26, '07) as a final tribute. "The influence of the Rawlinson Hackney ranch will be felt and remembered for all time to come . . . the achievement of which any two men may well be proud."

Unfortunately, the influence was not felt very long. Interest in Hackneys was maintained for some years but nobody followed with the resources and perseverance brought to the work of improvement by the Rawlinsons. And when automobiles became numerous and the Toronto business executive substituted a sedan with chauffeur for a carriage and coachman, the fortunes of the Hackney fell sharply. Indeed, few, if any, of the familiar breeds suffered such degree of depression, at least for a time.

Only twenty-one new Hackney registrations were entered in the Canadian Stud Book in the year 1931 and some people thought they saw the breed's extinction in Canada. But the pendulum swings one way and then the other and men becoming bored with the machine age sought relaxation in horses. The old English carriage breed was among those with appeal and Hackneys appeared again in the nation's showrings. The increase in numbers of pure bred horses was not spectacular but it was steady and in 1960, the new registrations recorded by the National Live Stock Records totalled one hundred twenty-six.

In their new role, the Hackneys—both horses and ponies—had slight claim to utility but all the arts of training and driving were revived to bring healthful pleasure to people who wanted to see and drive and feel fine horseflesh.

CHAPTER 23

Pacers and Preachers

U ntil gasoline motors brought more speed and more heart failures, roadster horses of Standard Bred type and breeding were considered as sheer necessities—like sheepskin coats in winter and sulphur and molasses tonic in spring. They pulled buggies and cutters over all sorts of roads, hauled doctors, farmers, machinery salesmen and ministers without discrimination. Farmers favored trotters; preachers preferred pacers.

To excel in road speed was everybody's aim. A good horse and shiny buggy with rubber tires placed an owner in a category identified in later years by a Cadillac. And if a man's driver was fast enough to pass other nags on the trail or in a matched race, so much the better.

Racing was a popular pastime in every community. In the absence of something better by way of race tracks, town and city thoroughfares were the scenes of rousing contests. Editors raised protests against street racing on the pretext of danger to pedestrians and local governments piously passed bylaws to make it illegal but policemen looked the other way and speeding continued. Anyway, who was to say that two trotters or pacers dashing up the Avenue—neck and neck— were not taking their drivers for emergency calls at the doctor's office?

Winnipeg's Main Street was a favorite meeting place for horse-men and warnings like the one issued by the *Winnipeg Sun*, August 17, 1881, went unheeded: "Some measures will have to be adopted to check driving in this city. Some gentlemen sporting fast horses indulge in a rate of speed on our principal streets which may be fun for them but terribly dangerous to pedestrians."

At Moosomin, ever a horse-loving community, the racing crowd practically took over the main street each day at noon, now and then varying the program, as on "Wednesday last" when, according to the *Moosomin Courier* of October 9, 1884, "Mr. Arnold of Ellice and a Moosomin sport got into a race, the Moosomin man betting $100 that Mr. Arnold's native pony could not trot to Ellice in three hours and a quarter, a distance of thirty miles. The Shaganappie took the money, with fifteen minutes to spare."

And at Brandon where horses ranked next to home cooked meals in filling men's lives, a race could start on Rosser Avenue at any daylight hour. Citizens would leave their work to watch the trotters and pacers display their courage and watch the horsemen add to their reputations. Sometimes the Brandon stakes were high, as when J. D. McGregor brought in the successful trotter, Dalton McCarthy. But pioneers recalled another McGregor horse which won more fame than success, this a California trotter with fashionable pedigree and pronounced disposition to laziness. The only command to bring unfailing obedience was "Whoa" which some transgressor on the sidewalk shouted in the middle of a Victoria Avenue race on one occasion to bring the high priced horse to a dead stop.

Dealing with heavy horses was a major Brandon industry and harness racing was clearly the chief entertainment. Children raced ponies as they drove home from school and fathers raced as they returned from church services or Christian Endeavor. And nobody had a stronger dislike to being passed by a faster horse than the country minister. Understandable was the satisfaction in being able to leave a boastful church elder or smug choir leader behind in dust.

One of those unscheduled races the local people could not forget, took place at a funeral. There were those citizens who considered it disgraceful that a funeral procession would arrive at the graveside in a cloud of dust and feigned a wish to suppress the story. Others, knowing how the deceased farmer loved a horse race, took the view that this manner of conveying the remains to its last resting place was, after all, entirely appropriate. But by whatever moral standard it was judged, it was the most exciting funeral in the history of that rural municipality, with preacher playing the leading role.

A certain Brandon livery firm commonly furnished the horse-drawn hearse for local funerals and one of the partners drove it. A reliable and slow-going team was kept for the purpose but on this occasion the team was not back from a trip to Rapid City. The hearse driver recognized no choice but to hitch a Standard Bred which had seen some racing along with a young broncho known to be without moral compunction.

The funeral service was to be conducted at the farm home of the deceased and burial at the country church cemetery another two miles beyond. With country road to himself, the experienced teamster had no difficulty in handling the obstreperous horses. At the farm, he might have stabled the team until the service had ended but hoping to eliminate unrest that could result from a strange stable, he decided to keep the horses hitched and simply drive them around the yard now and then to relieve excesses of nervous tension.

The service was long, or so it seemed to a man who had cause to be anxious about the behavior of his horses. With foamy sweat dripping from its overheated belly, the broncho member reared time and again but the driver consoled himself with the thought that when back on the road, the animals would settle down and show some semblance of respect for the occasion.

Finally the service ended and with proper solemnity the coffin was placed in the hearse. But the growing stir caused the unhappy horses to become more fractious. Then there was further delay while neighbors hitched to buggies, carts and democrats. The hearse would lead the slow-moving parade and the Presbyterian minister, driving his own horse, would be next in line, then mourners and others.

The hearse driver felt relief when the minister, with the air of a commanding officer, gave the instructions to move. The procession started with dignity befitting the sad moment although the hearse driver was not finding it easy to hold his team to a slow gait; the Standard Bred's instinct was to trot and the broncho's to run. Nobody in the long cavalcade of vehicles was worried however because the liveryman was known to be one of the best teamsters in the community.

But as events were to show, it was too soon for complacent thinking and at the moment the nervous young broncho on the off side turned his head to glance past bridle blinkers and see the great line of vehicles in pursuit, he reared and lunged forward while his Standard Bred mate showed no disposition to stay behind.

Despite the driver's best efforts, the hearse was now rolling forward at a disrespectfully fast rate. The minister's pacer, ever ready for a race and forgetting the funeral atmosphere, dashed ahead, overcoming any indifferent restraint from the reverend gentleman holding the reins. Those who followed could see no reason for a big gap in the procession and the pace quickened all along the line.

But the forward end of the procession was holding the centre of interest. With the minister's own horse gaining ground, the task of holding the hearse team became nigh impossible. The Standard Bred on the nigh side accepted this as a race; the broncho regarded it as a runaway and, either way, the teamster was having trouble. But the minister's noble pacer, knowing the shame of taking dust from other wheels on the trail, forged forward with the best of intentions. Torn between two instincts, the urge to race being slightly stronger, the churchman made an impressive show of inability to hold his fast horse. But how ineffective it was! Any way one looked at it, here was a horse race and those

who were far behind felt a strong desire to advance sufficiently to witness the finish. All along the line, buggy whips
were taken from their holsters and applied to horses showing signs of lagging. Nobody wanted to be left behind.

At the forward end, where the principal contestants were
now close together, dust was rising in generous clouds. As
the hearse sped over rough spots on the road, the coffin and
contents bounced until there was every prospect of it leaving the vehicle and coming to rest on the trail. The dead
homesteader had taken part in a fair number of races but
never one as closely contested or as eagerly followed by his
neighbors as this.

The hearse team had the centre of the road and was showing no inclination to share it. The minister's horse had the
left ditch, with two wheels on the unmarked sod. The buggy
was coming alongside. Now the three horses were exactly
abreast with still a quarter of a mile to the graveside.

By this time, no spectator could have been certain
whether the community's spiritual leader was pulling or
pressing forward on the reins he held, but with jaws
clamped securely together, lower jaw protruding slightly, his
august black beard swaying in the wind, plug hat tilted forward to anchor it on his head, and one foot braced against
the metal foot-rest, he was driving like a master and revealing as little as possible of what was passing through his
mind. It was a reasonable conclusion that he was not
rehearsing his graveside committal.

There were now two questions in every mind: who would
win the race and could the leading horses be stopped at the
cemetery? For answers, nobody would have long to wait.
The horses were tiring but if the drivers were suffering from
anything more than race track emotion, they were not
revealing it.

With a hundred yards to go, the wild pace was scarcely
slackened and the leaders were still travelling neck to neck.
But the experience of some other road-side races in which

the ministerial gentleman had taken part was not wasted and he and his pacer were saving something for the last dash. Smoothly and expertly, the minister moved into the lead, made a gentle swing into the graveyard, crossed an imaginary line beside the open grave and was undisputed winner by half a length. From those close enough to witness the finish came a shout which on such premises at any other time would have suggested nothing less than the resurrection morning. It was a cheer for the minister and his roadster.

If anybody had a fear about a crisis at the end of the drive it was quickly dispelled. The winner made a loop turn to the right and came to a stop beside the open grave. With the same sort of expert driving the hearse team made a loop turn the other way and stopped like gentle horses at the allotted spot.

There was still the burial. Some of those in attendance seemed to have lost interest. As the mourners and others assembled at the graveside it was not easy for the minister's admiring friends to contain themselves in silence while the last rites were performed. It was probably no easier for the minister to forget his roadside victory and devote his thoughts to the solemn responsibilities.

There were those who took a dim view of the day's events but before the drive home was commenced, the minister's pacer was receiving embraces rather than punishment. The reverend gentleman had no comment but when a horse trade was suggested, he replied: "No thanks, not even if you throw in the Pearly Gates."

CHAPTER 24

Battle Axe and His Kind

The preacher's pacer and, indeed, the best of all trotters and pacers were Standard Breds, tracing to one or all of three imported English stallions, Messenger, Diomed and Bellfounder—the first two being Thoroughbreds and the other a Norfolk Trotter or Hackney. But the real cornerstone of the American breed was a Bellfounder grandson, Rysdyk's Hambletonian 10, foaled in 1849. For a time prior to adoption of the now-familiar name, the young breed was known merely as Hambletonian because of the influence of that great sire. Here was the breed giving harness racing its popularity and importance; here the breed giving Ontario its Grattans, Saskatchewan its Battle Axe and Canada in 1960 a total of one thousand eight hundred and seventeen new registrations to surpass all other horse breeds.

The Hambletonians were strong and courageous horses, bold in gait, usually bay in color and from one thousand and fifty to one thousand three hundred pounds in weight. They were said to be "long livers." Symbolic of something in their nature, Hambletonian 10 lived to the age of twenty-seven years while imported Messenger, Justin Morgan and Peter The Great each lived to twenty-eight. Members of the strain seemed to enjoy racing as much as the men who drove them, confirming an old saying that "half the race horse is in its head."

In the year of Canadian Confederation, Dexter, son of Hambletonian 10, set a trotting record of one mile in two minutes and nineteen seconds, then sold for $40,000. The next Standard Bred sensation was Goldsmith Maid, granddaughter of Hambletonian 10 and one to lower the mile record to 2:14¾. After starting three hundred and eighty-two times and winning on three hundred and thirty-two of those occasions and gaining $365,000 in prize money, this notable mare was proclaimed the greatest trotting campaigner the breed had known.

The first pacer to make a mile in two minutes—the goal of all Standard Breds—was Star Pointer in 1897; and the first trotter to do it, Lou Dillon, in 1903. Skillful selection, better training, experience in driving, more perfection in tracks and superior sulkeys helped to achieve progressive improvement in speed. Although the first two minute mark wasn't made until 1897, some sixty-seven horses racing in 1960 did it or better.

About the time Canadians were displaying an interest in Standard Bred pedigrees, the fabulous Dan Patch was inspiring horsemen meeting at every livery stable on the continent to talk in superlatives. He was another "rags-to-riches" horse, one who came out of obscurity to gross close to a million dollars and pace a two-minute mile at least thirty times. He seemed to belong to Canada as much as to the neighboring country.

Dan Messner of Indiana bought the dam, Zelica, at auction for $255, then gambled $150 for service fee and got a crooked-legged bay foal. That foal of 1896 was named Dan Patch but nobody saw any future for the little fellow. Running his first race as a four-year-old, he still failed to impress anybody except his owner. But at Lafayette, Indiana, later in the year, he was entered in high class pacing company and began a distinguished winning record. Racing at Providence, Rhode Island, in 1902, he became the world's second horse to make a two-minute mark.

Months later, a Minneapolis manufacturer of patent stock food, Marion Willis Savage, bought the great Patch at the sensational price of $60,000. There had been nothing like that figure in horse circles before. But as the horse continued to race like a champion, his fame spread and sales of stock food bearing the Dan Patch association soared.

He was like a great international personality. School children were released from classes when he was to arrive in a town; brass bands met his train and town mayors presented beautifully phrased addresses of welcome. One man was said to have sold a thousand Dan Patch shoes to eager souvenir hunters at a dollar each—quite a few shoes for one horse to have had and discarded.

Retirement from the track came in 1910, the year in which the Canadian Standard Bred Stud Book was started. Thereafter, Dan Patch was used for breeding on the "International 1:55 Stock Farm," and there he died in 1916.

Canada too had some Standard Bred Wonder Horses, Grattan Bars in the East, Battle Axe in the West and some others. The Grattan family began romantically with Grattan Royal, bought by Charles P. Barrett, Parkhill, Ontario, in 1910. But the horse changed hands at $6000, won extensively on the Grand Circuit and made a mark of 2:06¼. Then he injured a ligament and was retired in the State of Iowa. In the meantime his Ontario offspring were maturing with unusual promise and Charles Barrett, his original Canadian owners, set out to find him. Now a derelict and almost forgotten, the horse was not easy to find. But Barrett advertised through the press and finally located him. After buying him for $200, Barrett brought the horse back to Canada. Next year, the Grattan Royal service fee was $100.

His most famous son was Grattan Bars with another perfect "success story," having changed hands at an early age in return for two pigs and two calves, then sold for $175. But Grattan Bars turned out to be a pacer of renown—loved to pace—made a mark of 1:59½ and then moved into a price range such as Canadians hadn't known.

Writing from Kerrwood, Ontario, under date of February 22, 1930, the owner admitted Grattan Bars could be bought but added that he had already turned down some big offers:

"I refused $100,000 three times one afternoon. And to give you a little idea of his value, I bred forty-one mares in 1929 at $500 service fee and I expect to breed over fifty mares in 1930."

Then there was Battle Axe, "the Great Miler from Melfort." Nobody looked for a harness champion to come out of Saskatchewan in the '20s but the West was making a reputation for surprise performances and the Battle Axe success was like Seager Wheeler's first international wheat championship in 1911 or Canary Korndyke Alcartra's four-year-old production of one thousand and eighty pounds of butterfat in three hundred and five days for Ben Thomson of Moose Jaw. Moreover, Battle Axe, being nine years old before his true capacity was demonstrated, almost missed the plaudits of the racing fraternity. Without inherited greatness along with the patience and skill of James Kealey of Melfort, the horse's name would have been unknown beyond the districts of Wilkie, Battleford, Lloydminster and Melfort. His entire career resembled a good pacer overcoming a poor start to win a race.

He was bred at Wilkie, Saskatchewan, by R. J. Speers, and foaled June 2, 1916. Like a bad penny, the horse had one Saskatchewan owner after another and as an eight-year-old came to Jim Kealey in return for an indifferent kind of colt and $50. Kealey raced the colt in the deal just once, winning $3 more than the animal had cost, so he figured "Battle Axe actually cost me $47."

Now a mature horse knowing little in the way of discipline, Battle Axe was a handful for a driver and Kealey did not race him until 1925. But 1926 was the big year for Battle Axe, then in the category known as "aged." On a half-mile track at Melfort he paced an exhibition mile in 2:03¼ with the last half in 1:00¼. That was the fastest mile paced over a half-mile track in 1926. And at Minneapolis, in 1927, he won the 2:08 pace in straight heats, time: 2:03¼, 2:02¼ and 2:01¼. They were the three fastest heats paced anywhere in the world in that year.

"I think the best race while I had him was at Davenport, Iowa, August 19, 1927, in the 2:10 pace, purse $2500," Kealey wrote. "The track was very muddy and he was seventh horse at the half in the first heat . . . He paced the last half in better than a minute, winning from a field of the best horses he ever started with."

About that race the Davenport press had something to say: "The 2:10 pace, the Hotel Davenport for $2500, had eleven starters and was distinctly tough sledding as there were a lot of good ones to face the starter and plenty of contention. Battle Axe took the race in straight heats, thereby ironing out the grievance of the previous week at Burlington and indicating that the Canadian horse is a hard-boiled customer once he gets underway. There was repeated scoring in the get-away for the first round, with Battle Axe at the rail and he got off to a slow start with a flock ahead of him. Little Elenor was the pace maker to the half, at which point Kealey let out a wrap or two and Battle Axe began easing to the front, with Walter Abbe and Atwood coming on at a wicked clip. They took the last turn together and there Battle Axe wound up for a whirlaway finish and came to the wire a half length to spare."

It had all the marks of a Saskatchewan farm boy who went to the big city and became president of his company.

In 1928, Battle Axe lowered his half-mile track record to 2:03, at the same time equalling the Canadian record which had been set by Remola. But in September of that year, Kealey sold the great horse in Minneapolis at a price said to be $10,000, then turned his attention to some Battle Axe sons and daughters which were coming along with the sire's great spirit.

Standard Bred horses, by this time, were well established in Canadian stables and Canadian hearts. The betting crowd had turned to Thoroughbreds but there were still the horsemen who loved a race for the joy of seeing a field of trotters or pacers straining every muscle in the most perfect unison.

They didn't have to bet to find thrill in the perfect display of equine rhythm.

Standard Bred fortunes did not escape depression as well as booms but the trend was upwards, both in track performance and public interest. The great Greyhound, trotting at Lexington, Kentucky, in 1938, made a world record of 1:55¼, destined to stand a long time. And among the pacers, it was Billy Direct with a mark of 1:55, also made in 1938, and standing until it was bettered by a horse which in 1961 looked like the "Man O' War" of the Standard Bred breed. That horse, Adios Butler, was a small and not very impressive yearling which sold in 1958 for $6000 and became the racing sensation of 1961, lowering the world pacing record to 1:54.6 at Lexington and bringing his earnings to over $350,000. With forty ownership shares in Adios Butler quoted at $15,000 each, the horse's book value was seen as $600,000.

With the introduction of the starting gate and resulting removal of monotonous delays in starting, Standard Bred racing found new popularity. By 1960, pari-mutuel betting in the United States reached $819,000,000—close to a billion because more and more people were attracted. Canadian racing was following the same pattern and during 1960 the Federal government supervised pari-mutuel betting at sixty racing association tracks; it represented four thousand one hundred and sixty-eight Standard Bred races with betting totalling $15,302,558.

And in 1960, exactly fifty years after a Canadian Stud Book came into existence, Standard Bred horse registrations far exceeded those of any other horse breed, heavy or light. While seven hundred and sixty-five Thoroughbreds were registered in Canada in that year, the Standard Bred total of one thousand eight hundred and seventeen was more than double. Ontario led the provinces in registration numbers with Quebec next and then the western province which produced Battle Axe.

CHAPTER 25

The Old Racing Breed

The old Thoroughbred—aristocrat among breeds—was England's finest contribution to the world of horses. The influence was like that of Shakespeare in the realm of literature and Pasteur in science. Thoroughbred association with western Canada began at the arrival of the Hudson's Bay Company stallion, Melbourne, in 1848, and with the East a short time later.

Although developed primarily for racing, the breed went to countries on every continent, bringing its refining influence to scores of lesser strains. Wanted and needed were the Thoroughbred quality of feet and legs, long pasterns, clean and flinty hocks, free action, high withers, long neck and trim head. Truly, the Thoroughbred has been the world's leading improver and benefits came to the United States and Canada as to other lands.

By the time of Melbourne's arrival at Red River, the Thoroughbred was already a mature breed in England where it had emerged from a foundation of Arabian and other North African stock. Already it was well established as a racing breed in Virginia to which state the stallion Bulle Rock by Darley Arabian and out of a Byerly Turk mare was taken in 1730. There in the southern states, as in England, human fondness for a horse race was the chief incentive to breeding, and the term Thoroughbred—English equivalent of the Arabian word "Kehilan"—became almost synonymous with racehorse.

In Canada, where enthusiasm for racing didn't wait for the specialized Thoroughbreds, a formal race meeting was held at Montreal as early as 1836. The breed's introduction in the East came after the middle of the century. The Queen's Plate, most important racing event in Canada and oldest fixture to be run continuously on the North American continent, was inaugurated in 1860. And the Ontario Jockey Club, of special significance in Thoroughbred promotion, was organized in 1881.

There in the eastern provinces the breed owed much to men like William Hendrie of Valley Farm, near Hamilton, Joseph E. Seagram of Waterloo and Commander J. K. L. Ross of Sir Barton fame, Montreal. The Hendrie family was for long a leader and the Martimas Wing of Hamilton General Hospital became a memorial to William Hendrie's noted horse bearing that name. After winning the Coney Island Futurity Stakes with Martimas, Hendrie donated the winnings to help finance the hospital extension and the wing was given the name of the horse.

And as the owner of Sir Barton, Commander J. K. L. Ross will always have a place of prominence in the annals of Thoroughbreds in this country. Canadian horses were not entered very often in the Kentucky Derby but Canadian delight knew no bounds when, on May 10, 1919, Sir Barton was the winner and another Ross entry, Billy Kelly, finished next.

Sir Barton, as the first horse to win the Derby, Belmont Stakes and Preakness in one year, was considered by many to have been the greatest horse of his breed in Canadian history—perhaps the equal of Man o' War. Inevitably, there was a clamor for Sir Barton and Man o' War to meet and, sure enough, it happened—and on Canadian soil, October 12, 1920. It was a match race at Kenilworth Park, Windsor, Ontario, the last race for both great horses before their retirement and the purse was $75,000 supplemented by a gold cup said to be worth $5000.

It was Canada's most famous race, one of which horsemen will never cease to talk. Special trains ran to Windsor and interested people of two countries awaited the outcome as though their national self-respect was at stake. Man o' War's reputation was formidable, having been made by twenty wins in twenty-one races in the two previous years; and Sir Barton was fresh from major successes. Strangely enough, the two famous horses had never met until this time.

Sir Barton led in the early part of the race but it wasn't the Canadian horse's day and Man o' War came roaring forward to win by seven lengths, at the same time making a new Kenilworth Track record for a mile and one-quarter. Having won the handsome prize, Man o' War was accorded the honor of taking the first drink from the gold cup. But many Canadians were still unconvinced that Man o' War was any better than the Canadian horse.

Western racing began, as elsewhere, in a strictly informal and unorganized manner. A race could be arranged at any time two horses and two horsemen met and started in the number of minutes it took to tighten saddle girths. Newspapers carried challenges. Edmonton people with eternal eagerness for a race, read in the *Bulletin* of December 27, 1880: "Challenge—I will run my horse within fifty miles of Edmonton for any amount, within one month. Put up or shut up. J. Campbell, Edmonton Hotel."

A few weeks later, January 24, 1881, the same paper intimated that: "E. Brazeau has bought the running horse, Big Knee, from Abram Selwyn for $200. He is prepared to run anything around Edmonton a ¼ mile race at any time." And the *Winnipeg Sun* of November 22, 1881, complained: "Main Street every afternoon is turned into a race course and several narrow escapes have occurred."

Oval race tracks were still uncommon and when they did become a reality they presented some new and confusing problems if one may judge from the experience of two cowboys from the first town south of Calgary to have such a course. It was a town in which the lights were turned off at midnight and on again at 6 A.M. The two men from the hills, after sitting too long at the bar, hitched their team to democrat and started for home. But the trail led across the new race track on the west side of the town and in crossing the track, the horses took the best road which was the race course itself. Men and horses continued to travel all night and at 6 A.M., when the town lights came on, the two sleepy riders decided to turn off the road to see what strange town they had come upon. Great was their dismay when they discovered they were still at the town of their evening pleasures, having driven all night on the new race track.

But with country-wide interest in racing, it was natural that attention would be directed at Thoroughbreds and the late '80s saw at least three high-class breeding studs started in the North West Territories by the Quorn Ranch in the foothills, Beckton Brothers at Cannington Manor and Michael Oxarart on his ranch in the Cypress Hills.

The Quorn, west of Okotoks, was started with English capital in 1885 and received its first breeding stock in '86. A herd of cattle was driven from the South and five hundred broncos, also from Montana and neighboring states. Then, in time for the breeding season, twelve super-quality Thoroughbred stallions from England were unloaded at Calgary and delivered in safety at a new barn on the ranch. The high calibre of the imported horses brought surprise to everybody on the frontier and the first reaction on the part of horsemen was that such excellent sires would be wasted on the kind of mares available thereabout. The centre of attraction in the group was Eagle Plume, a big and stylish bay of which E. D. Adams said: "The best Thoroughbred I ever saw." Included, also, were Acostic who had been a track winner in England, Grand Coup and Yorkist.

Then, in the spring of 1887, while cattlemen were counting their disastrous losses after a severe winter, a large band of Thoroughbred mares from Ireland and England came to the Quorn to place the foothills ranch in a still more distinctive position.

152

With the great Negro stockman, John Ware, in charge of the Quorn horses, the stallions were kept in show shape at all times and young animals given good care. When the offspring from the imported stock began to mature, the quality attracted buyers. The first horses to pull the Town of Calgary firewagon were bought from the Quorn and men responsible for the buying of cavalry horses and police mounts found the Quorn halfbreds to be most suitable. These hardy young horses with substance and hardiness from semi-native dams and quality from imported sires were good enough that the Mounted Police Commissioner announced the force would cease to look to Ontario for its needs.

The Quorn experience proved quite conclusively the Thoroughbred's exceptional worth for crossing, not only in getting police and army mounts from common mares but in producing general purpose and light delivery horses from heavy mares. Farmers, in many cases, found those middleweight crossbreds to be their handiest workers and some of those animals became heavyweight hunters.

While the Quorn was making Thoroughbred history, imported stallions of the breed were brought to Fort Macleod by Frank Strong and High River by the High River Horse Ranch, but in these cases, also, the production of utility horses rather than racing stock was the purpose. Michael Oxarart, the colorful Frenchman who created a chain of police problems following his arrival with horses from Montana and Oregon in 1884, later imported and bred for racing purposes on his ranch in the Cypress Hills.

But the best known early breeders of the West specializing in racing stock were the Becktons of Cannington Manor. The Cannington community, with an intensely English character, was the brainchild of Captain Edward M. Pierce and started in 1883. Fox hunting and racing were pastimes for which the English settlers had no trouble in finding time. The Cannington Manor Turf Club was formed quite early and a race track was constructed. A race meet held there in 1887 drew horses of one kind or another from farms and home-steads for a hundred miles around. Thereafter, the Beckton Brothers—William, Ernest and Hubert—were the undisputed leaders on local tracks. Having come into a fortune, they set about to erect elegant farm buildings, entertain lavishly and own the best Thoroughbreds obtainable. Eight high class mares were brought directly from England in 1889 and a Kentucky-bred stallion, Jase Phillips, was bought to go with them.

"The best appointed stable west of Winnipeg," an editor conceded after visiting the Beckton farm. The racing barn, one hundred and twenty feet long, housed many animals with track reputations, Jack Daw, Miss Tax, Picininny, Imogene and Cloe Martin among them. Didsbury and Picininny were winners at the big Territorial Exhibition in Regina, 1895.

But that was only the beginning. East and west there came better tracks, more skill in training and many more of the good horses. New Thoroughbred names appeared to win public praise. The United States had its Thoroughbred Great—Man o' War, described as the best bargain in turf history, bought by Samuel D. Riddle for $5000 and ultimately declared "The Horse of the Century"; Citation with a one-mile record of 1:35.6; Alsab which was bought by Al Sabath at Saratoga Sales for $700 and then won $350,000, and others. Canada's list of "Greats" was not quite as spectacular but it holds significance—great sires like Yorkshire Lad, foaled in 1902; Will Somers, imported by the Duke of Windsor when he was Prince of Wales; Craigangower, imported by James Speers; Marine by Man o' War, and so on.

And in 1960—exactly one hundred years after the first Queen's Plate event—Canada's leading sire was another "Great," Chop Chop owned by Mr. and Mrs. E. P. Taylor, Windfield Farm, Ontario. At the same time, Victoria Park by Chop Chop and bred by Mr. and Mrs. Taylor, was the Horse of the Year in track performance, also pronounced "the best ever among Canadian-breds."

CHAPTER 26

Mr. Racing

"A race horse," somebody remarked, "is an animal that can take thousands of people for a 'ride' at the same time." Somehow, the "riders" love it, love the legalized betting, and their enthusiasm has made Thoroughbred racing a major sport and major business across Canada.

But racing wasn't always on the high plane now taken for granted and for the order brought ultimately to it in western Canada, the race-loving public can thank the pioneer efforts of the late R. James Speers, Thoroughbred breeder with outstanding successes and distinguished leader in racing organization.

When he took a Thoroughbred mare to settle a debt of $200, many years ago, it may have been the most important single transaction in western racing history, inasmuch as it led to the founding of Whittier Park Stock Farm near Winnipeg and the most imposing breeding record between the Atlantic and Pacific Oceans up to that time. As determined from annual track performances, Speers qualified to be named Canada's "Leading Breeder" in 1939 and each of the six consecutive years, 1946 to '51, inclusive. In eight other years, he was the runner-up for the same All-Canadian distinction, making a record no other western breeder had approached and none in the nation had surpassed.

This man, virtually the czar of western racing for a quarter of a century, loved a good horse of any kind—and loved to gamble. A chart showing the fortunes and reverses in his career would look like Rocky Mountain peaks against a sunset sky.

The Speers association with racing began the day after his arrival in the West. Sensing only limited opportunity with his father's blacksmith shop where Malton Airport stands today, the young fellow resolved to see the West. He arrived at Winnipeg with a bicycle and $4. When he reached Regina, assets were reduced to the bicycle without dollars and in order to extend his journey, he was obliged to take to the trail. Pedalling all the way to Battleford, his arrival coincided with the payment of Treaty Money to the Indians and pony races were being arranged to make it easier for the betting Crees to part with their cash. Speers had no money but he sold his watch for $2 and after betting on Albert Champagne's Thoroughbred mare, Minuette, he ended the day with a profit of $80.

Battleford was a community of horsemen, with interest slanted strongly toward Standard Breds, and the 18-year-old Speers decided to stay. His first job was with Ben Prince— later Senator Prince—building a mill. That completed, he and Albert Champagne and Métis John Todd took a holiday, drove over three hundred miles by buckboard to attend a harness race meet at Calgary. The pleasure of the races more than justified the effort, at least until the way home when Todd forgot to hobble the team as camp was being made for the night. In the morning, the horses were missing. The men searched in vain and finally completed the journey from Sounding Lake to Battleford on foot, with no rations except a cold prairie chicken and bag of sugar.

In 1908, Speers began farming at Wilkie and at the same time started building flat warehouses for grain storage. Two years later this sideline enterprise included ten country elevators, all full of wheat. But misfortune wouldn't leave him alone and when the price of wheat crashed, Speers was ruined, temporarily at least. He turned to horses. It was instinctive. Nobody could fool him on a horse and between 1910 and 1912, when farmers had big needs for power, Speers handled and sold five thousand head, "$225 for the sound horses, $150 for the cripples."

Anyone who loved the uncertainties of a horse race or the horse business might have been expected to try politics and Speers accepted a Conservative nomination in the rabidly Liberal Constituency of Tramping Lake. Harry Rudd, a young Englishman who had been working with Speers continuously from the time of coming to the country, was his agent. Together they worked hard against Liberal Jim Scott but it was a lost cause and on the morning after the election, Speers called for a general report. Employing the eloquence of brevity, Rudd replied: "You've lost five months of your time; you've spent $10,500 of your own money; you are charged with eleven hundred gallons of beer for the picnics; three of your workers have been arrested and one is still in jail; you're faced with a $12,000 libel suit and you're licked by two hundred and thirty-nine votes." Otherwise, everything was fine.

When the First World War broke out, the Canadian government wanted cavalry horses and Speers undertook a task of buying and assembling. On February 20, 1916, while on a horse buying journey in the Western United States, a locomotive plowed into a sleeping car of another train, killing outright five of the six men in it. Speers was the sixth and at first he too was thought dead. At best he was wrecked about as badly as the sleeping car telescoped by the awful impact. Rescuers rushed him to hospital and attendants there sent messages to all the relatives who should be with a dying man.

But Speers didn't die. Fractures were numerous and doctors put him in a cast where he remained for weeks and weeks. The stay in hospital lasted thirteen months and for another year the man didn't walk. Nor did trouble come alone. While in hospital, a lien note against his elevators came due and before he could satisfy the creditors, the elevators were sold.

But those months in hospital were not a total loss. They offered time for an analysis of mistakes and plans for the future. As soon as he was able to walk, Speers started a livestock commission business in Winnipeg and declared his intention of doing something about organized racing. There had been practically no racing in the city since 1914 and the sport was in disrepute. But he knew the public would still foresake all other recreation to enjoy the horses. Had not the races at Old Battleford attracted settlers for fifty miles? And had not John Todd and Albert Champagne accompanied him all the way from Battleford to Calgary by buckboard, expressly to see the races?

Speers started things by organizing the Winnipeg Driving Club in 1921 and holding a three-day meet at which pari-mutuel betting was introduced at wickets cut in a board fence. To liven things up some saddle horses were brought from the Sumner Riding Academy and given fancy names while their riders were decked out in silks. "To my amazement," said Speers, "more money was bet on these running horses than on the match harness races." But apart from the practical lesson about the popularity of the runners, things didn't go overly well; on the first day, tickets were cashed before the cashiers learned that a winning horse had been disqualified. Next day somebody stole the cash. But Speers was getting experience.

The fact was that racing in Winnipeg needed strong leadership to take it out of the hands of sharps and bookmakers and give it an air of regularity. His next move was to take over Winnipeg River Park and this led to the building of Whittier Park on the St. Boniface side of the river. Whittier opened in 1924 and in the next year, Polo Park was built, also Chinook Park in Calgary. Now, sensing the need for a strong organization to control the expanding sport for the protection of both horse-men and public, he formed the Prairie Thoroughbred Breeders' and Racing Association.

The new organization was exactly what western racing needed and, looking back upon its first five years, F. L. Smith, an observer from the beginning, wrote: "As a result, racing has undergone a vast change for the better, to such an extent that an appreciative public now regards racing as the major sporting event . . . The association has been conspicuously successful in stimulating interest in the breeding of light horses of all classes."

"That's what we want," Speers repeated, "an interest in breeding better horses right here." He was now devoted to Thoroughbreds and with an urge to have his own breeding farm where he could enjoy good horses twelve months of the year, he bought a nine hundred acre place close to Winnipeg and proceeded to stock it with the best he could buy in Kentucky. As Whittier Park Stock Farm, it quickly became a place of beauty and productiveness, and the nursery of many of Canada's best Thoroughbreds.

Conspicuously, Whittier became the home of some of the best sires of the breed. Craigangower—once a $30,000 purchase—was bought in Kentucky in 1933 and his arrival marked the beginning of better Thoroughbreds for all Canada. Then came Cudgel, the greatest handicap horse in Canada and Leading Sire in 1939; Brooms, a winner of the Hopeful Stakes; Marine, by Man o' War; and Osiris II, a gift from R. S. McLaughlin of Oshawa.

Late in 1949, after Speers won Canada's "Leading Breeder" distinction for the fifth time, it was announced that Whittier Park Farm had gone over the top with track winnings at more than a million dollars for horses bred there. Speers was the first Canadian breeder to do it.

And while he was helping himself, he was assisting others. Money wouldn't buy the famous stallion, Brooms, but with assurance of a good home for the rest of his life, the lovable old horse was shipped to University of Saskatchewan, freight prepaid.

And the story of Omar's Gift has been told many times. As A. G. "Scottie" Kennedy and Speers watched the two-year-olds working at Whittier Park one morning in April, 1942, the older man knew how much the younger one longed to own a good Thoroughbred. "If you'll make your choice before the two on the track reach this point, you can have it for the cash in your pockets," Speers offered.

Kennedy was all attention. "It's a bargain," he shouted. "I'll take the light bay filly." Then, turning his pockets inside out, he exposed a total of 37 cents. But he bought a Thoroughbred mare and a few weeks later the 37 cent mare won the Winnipeg Futurity and a purse of $2205. Speers sold one Thoroughbred for 37 cents and another at almost the same time for $3700.

The name of Speers became known wherever there were Thoroughbreds and racing on the continent, even in Hollywood circles. When he sat in a friend's box at Santa Anita track, a stranger took a seat beside him, saying: "I hope you don't mind if I sit here a minute."

"I don't mind," Speers answered, "but this is my friend's box and he just asked me to keep any bums out. But my name's Speers. What's yours?"

"Oh, I thought you were Jim Speers," the other replied. "I'm Don Ameche."

"Glad to know you, Mr. Ameche," Speers said. "And what line of business are you in?"

After that they were friends.

Under his guidance, racing became ever more popular across the country and pari-mutuel betting on Thoroughbreds became bigger and bigger. In 1960, an even hundred years after the first running of the Queen's Plate in Canada, the money wagered at seventeen Canadian tracks totalled $126,117,121. Government taxes on it came to $8,393,439 and prize money to horsemen was $5,772,100. And there was another annual payment which brought special satisfaction to Jim Speers; it was the five percent of purses paid to breeders of winners and administered by the Speers-created Prairie Thoroughbred Breeders' and Racing Association. In 1959 the payments were $21,938, bringing the total in all years since it was started in 1926 to $251,470.

Speers, somehow, couldn't do things on a small scale. Profits were big; losses were big and so were his benefactions. And what he did for Thoroughbreds was to build a well-ordered racing empire and give it the best of horses.

CHAPTER 27

Here Comes Joey

Nearly every breed has some horse or horses with special gifts in capturing human hearts—a Bouncing Buster, a Robin Adair, a Speckle Boy or a Rex Stonewall. Such was the American racehorse, Exterminator—familiarly known as Old Bones—and such was the unprepossessing little black gelding, Joey, whose spirit and track performance made him the best known and most widely loved Canadian horse of his time.

Joey was an Alberta-raised Thoroughbred with great racing names on his family tree. As with other representatives of that old breed, ancestors fraternized with English kings and queens and brought national importance to the racetrack. Great Thoroughbreds have been great racehorses and Joey, as one of them, succeeded in winning more money than any other Canadian-bred during the '30s. But it wasn't just the capacity for speed in his limbs that touched the race fans; it was largely a matter of inherent perseverance and fighting spirit. As an eight-year-old, when he had his least successful season, the racing scribes said: "Joey is through." But the stout-hearted little gelding defied a saying in sporting circles, that "they never come back," and gallantly fought to regain his finest racing form. Joey was a "comeback horse."

Even before his death, Joey was becoming something of a legend and when he died in 1941 he was accorded a hero's burial beside the Elbow River, right in Calgary's Exhibition Park.

But what adds extra lustre to the story of Joey's successes is that nobody expected him to amount to anything. He was the scrawny young horse in which no owner could find pride. He was the "ugly duckling," foaled near Calgary in 1930.

Good Thoroughbred horses had often changed hands at from $5000 to $50,000, and Samuel D. Riddle was said to have refused offers of $260,000 and $400,000 for the celebrated stallion, Man o' War. Joey, by contrast, was a "two-bit" horse, actually sold with his mother on the first and only bid of $185. It was late in the spring of 1930 and Arthur Layzell whose horse breeding farm was on the Chestermere Lake side of Calgary, was offering a cut of Thoroughbred mares and foals by auction at the Calgary Exhibition Grounds. Among the local breeders of Thoroughbreds, Jacques Brothers—Leonard P. and C. L., whose farm was on the west side of Calgary—were interested in adding a mare or two. Leonard phoned his brother to say he was going to the sale with the idea of bidding on a mare, Juanita Parks, and her filly foal. The brother's reply was: "Better buy two mares and there'll be one for each of us."

Depression was beginning to be felt across the country at that time, and bidding was slow, discouragingly slow, as Arthur Layzell saw it. Jacques bought Juanita Parks and her filly foal for $185. It was his main reason for coming to the sale although he expected to pay more. With such slow bidding, Arthur Layzell decided against bringing the thin mare with the poor colt into the ring because, as he was heard to remark: "These people will take a look at that foal and refuse to bid. I'll take them back home."

The mare in question was Aileen Hoey and her three-weeks-old foal by Dr. Joe was the young thing later given the name of Joey. Leonard Jacques heard the owner's remark about taking the last mare home and, knowing she had good breeding, he interjected a suggestion: "My brother would take a mare. If you'll put that mare and foal up I'll start them at $185."

Mr. Layzell accepted the proposal and mare and foal were brought into the ring. The auctioneer said something complimentary about the mare's breeding; there wasn't much else to say. "The mare and foal looked terrible," Leonard Jacques recalled. But, good as his word, Jacques made the starting bid of $185 and the auctioneer called for "any advance on $185?" Minutes passed and the original bid was not raised. Finally, the auctioneer said: "Sold—to Leonard Jacques—$185."

It might have been a time to recall that a big price will not make a Thoroughbred run any faster, nor will a mean price prevent one from breaking a track record. There have been those high priced colts which never won a contest, just as there were horses like the American Thoroughbred, Alsab, which sold at $700—a mere nothing in Thoroughbred trans- actions—and in 1941 made some of the horsemen say: "Best since Man o' War."

The two mares and foals were taken to their new home and C. L. Jacques, with obvious disappointment, inspected Aileen Hoey and her black colt. The mare might be a fair investment, he reasoned, but "that youngster looks like a misfit." To be gracious, however, he said: "All right, I'll take them, even if the foal is no good."

Time passed and Joey looked no less like a scrub. If any- thing, he looked worse, being small and thin. C. L. Jacques grew more unhappy about owning such a specimen and offered his brother $200 to exchange mares and offspring. The brother declined and C. L. Jacques was stuck with the poor colt.

Late in 1931, plans were being made for the training of any rising two-year-olds good enough for the racing season. Juanita Park's filly and one or two others would be taken to Victoria Park in Calgary and there trained by "Doc" Ronald. But what should be done with the runty black gelding? It was clearly evident that Joey would never win anything on his appearance. A general plainness coupled with his small size and perpetually thin condition would go against him in the show ring. If he were to pay for his oats he'd have to do it on the track. Altogether, he looked too much like the depression then spreading itself across the country. But Trainer Ronald suggested it would be about as easy to take the colt along as to leave him behind where he'd require separate care. "We might as well break him," he said, "then you can decide if he's worth keeping."

And so, Joey went to Victoria Park but attracted no attention—at least not until the following April when Trainer "Doc" Ronald showed a sudden desire to buy a half interest in him. He had clocked the unhandsome colt's performance and was startled at what he discovered. Moreover, here was gameness and determination as well as amazing speed. "You've got something there," Ronald confessed. "Might be we'll be reading about that little fellow someday. He makes me think he really wants to be a racehorse."

Joey's first race was at Winnipeg on May 23, 1932. He was the smallest horse in the race—barely 14¾ hands—and hardly anybody picked him to win. But, sure enough, he romped home a winner and Trainer Ronald repeated: "That little cuss has something you don't see every day." In that two-year-old season, Joey started six times, was a winner on four occasions and was second and third in the other events. One of those winning races was the Winnipeg Futurity and before the season ended he was being acclaimed the best two-year-old of the year. Leonard P. Jacques was present to see the colt win the Winnipeg Futurity and get one of the thrills of his life. Jokingly, he then asked his brother if he was still interested in giving $200 to exchange mares and offspring bought at the Layzell sale.

Joey continued to win. At three years of age he was up to fifteen hands, still no beauty, but his courage and driving determination were beginning to appear as handsome qualities and the horse was winning friends wherever he went.

In 1935, he started in eighteen races, was the winner nine times, second four times and third four times to qualify for $10,630 in purse money. Then, in the next couple of years, Joey's racing fortunes slumped for some reason and it was in 1938 that the pundits said he was finished as a winner. In that season, too, he was taken in a $700 Claiming Race in Winnipeg and lost to the Jacques Stable. After a short rest, Joey, carrying the colors of H. A. Bruns, came back stronger than ever. Horsemen still talk about his performance in the Western Canada Handicap at Winnipeg on June 22, 1940, as the greatest race of his career. He was now ten years old and running against younger horses. Heavy rains converted the track to a mire and rain was still falling when six Thoroughbreds went to the post. The fans made Joey their favorite but he started poorly. He had an annoying habit anyway of failing to find his stride until the last half of a race, something which must have aggravated heart-failure among his supporters. At the end of the first half of this race he looked like nothing better than a third or fourth prize winner. But then Joey, with resolve to win, presented a display of effort the spectators couldn't forget. Plastered with Red River gumbo, Joey passed one horse, then another and finished with a comfortable lead, just as thousands of his racing enthusiasts in the stands should have expected him to do. It was Joey's undying will to win that made people so fond of him.

It was now wartime and in 1941, Joey was drafted for a new and auspicious role, that of officially opening the Victory Loan Campaign in Winnipeg. As the leading Canadian-bred winner of the decade, he was brought from Vancouver by special train and at the Winnipeg City Hall, was given a formal civic welcome by Mayor John McQueen. Then, on his behalf, a cheque for $18,500—half of the eleven-year-old's track winnings—was turned over in payment for the first Victory Bonds in the drive. The purchaser was R. James Speers, honorary secretary of the Prairie Thoroughbred Breeders' and Racing Association. And during the race meet at Polo Park in the weeks following, horsemen were given opportunity to purchase portions of the bonds taken temporarily in Joey's name.

Joey was returned to Victoria Park in Calgary and there, on August 15, 1941, the famous campaigner died. Horsemen were saddened as though they had lost a friend. Manager Charles Yule of Calgary Exhibition and Stampede agreed that burial might be right there on the grounds where Joey lived much of his life. The necessary digging was completed and with a group of horsemen present, they buried Joey, close to the Elbow River. Said one of the men present: "I never saw more wet eyes at a funeral."

Nor did Joey's part in raising Victory Loan funds end with his death. The horsemen did not forget and on October 16, 1944, three years after his death, there was an auction sale at Calgary at which the racing shoes of Joey, Whirlaway and Seabiscuit were sold. There was one unusual feature of this sale: the bids taken were pledges to buy Victory Bonds.

It was like another contest between monarchs of the turf and in this one, Joey won by a long length. Bidders with strong sentiment wanted Joey's last racing plates, silver mounted on pieces of aeroplane propeller wood. The shoes of the mighty Seabiscuit brought $10,000 in Victory Bond purchases and Whirlaway's went for $6000. But Joey's shoes accounted for a total of $40,000. Mervyn "Red" Dutton of National Hockey League fame got one on a bid of $15,000, while the other three of the little horse's last shoes were knocked down at $10,000, $10,000 and $5000 respectively.

It was the gallant Joey's last race and, because his friends were loyal to his memory, he was the winner.

CHAPTER 28

Reminiscing with Rex

R ex Stonewall was a chestnut American Saddle Horse stallion with an amiable personality and a storybook career. Just about everything, it seemed, happened to Rex. He was in so many city street parades that he knew all the popular routes; he won showring honors at Calgary and Edmonton, was in the cold clutches of horse thieves, pranced with the Mayor of Toronto in his saddle and, only by the most uncomfortable margin escaped an undignified end in foxmeat. But, finally, as an old timer, he lived in comfortable retirement with all the Welfare State security his owner, the late Archie Currie of Calgary, could provide.

Even being a representative of the American Saddle Horse breed would have been enough to bring some distinctiveness. If the horse species was God's finest creation, surely the high-stepping Saddlebred with animation, symmetry and quality was one of the crowning achievements in human effort to make a good thing better.

Breed origin was mainly in Kentucky where riding horses commanded much of men's time and thought. Wanted were animals which would be useful as well as graceful and beautiful. Thoroughbred sires on pacing and racking and ambling mares used on plantations gave rise to elegant saddlers with predisposition to racking gaits.

As in the Standard Bred and Morgan breeds, one founding sire was more influential than others; in this case it was the Thoroughbred called Denmark, foaled in 1839. From a mare described as a "Canadian pacer" came Denmark's greatest son, Gaines' Denmark, and with a blend of the best characteristics from various strains, the most striking of all American breeds emerged. Some specimens were described as three-gaited like the more conventional riding horses, while others showed a peculiar capacity for additional gaits—rack and single-foot or running walk—to be classified as five-gaited. By the time of the great Rex McDonald—black stallion foaled in 1890 and sired by Rex Denmark, by Crigler's Denmark, by Washington Denmark, by Gaines' Denmark— the breed was unsurpassed in style and finished beauty. It looked like something created for showring and boulevard.

Such was the background of horses like Rex Stonewall, bred by Western Canada's leading champion of the breed, Joe Fulkerth, Didsbury, Alberta, and foaled in July, 1937, when Western Canada was feeling the worst drought in its history. Actually, there wasn't much interest in the American Saddle Horse breed at that time of adversity although Fulkerth's pioneer devotion was unwavering.

Born in Iowa, December 18, 1884, Joe Fulkerth was raised in Missouri where the new breed was gaining a foothold. As a farm boy, he enjoyed the luxury of riding a horse of this breed to Sunday School and racing it against neighbors' nags on the way home. In 1907, the family came to Alberta, settling at Didsbury and bringing ideas about raising Saddle Horses and mules.

By 1928, Joe Fulkerth was able to give expression to a boyhood ambition; returning to Missouri, he invested in the best possible foundation of American Saddle Horses, four high class mares and a three-year-old stallion called The Dare. It took courage to buy into a breed which was still practically unknown on the Canadian side. Alex Galbraith of Edmonton had imported a few individuals but nobody was breeding horses of this kind with any show of determination and only a few people were really conscious of their existence. In the hope of gaining a quicker return from his breeding enterprises, the man added a jack to his list of purchases and resolved to raise mules.

The mule market was good and Fulkerth shipped carloads of them from his Didsbury farm to Kansas and Nebraska. The interest in American Saddle Horses came more slowly. Western Canadians had shown an interest in Rawlinson's Hackneys but they were reluctant to do as much for the American Saddle Horse breed, the only one which could equal or outstep the Hackney in the showring.

In 1929, Fulkerth took his Saddle Horses to Calgary Horse Show and received a cool reception. It was the first time representatives of the breed appeared publicly in the West and the Calgary management refused to accept the entries. But upon second thought it was decided that the man from Didsbury might be allowed a few minutes in an afternoon to stage a demonstration, "at no cost to the show." Fulkerth rode The Dare, demonstrated the five gaits and spectators were delighted. The show manager came offering fifteen minutes for a similar exhibition each remaining evening but everything about the week's performance was still at the horseman's expense.

Before the week ended, an Edmonton Horse Show official who had been in the audience invited him to bring his horses to the northern city in the following week, promising a cash bonus if he'd repeat the demonstrations of slow gait and rack as well as walk, trot and canter. Fulkerth accepted and the Edmonton committee not only paid $75 in bonus but accepted late entries in regular classes and he was $185 richer at the end of the week.

Still pioneering with the breed, Fulkerth went back to the United States for more horses. The good sire Dempsey's McDonald was imported in 1934, then Kalarama Rex A, by Kalarama Rex, by Rex Peavine, by Rex McDonald. In 1943, Edgemorr's Star Genius was imported, this high quality chestnut being by Fair Acres Genius, by King's Genius, by Bourbon King, by Bourbon Chief—some of the greatest names in the American Saddle breed. After being used for some years, Edgemorr's Star Genius was sold to Montana where he came to be regarded as one of the best sires of his generation.

Gradually, the admirers of fancy horses were beating a path to the Fulkerth farm and horses were being shipped to points extending from Victoria to Halifax. Some of those horses found their way to the Royal Winter Fair and United States shows and won high honors.

As part of the Fulkerth importation of 1934, there was a good mare, Tishie Anne, and she, to the service of Kalarama Rex A, produced the subject of this sketch, Rex Stonewall. While still a colt, he was sold to Jerry Puckett of Calgary and in 1944, became Archie Currie's property, Archie Currie's riding horse and Archie Currie's companion. With Currie in the saddle, Rex distinguished himself in parade and glamor classes which he loved and was repeatedly called upon to lead street parades.

When a trainload of Calgarians went to Toronto to see their Stampeders win the Grey Cup in 1948, Archie Currie and Rex went along. There would be some parading and what would a Calgary parade be without Rex? But instead of carrying Currie in the Toronto parade, Rex carried Mayor Hiram Walker who said he hadn't been in a saddle for 25 years. It happened this way: the mayor made the mistake of looking admiringly at the noble Rex and almost immediately found himself in the saddle, with no easy way of getting down. And so, Rex and His Worship paraded their way from the Royal York Hotel to Toronto's City Hall.

But the manner in which Rex made friends in the East only added to Currie's disappointment in being separated from his horse in the weeks following. A rancher from the foothills asked: "What will you take for him?" Currie, thinking the conversation to be so much banter, replied: "About ten of your young horses." To Currie's surprise and horror, the other party said: "That's a deal." According to a horseman's ethics, a verbal deal is as binding as a written contract. Currie couldn't back down and he parted with his horse.

But the stallion's adventures were only beginning. In 1950, when the foothills ranch to which Rex went was sold, the horses on it had to be moved, and quickly. A message was sent to Currie: "If you want your pal Rex back at no cost to you, come and get him at once." The message, however, became delayed or lost in its transmission and when Currie failed to make reply, a cut of two hundred and fifty ranch horses—Rex included—was shipped to the horsemeat plant in Calgary. The noble Rex, it seemed, was on his way into fox rations.

When the message finally reached Archie Currie, he rushed to the slaughtering plant as though goblins were chasing him. On his arrival at the plant, he searched eagerly through the holding yards but Rex wasn't there. He was nowhere to be found. A check with the records and workmen showed rather conclusively that the horse had not been driven into the plant for slaughter. And the fence was too high to allow a horse to escape by jumping. There was just one other possibility, that the horse had been stolen. The police were notified and a search was started with Currie taking part.

Five days passed and there was no word about the lost stallion. Then a mail carrier from Bowness reported seeing a horse meeting the description in a stable out his way. The animal, he had learned, was found in a town garden and an irate householder caught and stabled it there. Currie rushed to Bowness and, sure enough, identified the stray as Rex. The evidence pointed to only one conclusion: the stallion had been taken from the corral at the plant and whisked into the country by thieves who knew a good horse when they saw one. Then, however, Rex gained his freedom and was on his way back to Calgary when caught in the act of lunching in an urban garden.

From Bowness, Rex was brought back to the quarters he had occupied in earlier years and Archie Currie vowed the horse would have no more worries about sale or slaughter plants or horse thieves. Sharing a barn with the big black Clydesdales which pulled the Burns and Company wagons, Rex had a box stall, a dry bed and all he could eat until overtaken by death from old age.

In the meantime, the imported mare from which Rex came was bought by a Fraser Valley breeder and after he sold $8500 worth of her offspring, he sold her as a nineteen-year-old for $650.

And as for Joe Fulkerth, he continued to be Canada's biggest and best known breeder of American Saddle Horses— at least until 1951 when at the age of sixty-seven he considered retiring. Accordingly, there was a dispersal sale with forty-eight of the good horses coming to the auction block.

Naturally, it was a bad day for the pioneer and as the horses for which he had strong affection began leaving the farm, he was so moved with regret that he wanted to buy back some of the mares. One man accepted $50 more than he had bid for a mare and left her on the farm and, later, Mr. Fulkerth was able to buy back several more of the good mares. Before long, he was again in business, doing chores through long hours, showing visitors his favorites and watching foals grow into horses.

At the age of seventy-seven, ten years after his "retirement sale," Joe Fulkerth, having abandoned all thought of retiring, said: "When a man is doing something he enjoys, he'd be foolish to quit."

When Joe Fulkerth imported his first Saddle Horses, there was no Canadian Stud Book for them and he was obliged to register everything in the United States. For a time horses of the breed were recorded in the General Stud and Herd Book of Canada and only in 1948 was the Canadian American Saddle Horse Breeders' Association incorporated under the Live Stock Pedigree Act. As late as 1961, annual registrations were not numerous but, nevertheless, this breed with which Joe Fulkerth pioneered in the West—or in Canada as a whole—had an unchallenged place in almost every horse show program.

CHAPTER 29

Arabians Rediscovered

Polished with the sand of centuries and swathed in desert legends, the small but vigorous Arabian is like a rare jewel among horses. The proudly-arched neck, gay carriage of tail and triangular shape of head with dished profile and fine muzzle, combine to give this horse of the desert a saucy style and loftiness. Indeed, it should not be forgotten that other breeds owe much for their acquired quality to infusions of Arabian, the horse with refinement as its hallmark.

Here is the oldest of all present-day breeds. England's Lady Wentworth, uncompromising authority on the breed, contended that Arabian pedigrees could be traced back four thousand years to the great-great-grandson of Noah. However this may be, Bedouin masters selected with care and so treasured the good ones that not many were permitted to leave Arabia. A few taken to England during the 17th century furnished foundation upon which the Thoroughbred breed was built and a stallion known as Ranger, imported to the United States in 1765, sired the grey horse George Washington rode in the Revolutionary War. But until after the beginning of the present century, only a few individuals were brought to North American shores.

Not until 1908—two years after Homer Davenport of New Jersey brought twenty-seven head from native land— was the Arabian Club of America started, with headquarters at Berlin, New Hampshire. For many years, pure bred Arabians could be registered in the Arabian section of the American Thoroughbred Stud Book; and Thoroughbred-

Arabian crosses, known as Anglo-Arabs, could be registered in the Thoroughbred section of the same book.

But strangely enough, that most ancient of all horse breeds, was much later in making its appearance in Canada. Boasting horsemen often pointed to a high quality animal of uncertain breeding and said: "It's part Arabian." But such was generally wishful thinking because, even when Canadian horse numbers reached their highest point in 1921, the West had only one pure bred of the race and pure specimens in the East could have been counted on the fingers of one hand. Even in 1950, only twelve new Arabian registrations were entered in the National Live Stock Records at Ottawa. But at that midpoint of the present century, Canadians seemed to rediscover the Arabian horse as they might a priceless heirloom long in hiding. Interest mounted, especially in the West. Chilliwack Agricultural Association sponsored an All-Arabian International Show in conjunction with its August exhibition in 1956. And Calgary, in 1958, held the first All-Arabian Show on the prairie side of the Rockies, making it an annual event thereafter.

When did the first representatives of the ancient breed come to Canada? The first of which there is record was brought to the East, a chestnut stallion, Bara, imported from England as a foal in September, 1909, by H. H. Miller, Hanover, Ontario. The stallion's breeder was Sir Wilfrid Scawen Blunt, Sussex, England, and the granddam was a mare brought from the Euphrates. There being no Arabian Stud Book in Canada, the horse's registration was entered in Volume I of the Canadian Thoroughbred Stud Book, with number -209-.

The next Arabian to be recorded in the Thoroughbred books was Narda -1175-, bred by Lady Anne Blunt of England, foaled in 1902 and imported to the United States by F. Lothrop Ames of Massachusetts in 1910. Making her a much-travelled mare, her fourth owner was Simmons Brown of Quebec City. Nor was there anything dull about her family history; her great granddam, Dajania, foaled in 1876, was bred by Mohammed Pasha "who stole her dam from the Sebba . . . Dajania was in turn stolen from her owner and sold to Mr. Blunt at Aleppo in 1877." Several horses bred at Lady Wentworth's Crabbet Arabian Stud in England were brought to Canada; one of them, a stallion, Rajafan, foaled in 1915, was taken to the United States and then imported to Canada by Norman Brown of Quebec City. Volume 3 of the Canadian Thoroughbred Stud Book carries the names of three Arabian horses acquired by Allan K. Foster, Knowlton, Ontario, one being the Crabbet-bred mare, Rokhsa, foaled in 1915. And more Crabbet-breds came to Septimus Thompson of London, Ontario, notably the grey mare, Namilla, foaled in 1929 and imported to the United States by Roger Selby, and the chestnut mare, Jerama, foaled in 1930, and also taken to the United States by Roger Selby before being brought to Ontario.

The first Arabian in the West was a bay stallion, Osolette, foaled April 15, 1915, and imported in the next year by Charles Furman of Taber, Alberta. Furman, from Eastern Oregon, came to the North West Territories in 1889, settling near Boundary Creek, south of Cardston. As a particularly imaginative horseman, he searched widely in the United States for an Arabian stallion, his motive being to breed polo ponies of 14½ hands.

Story had it that Osolette or his mother was stolen out of Arabia to become a star performer in an internationally known circus. It's too bad to spoil a fascinating fable but the truth is scarcely less significant; the horse was completely the product of the desert-bred horses imported by Homer Davenport in 1906. The sire, Hamrah, was one of the Davenport originals, as were both grandsire and granddam on the mother's side.

With aristocratic blood lines, Osolette might have been seen as wasted in the Canadian West at that period, "born to blush unseen, and waste its sweetness on the desert air." But the stallion's influence was not wasted. For Charlie Furman this Arabian pioneer, when mated to light mares of mixed breeding, left many high class mounts suitable for polo and range work. Then at the age of thirteen, the horse went to the foothills ranch of Streeter Brothers and, finally, to the Cartwright Ranch where he died in 1934.

"He was a tough little horse," Allie Streeter said, "about 14½ hands and always fat. A man on him knew he'd never be afoot. You couldn't tire him on a long ride." Osolette was demonstrating something about the Arabian fibre.

With more glamor and prestige, Aldebaran came to Western Canada, property of H.R.H., Edward, Prince of Wales. This Arabian stallion, first western-owned member of the breed to gain Canadian registration, was foaled in England in 1919—same year as the Prince of Wales saw Alberta and decided, more or less on impulse, to buy the foothills ranch west of High River. Cattle, sheep, Thoroughbreds and ponies were imported to stock the ranch and in August, 1929, the chestnut Arabian stallion was brought to Canada.

Horsemen drove hundreds of miles expressly to see a real Arabian and were pleased with the high quality and proud air of antiquity they saw. But, there being no Arabian mares in the country, Aldebaran had no chance to leave pure bred offspring. He was mated successfully with Thoroughbred mares and Dartmoor ponies and many of the offspring appeared in western showrings, the first half-Arabs many Horse Show patrons had seen. But in September, 1938, with a new name, Aldebar, the aging horse was sold to go to the United States.

In British Columbia, where the breed could later show its best Canadian progress, the pioneer stallion leaving the most vivid mark upon light horses generally was Adounad by Hanad and bred by Kellog Ranch in California. This brown horse was imported by Charles J. Taylor of Vancouver in 1932, and after changing hands several times, came to

Mr. and Mrs. C. E. Latimer of Chilliwack—later Vernon. While owned by the Latimers, Adounad left many of the best Anglo-Arab show horses seen in the country, the gelding, Fargo, for example.

Adounad was destroyed in 1957 at the age of twenty-six, after adding to the Arabian reputation for longevity. Some Canadians could recall seeing Adounad's sire at the age of twenty-seven and sharing stable quarters belonging to Mrs. Alice Payne of Whittier, California, with other distinguished patriarchs of the breed. There was Poka, a twenty-eight-year-old mare heavy in foal, the twenty-three-year-old desert-bred Aziza with husky foal at foot, and the twenty-six-year-old Raseyn, bred by Lady Wentworth and sired by the incomparable Skowronek for which Lady Wentworth was reported to have refused a Russian offer of $250,000. Later in the year, another old timer of the Arabian breed came to join the distinguished group at the Payne stable, this one the twenty-three-year-old Raffles, also by Skowronek. And all of these remained active to add more years to their lives.

What may have been the first pure bred Arabian mare in the Canadian West was a bay, Al Hamseh by Raseyn, foaled in 1936 and brought to Chemainus, British Columbia, by Godfrey Lomas. A stallion, Jamil Abdullah Azam, was imported at the same time and these two gained numbers -1- and -2- in the Canadian Arabian Stud Book. But they did not remain in Canada and their contribution to breed progress on the Canadian side was unimportant.

One of the most important Arabian foundations in Western Canada was laid by George Iverson of Prince, Saskatchewan. In 1944, he imported a grey stallion, Sibari, and two chestnut mares, Kashira and Khivane. The mares, first of their breed in Saskatchewan, presented their owner with two fillies annually for three consecutive years and George Iverson soon found himself with the biggest band of pure Arabians in the country.

It was a late start. It was surprising that the breed recognized as the world's oldest was so late in gaining a Canadian foothold. Then, suddenly, there was an enthusiasm among people who seemed to see Arabian horses as the Creator's crowning achievement. At the Calgary Spring Horse Show in 1955, a class for Arabian stallions of three years and over brought out ten entries. Nothing like that had happened before and horsemen waxed eloquent about the display of symmetry, alertness and winning breed personality. There, Horse Show visitors saw the Bedouins' ideal with "flanks of the gazelle, the legs of the female ostrich and the straight back of the wild ass standing sentinel on a hillock."

In less poetic terms, they saw the picturesque Arabian head, trim and graceful neck, short back, high setting of tail, long and level croup, clean and dense bone and height of 14½ to 15 hands. The person who said he wanted a bigger horse was told to choose another breed. And that head, with big eyes, small ears, dished face and tapering shape was something to dwell upon as one would a great picture from the brush of a master. If, as Lady Wentworth suggested, they were the horses which occupied King Solomon's stables, it becomes easy to understand how they could captivate him and draw the wrath of jealous wives.

With the sudden enthusiasm came organization. Breeders in British Columbia met in 1950 and formed the Arabian Horse Association of British Columbia, with thirteen charter members. In time, the organization was extended to become the Arabian Horse Association of Western Canada. The first Arabian horses in Canada were admitted to registry in the Canadian Thoroughbred Stud Book, then in the General Stud Book; but in 1958, the Canadian Arabian Horse Association was incorporated under the Live Stock Pedigree Act and registrations thereafter were in the breed's own Stud Book. New registrations in 1960 numbered one hundred and four, with forty-one of these coming from British Columbia, thirty-five from Alberta, twelve from Ontario, nine from Saskatchewan, five from Manitoba and two from the province of Quebec.

CHAPTER 30

Coat of Gold

In the Palomino, Canadians found a fascinating demonstration of processes in breed building. It was the case of a distinctively colored strain of horses having a four hundred-year association with North America before there was any organized attempt to bring it to the rank of breed. But when the effort was put forward, progress was strikingly rapid. Even in the early years there was no lack of admiration for those horses with the romantic gold-colored coats; only the incentive to ensure permanency for the strain was missing.

Without inherited tenacity and vigor, the color would have become extinct long ago. But the Palomino color refused to be exterminated and ultimately men recognized purpose in combining the glamorous coats with approved saddle type and advancing the strain to status of breed. It began in the United States in 1932 and in July, 1944, a little group of horsemen met to organize the Canadian Palomino Horse Association and take steps to record foundation stock with the desired colors and refined saddle type. It was an essential step in breed building. The methods fixed upon at that time proved effective. According to the plan, no horse would be accepted for foundation purposes without on-the-spot inspection and approval for type and soundness as well as color.

As a result of the manner in which horses were admitted to record, advancement was rapid. At the first of January, 1953—just eight and one-half years after the Canadian association was formed—the new breed was formally recognized by the Department of Agriculture and the responsibility for keeping stud book registrations placed with the National Live Stock Records, Ottawa. Achieving the rank of breed in less than ten years after the records books were opened was the best possible endorsement of methods employed by the association, whose secretary throughout the formative years was Thomas P. Devlin, Winnipeg.

Making this new stand, then, was an old strain with history as rich as the pigment in its coat. Here was manifestation of triumph over harsh tests in strange and varied forms. To have been rejected by the Arabs, treasured by Spanish royalty, carried to this continent and lost by gay conquistadors, redomesticated by Indians, rediscovered by modern horse lovers and adopted by Hollywood, was but part of the amazing record of those horses with coats of gold.

No doubt Spanish horses at the time of Columbus were descended largely from North African and Arabian stock which had carried warriors to one victory after another in former years. Spain became known as a nation of horsemen and animals with the brilliant gold coats enjoyed the special patronage of royalty. When Spanish colonizers were setting out for the new world, horses of quality were selected to be taken along. Of the eighteen horses to be landed by Cortez in Mexico in 1519—first horses to set feet on North American soil following disappearance of the native races at some prehistoric stage—at least one possessed Palomino colors, the richly colored coat with white mane and tail.

In the years following, more selected Spanish horses were taken to North America. Legend tells of a special gift of a stallion and five mares, "the color of the setting sun," from the Royal Stables of Queen Isabella of Spain. There can be no doubt about that Queen's fondness for horses possessing this particular color but history has ungraciously repudiated the gift story by recording the good Queen's death a few years before Cortez went to Mexico. It could, however, have been a gesture on the part of her successor.

In any case, horses having the color were introduced by Spanish adventurers and they were unquestionably the ancestors of Palomino colored specimens which survived in Mexico, became fashionable in early California, won favor with the color-conscious Indians and found their way into Canada.

Prairie homesteaders saw them and, without regard for technical differences, called them buckskins, then added: "You can't kill a buckskin." But unlike the real buckskins, these horses which were to burst into popularity, had white or silver manes and tails along with rich coats approaching the color of a new minted gold coin.

Indians and settlers prized these horses with the glamorous appearance but with government organization came restrictive stallion enrollment laws which placed extreme emphasis upon pedigrees and orthodox breeds and prevented planned propagation of uncommon types. California could claim the first organized promotional effort; there, in 1932, the Palomino Horse and Stud Book Registry was started, with an internationally known enthusiast, Dick Halliday, as secretary. A subsidiary organization emerged in Texas and then, in 1941, it became the Palomino Horse Breeders of America.

The first Canadian Palomino to be recorded anywhere was the Saskatchewan-bred stallion, Laddie, entered in the books of the Palomino Horse Breeders of America. This stallion, bred by Mrs. Anne Naismith of Maple Creek and foaled in 1940, was used in the Saskatoon and Lloydminster districts throughout a long life and was described as the most influential sire of the breed in the years before the Canadian National Live Stock Records took over registrations. When the Canadian Stud Book came into existence, Laddie was entered with a new name, Jungle Gold.

Even before the Canadian association was founded, the Palomino was booming in the West. The results were not all good. So great was the sudden demand that any horse or mare with the approved and fashionable colors—regardless of quality or lack of quality—was immediately able to command twice or three times what an animal possessing similar conformation and more common color would bring. Some horses with draught type, some with unsoundnesses, some totally lacking in refinement were sold at prices far beyond their reasonable worth.

The first task facing the Canadian Palomino Association when it was formed in 1944, was to make it clear that saddle type and quality were positive prerequisites in animals to be classified with the good name of Palomino, written with capital P. In providing a stud book for foundation stock, the association, from the very outset, required that all candidates for entry had to pass inspection before being accepted. The organization officers were determined to exclude individuals whose influence would be harmful to a breed. It was the insistence upon pre-registration inspection, coupled with high standards, which led to the official recognition by provincial and federal governments. Saskatchewan was the first province to make provision for the licensing of Palomino stallions under the Stallion Enrollment Act.

The new association attempted, also, to declare Palomino type in specific terms and rule on the relative importance of conformation and color. Somebody had to decide if the Palomino breed was to be, fundamentally, a pleasure horse, driving horse, stock horse, parade horse or fine harness horse. It couldn't be expected to combine all types. It was conceded that some flexibility is necessary but opinion decreed and the association confirmed that the Canadian Palomino should be, first of all, an animal with refinement of body and bone and, after that, essentially of a type to carry a western saddle.

A good Palomino, the Association ruled, must in all cases possess the conformation to be a good saddle horse, 14½ to 16 hands high, have good feet and legs, show straight action and display refinement and grace in body.

At first, with the unwarranted emphasis upon color, some exhibitions ruled for the guidance of judges making showring decisions that consideration be based, twenty-five percent for conformation, twenty-five percent for manners and action, and fifty percent for color. The Association officers were quick to rule a more sensible division of points—fifty percent for type and quality, twenty-five percent for manners and action, and twenty-five percent for color. Said the president in reporting to the annual meeting in 1954: "I see no reason for relaxing color standards but even in the showring there should be no suggestion that coat color is as important as refinement and general saddle quality."

The color, first characteristic to make the strain distinctive, presented other problems: it didn't breed true and refused to become a fixed entity like Yorkshire white or Aberdeen Angus black or Suffolk Punch chestnut. There were disappointments when Palomino to Palomino matings produced a color unacceptable to the breed association. As experience demonstrated clearly, such matings could give Palomino, sorrel or albino.

A few Palomino stallions seemed to demonstrate unusual prepotency in getting true colors but some of the success was no doubt explained by coincidence—like tossing a coin five times and getting heads on all occasions. From matings of Palomino to sorrel, the foal crop should be fifty percent Palomino in color. And backed by both theory and practice, the best assurance in getting the wanted color follows matings of sorrel and albino.

Palomino horses very quickly found a place in Canadian showrings. Such followed an obvious public interest in the breed and nothing pleased Horse Show spectators more than good and stylish Palominos carrying parade class equipment and colors. The first Canadian classes specifically for Palominos were offered at Nanton, Alberta, and, writing in 1947, Association Secretary Thomas Devlin said: "The three best centres for Palomino showings have been the Horse

Show at Nanton, the Spring Show at Edmonton and the Royal Agricultural Winter Fair at Toronto."

As with styles in clothing, breed popularity never follows an entirely steady course. The Palomino craze of the '40s was too good to last. In 1954—year following recognition of Palominos by the National Live Stock Records—the Association had one hundred and forty-five members in Canada and registered fifty-seven new horses, bringing the total registrations at the end of that year to four hundred and fifty-five. For 1960, there were one hundred and twenty-eight members and sixty-five new registrations. More than one-third of the year's registrations came from the province of Saskatchewan.

Great, indeed, were the changes which came over the horses called Palominos. Not only did they multiply rapidly but they moved ahead at the same pace in point of quality. And convinced that the largest measure of improvement was due to the policy of accepting only horses passing the tests of inspection, the same qualifying conditions were continued after the Palominos gained admittance to the National Live Stock Records.

There was no doubt about it being worth while; a strain was saved from possible oblivion and a breed created. And the name, Palomino, strange to most Canadians in 1940, was commonplace twenty years later.

CHAPTER 31

Spots on the Rump

The Appaloosa horse, sharing color distinction with the Dalmatian dog, stands as the sole example of livestock improvement by North American natives. But the effort by the Nez Perce tribesmen living in the Idaho country was a good one. For a time, these horses with spotted coats and built-in hardiness were called Nez Perce and there would have been the best of reason for retaining that name as a tribute to the breed's creators.

Much will be heard about rapid advancement to breed recognition after the Appaloosa Horse Club of United States was formed in 1938 and the Canadian Appaloosa Horse Club in 1954, but recent success was mainly in the nature of recovery of something nearly lost, because the Nez Perce horses of 100 years ago had attained the maturity and character of a breed. Alone among the North American tribesmen, the Nez Perce—meaning "pierced noses"— brought purpose and the principle of improvement through selection to horse breeding.

Employing the modern stockman's chief means of bettering his flocks and herds, the Idaho Indians gelded all but the best males and traded off their poorer mares. Distinct superiority in their riding stock was the reward. Eastward on the Montana plains, their horses proved to be the best buffalo runners and in time of war, the extra speed and endurance brought definite advantages to riders. That the horses had unusual colors and spotted rumps was pleasing to the Indian owners but more important was performance on long and hard trails. Probably it never occurred to those early breeders that there was a hereditary relationship or linkage between the Appaloosa coat and thin mane and tail on one hand and the extra hardiness on the other. But what was the earlier source of horse stock with spotted coats? The pages of history show the Appaloosa markings to be very ancient. Oriental art depicts spotted horses as early as 500 B.C. and it is evident that Chinese rulers of two thousand years ago, seeing their destiny likely to be determined by the speed and worth of their cavalry, sought the highly-rated, "blood-sweating" or spotted horses owned by tribes of the Asiatic Interior. The endurance and general superiority of those spotted horses from the Interior, according to legend, was explained by crossing with a cave-dwelling monster of the dragon type.

The great Persian warrior hero, Rustem, was carried to victory and fame by his spotted horse called Rakush, a noble steed whose pedigree was likewise unusual; the horse's mother was described as a "man-eating mare" and his father an "evil spirit." Presumably, nothing less would explain the Rakush power and courage.

With passing generations, spotted horses were taken westward along Mediterranean shores and beyond. A rump-spotted stallion called Bloody Buttocks was sent from Turkey to England in the 17th Century and spotted horses found in the British Isles today are believed to owe their colors to him. And Spanish adventurers who followed Columbus to the New World brought members of the spotted race, just as they brought the ancestors of today's golden-coated Palominos.

Horses from the Spanish introductions reached the Columbia River Basin about 1730 and were adopted eagerly by Nez Perce Indians in that part. For people who were quick to acquire high ideals in horse breeding, the region affords advantages. As an inter-mountain territory, the range was limited by barriers; peaks and canyons afforded some protection from marauding enemies. Thus the Nez Perce people were shielded somewhat from the great Indian sport of horse stealing and their breeding program progressed.

Having become the proud owners of spotted horses, the Nez Perce Indians had the good judgment to recognize inherent merits. Moreover, they set out to make their horses still better. Selective breeding, coupled with the forces of natural selection which effectively eliminated weakling stock, gave the Nez Perce strain more and more of the character of a breed.

When Lewis and Clark travelled through that section of the Northwest in 1805, they noted the spotted markings and high quality of Nez Perce horses. But not all the good ones with spots were confined to the Columbia Basin at that time. Thefts and trades led to wider distribution. In 1807, when Alexander Henry the Younger, who contributed much to the history of Western Canada's fur trade, was travelling through Mandan country in the Dakota Black Hills, he came upon a spotted stallion which filled him with an urge to own it. In conformation and speed, this four-year-old was the best Henry had seen. Accompanying the trader at the time was a Gros Ventre chief displaying the same ambition to own the stud with Appaloosa coat. Henry offered his own horse and a hundred beaver skins worth of trade goods but met with refusal. The Gros Ventre chief raised the offer to two horses, one of his wives and other assorted treasures to the value of fifty beaver skins but the owner would not be separated from his handsome stallion.

The best horses were still in the hands of the Nez Perce Indians and gradually they were becoming known as Palouse, a name originating with a small river rising in Idaho and flowing into Southeastern Washington and along which many of the best horses grazed. From that name came Apalouse, Apalousy and, finally, Appaloosa.

But the white man dealt harshly with Nez Perce Indians and their horses. Discovery of gold on Indian land in 1860 brought natives and gold-seeking whites into direct conflict and one encounter led to another until there was open warfare.

The Indians, with better horses, outfought the pale-faces for awhile. But there came the great tribal tragedy. It was 1877, year in which the last of the major Indian treaties was signed on the Canadian side and year of disaster for Chief Joseph's Indians and their good horses on the other side. The government was mustering bigger and bigger forces and gradually the Nez Perce people were being worn down by fighting. Under Chief Joseph's able leadership, they were fighting a rearguard action and moving eastward on the Montana plains. Their hope was to join forces with prairie tribes or, if all else failed, to cross the border to Canada and take refuge there as Sitting Bull's fugitives had done.

Burdened with women, children, old people and belongings, Chief Joseph was terribly handicapped. In the face of increasing pressure from the United States army, he turned northward, finally relaxing in the Bear's Paw Mountain country of Northern Montana, believing he was then in Canada. But he had miscalculated and had a major battle on his hands. There in the Battle of the Bear's Paw, his Indians were overwhelmed and the Chief finally surrendered to Colonel Nelson Miles and parted with eleven hundred of his good war horses—nearly half of which were Appaloosas. Those animals, prizes of war, were soon scattered, falling into unappreciative hands. Crow Indians were allowed to take many.

It was an equine tragedy of the first order. The stuff from which a breed was made was all but lost. The loss might have been complete were it not for the spirit of the strain, a spirit refusing to be expended. The attractive coat and characteristic stamina persisted in successive generations until some students of animal breeding awakened to the unusual worth and set about to make recovery.

Retrieving an almost lost breed wasn't easy. Only little remained with which to work—a pocket of breeding stock on the Pine Ridge Sioux Reservation in the Black Hills of South Dakota and an undetermined number of widely scattered individuals in United States and Canada having the characteristic markings. But farmers and cowboys who happened to own them said almost invariably that they were hardy and good. Under the Appaloosa hide, it seemed, was a horse capable of going farther and easier than an ordinary specimen would do, as the cruel thirty-mile stock saddle race held in Alberta in 1946 helped to confirm. Of forty-one starting horses, one was an Appaloosa; it didn't win the race but it did qualify for an award offered to the horse finishing in the best condition.

Just as the thin mane and tail, laminated or vertically stripped hoofs, mottled skin around the muzzle and white sclera or outer ring of the eye gave clear evidence of genetic linkage, so hardiness and stamina appeared to be associated in a hereditary way with the Appaloosa coat—whether that coat showed typical rump spotting, leopard markings, raindrop pattern or snowflake pattern.

In any case, it was all too good to be lost. Before it was too late, horsemen heard a call to save the remnant and give the old strain a permanent place among the breeds. South of the border, the Appaloosa Horse Club, formed and incorporated in 1938, set about to collect historical data, record animals considered suitable for foundation and establish standards of type and quality. Twelve years later, the National Stallion Board of the United States extended official recognition, thus acknowledging the Appaloosa as a breed.

North of the line, the Canadian Appaloosa Horse Club was formed at a meeting on April 16, 1954, with James Wyatt of High River as president. Here, too, the objective was to preserve the best of an ancient strain, advance its quality according to modern concepts and open a stud book for animals suitable for breed foundation.

But certain Canadians, catching early visions of breed potential, did not wait for the opening of a stud book. One of them, Ed McCrea of McCord, Saskatchewan, bought a snowflake mare in 1928 and in the next year got a stud foal he named Rainbow. This stallion proved to be an excellent sire and a son called Checkers was retained by Mr. McCrea. From Checkers came Polar Star which the Saskatchewan man took along with four other horses to the first National Appaloosa Show at Lewiston, Idaho, in 1948, there winning third prize in the open stallion class and third in sire-and-get class.

Calgary's Spring Horse Show of 1954 provided special Appaloosa classes for the first time and among the winners were two of the West's best known stallions: Jim Wyatt's Speckle Boy which won the saddle class and Mrs. Lois McLeod's Polka Dot Prince which won the halter competition. Indeed, Speckle Boy provided some of the best publicity for the breed, having been a perennial winner in open stock horse classes. When he won at Edmonton Spring Show in that year, it was his 26th triumph in twenty-eight stock horse contests in Canada and United States.

The leadership provided by the Canadian Appaloosa Club was practical and progressive and the reward came with the official breed recognition by federal authorities on January 19, 1961. The Nez Perce horses had now come of age. James Wyatt, the club's first president, was still president when the goal of breed acceptance was reached. By that time, the club could report a Canadian membership of three hundred and a stud book with over nine hundred entries. In winning breed recognition in Canada, the Appaloosa was following hard upon the heels of the Palomino, although the spotted horses, bred and improved with a clear purpose by Indian tribesmen, had the better claim. In any case, the new breed established on an old Indian foundation, was assured of support, mainly from people who employ stock saddles.

Nothing told more clearly of recent improvement than the International Appaloosa Shows held in United States and Canada. An observer who attended the first Canadian International Show at High River in 1957 and then the fifth at Lethbridge in 1961 said: "The spots were the same but the quality was unbelievably better."

CHAPTER 32

Sleepy Cat's Breed

Sleepy Cat, dun stallion imported from the United States in 1940, was about the best possible advance agent the Quarter Horse breed could have had in Canada. There had been grade and non-pedigreed horses bearing Quarter Horse type before him—some brought by Tony and Ad Day and some by itinerant cowboys following the rodeos—but Sleepy Cat was the first of confirmed pure breeding. And when he was paraded around the ring at Calgary Horse Show in 1942, many westerners leaned forward and remarked: "So that's a Quarter Horse! First one I've seen."

But even at that rather late date, horsemen were enquiring: "What's so unusual about the breed?" and "How does it come by that name?" When informed about a certain Quarter Horse in the United States selling for $10,000, an observer with a better grasp of mathematics than horse history, inquired: "What'd the other three-quarters sell for?"

The breed, seen as the answer to the cowboy's prayer for stock horses, developed in the older sections of United States. Taking shape two or three hundred years ago, speed and utility were the motivating prerequisites long before there was a western cattle range. Hence, Quarter Horses may be seen as an old North American breed, even though breed organization is very recent.

Not until January 15, 1957, was the Canadian Quarter Horse Association incorporated under the Livestock Pedigree Act, permitting it to maintain a Stud Book within the frame-work of the Canadian National Livestock Records at Ottawa. Prior to that time, Canadian-owned Quarter Horses had to be registered with the American Quarter Horse Association—likewise a youthful organization.

The annual report of the Canadian Record Office for the year 1957 showed sixty horses of the breed as having been admitted for registration in the twelve-month period. But as an indication of a mushroom-like growth of interest, the members in that year outnumbered horses registered; there were ninety-nine members in the Association, forty-four of them in Alberta and sixteen in Saskatchewan. Three years later the membership had jumped to one hundred seventy-one, with the biggest provincial group then in Saskatchewan; that province had sixty-three members while Alberta had fifty-eight and Ontario thirty-six.

But what was behind the spectacular rise in public interest? The breed's peculiar worth for racing on short tracks had something to do with it but that was not the principal reason because many people who became enthusiastic, admitted no interest in racing. Probably the answer was to be found in the breed's "built-in" utility. In handling cattle on farms and ranches, nothing would take the place of a good horse and here, in the words of a Saskatchewan cattleman, was a breed "created for cowboys."

In origin, the Quarter Horse goes back to early Colonial days in the Eastern States, where handy saddle horses were essential in the lives of settlers. Speed was desirable and if a horse had enough of it to win a roadside race, so much the better. Horse stock brought from England blended with semi-native mares tracing to Spanish importations to produce versatile animals with abundant muscling and stamina and that extra measure of speed. Virginia, where short racing was popular, saw the most evident progress in improvement.

By the middle of last century, Virginia claimed the best and fastest saddle horses. Although the Quarter Racing Horse was showing signs of individuality almost three hundred years ago, it wasn't until the time of the famous Steel

Dust—bay stallion foaled in 1843 and taken to Texas—that men were getting a clear vision of breed formation. By this time, Virginians were sure they had the fastest things inside horse-hides for quarter-mile courses; hence the name, Quarter Horse.

As in most breeds, certain stallions proved especially influential in advancing the strain; to name a few, there were, in addition to the famous Steel Dust, Copper Bottom, Shiloh, Old Sorrel, Joe Bailey, Traveller and Peter McCue. Peter McCue was supposed to have made a quarter mile mark of twenty-one seconds, remarkable if correct.

Even though the breed's roots penetrated deeply in the continental soil, organization came slowly. The American Quarter Horse Association was organized at Fort Worth, Texas, in 1940. In the next year, the breed's first volume of the Stud Book was published, with the King Ranch stallion, Wimpy, being accorded the honor of the first registration. Since that time, the increase in registrations has been quite spectacular.

The Quarter Horse to emerge as typical was a stoutly built fellow with mild disposition and unbeatable breakaway speed. Color could vary widely through chestnut, bay, dun, brown, black and palomino. Thigh and gaskin muscling was and is most pronounced, although the "bulldog" type with poorly developed withers and short pasterns failed to gain more than brief popularity. That chunky type had ardent supporters for a time but horsemen wanting good withers to hold saddles, flat bone as a mark of quality and reasonable length of pastern to ensure easy riding, won the argument.

Canadian critics, with time-tested ideals about quality, said they would gladly exchange a measure of the bulging Quarter Horse muscling for more of those feet and leg characteristics which were long the hallmarks of equine excellence—sharp hocks, flinty bone and generally good wearing capacity. But as in all breeds, type ideals change and for a time the American Quarter Horse breeders would be permitted to resort to Thoroughbred outcrosses from which added grace and quality could come. For the old Thoroughbred, it was repetition of a role it filled in breed building throughout the history of horse improvement. Clearly, the Quarter Horse could tell a story of striking success. It was not because of any simple and visual characteristic like fancy showring performance or super-refinement; rather, the explanation was to be found in a combination of utility, versatility, reliability and temperament.

And although the breed was slow in gaining recognition in Canada where there was strong loyalty to Thoroughbreds and Thoroughbred crosses, its ultimate rise in popularity seemed to bear a striking resemblance to Quarter Horse speed on a short track. Farmers, cowboys and dudes decided they wanted horses of the breed and it appeared that Canadians in 1960 invested more money in them than in stock of any other horse breed.

How much of that recent Quarter Horse popularity could be attributed to the influence of Sleepy Cat is difficult to determine but, certainly, he could take some measure of the credit. In addition to leading the Quarter Horse parade in Canada, the stallion was used extensively for breeding through his long life and left hundreds of useful horses. It should be mentioned, however, that he probably did not sire all the animals said by ambitious owners to be his offspring. Horse Show judges have been impressed by the number of stock saddle contestants in widely scattered parts of the country which were alleged to be "Sleepy Cats."

Sired by Red Dog and bred by Jack Casement, Whitewater, Colorado, Sleepy Cat was foaled in 1938. As a two-year-old he was brought to Canada by the Streeters of Stavely who had previously used Arabian and Thoroughbred stallions to secure horses for ranch use. As time was to prove, the Streeter selection was a good one; Sleepy Cat demonstrated his greatness both as a breeder and performing stock horse.

After making his initial public appearance at the Calgary Horse Show in 1942, he was seen rather often, in cutting contests and as a roping horse in rodeo events. In 1945, he was the Best Roping Horse at Calgary Stampede, having won the distinction the same day his owner, Jack Streeter, was married.

With dun colored coat and pepper colored mane and tail, Sleepy Cat was a distinguished fellow, even in appearance. He was fifteen hands in height and had the disposition of a gentleman.

How he was regarded by the Streeters is shown clearly by the fact of being retained in their ownership for exactly twenty years, or until death by what seemed like heart failure overtook him. He was twenty-two years old when he died on pasture in 1960.

And so, Sleepy Cat, the Quarter Horse pioneer in the Canadian West, lived to see his breed making friends and the breed Association flourishing.

John G. Millar, Milestone, Saskatchewan, became that Canadian Association's first president. He was followed by Calgary's George Cheatham, a Missourian who brought some inherited convictions about horses to Alberta and became a leading breeder of Quarter stock. The stallion, Sobre's Red Chubby, and mare, Punkin Jones, were Cheatham importations in 1953 and before very long, the latter was rated among the four top cutting horses in Canada.

Importations became more and more numerous, with many outstanding stallions being introduced to Canadian breeding farms, sometimes at extremely long figures. One of those stallions, Beaverdam Beaver, rich in the blood of Old Sorrel, was bought by C. and A. Bohomolic of Arrowhead Ranch, Kevisville, Alberta, at the Utter Ranch sale, Spokane, in June, 1960, for $22,000. Canada, it was said at that time, was getting one of the greatest sires of the breed.

Then, early in 1961, Ken Paget of Two Rivers Ranch, Cochrane, Alberta, imported the outstanding young stallion, King Leo Bar, at a price understood to be $45,000. Such a purchase would make him the highest priced horse ever brought to Canada. Plans, as announced, were to allow the horse to stand for limited public service at a fee of $1000, and by April it was reported that the service book was full for 1961.

This horse, a chestnut with refined type and distinguished racing record, came as a rising four-year-old. Having been entered in fourteen races as a two-year-old, he never failed to place and completed the season with seven first prize awards and four seconds—also $4700 in purses. The young horse's grandsire on the sire's side was Three Bars whose get had won over a million dollars in racing prizes and was the leading sire of money winners for eleven consecutive years.

By 1962, just twenty-two years after Sleepy Cat's arrival on Canadian soil, it wasn't easy to keep abreast of the rapid-fire Quarter Horse transactions across the country.

CHAPTER 33

Morgans, Tennessees and Pintos

Originating with a single stallion which legend says was a "catch colt," the Morgan was for half a century the most versatile breed of horses on the continent. Here were the horses New Englanders used for driving, riding, racing and even farm work. Eventually, small size reacted against the Morgan and the stout-hearted breed with endurance and beauty of form was threatened with extinction when the United States Bureau of Animal Industry took steps to save it.

In Canada, numbers were never high but a few loyal horsemen with good memories continued to talk about Morgans. Canadian Rancher C. H. "Chay" Gilchrist, with a lifetime experience in breeding horses, recalled the many breeds he had used since riding his first Morgan on the Montana range fifty-five years earlier and said: "If a man hasn't got a Morgan under him when he's got work to do, he isn't really mounted."

In its origin, the Morgan was as American as corn pone and had the unique distinction of springing from one stallion, the immortal Justin Morgan, foaled in 1793. The dam was at least part Thoroughbred but the sire remained anonymous. And the name given to the young stallion was that of his owner, a school teacher at Springfield, Massachusetts. But when the dark bay horse was a five-year-old, the school teacher owner moved to Vermont—a fortunate event for horse breeding in that state—and there Justin Morgan won fame.

It wasn't his size that made him the idol of that part; at maturity he stood little if any more than fourteen hands and weighed only nine hundred and fifty pounds. He was long in the underline, short in the back, heavily muscled, beautifully turned and favored with hard and clean bone. His proud bearing was that of a good parade horse and in action, he was fast at a walk and a racehorse at other gaits. Of this stallion with versatility and gentlemanly personality, folks said he could out-walk, out-trot, out-run and out-pull any horse in Vermont.

Even in span of life, Justin Morgan was unusual; he lived to be thirty-two years of age and then met death following a kick from another horse. But people who saw him said he was active, sound and clean even at that advanced age. And best of all, his offspring were consistently good, especially as roadsters. Some like the great grandson, Ethan Allen, made world trotting records. Until the Hambletonian 10 stock came to public attention, Justin Morgan offspring were regarded as the finest treasures with owners, traders and horse thieves. It explained why the Morgan horse was used extensively and effectively in building other breeds like Standard Bred, American Saddle, Quarter Horse and Tennessee Walking Horse.

For a long time, the Morgan was a family horse, the kind that did some form of farm work all week and then hauled the family to church on Sunday. And on fair day, according to one who grew up with the breed, "You could use him for chores in the morning, hitch him to a buggy to get to the show, and then enter him in the harness races and see him go like a fiend."

But in time, the old breed with romantic New England background suffered domination by horses with more size— at least until there was an effort to bring the Morgan back with some added stature. In remodelling the Morgan to meet changing times, the United States Department of Agriculture could take a lot of the credit. For a breeding program started in 1905, mares and stallion were chosen with extreme care. The stallion selected was General Gates and the influence was encouraging. From the beginning all horses raised at the government station were systematically tested at walking, trotting and cantering gaits. For measuring endurance, horses hitched to two-wheeled vehicles and pulling sixty percent of body weight were worked on five-mile courses. Under saddles and carrying twenty percent of body weight, they worked on 11½-mile courses, doing 4.7 miles at a walk, 5.7 miles at a trot and 1.1 miles at canter. Changes in respiration and heart beat, also signs of fatigue, were noted. Planned testing furnished a sound basis for improvement and bigger and better Morgans came from the government experiment station in Vermont.

The re-made Morgan was a horse with its former symmetry of body, crested neck and traditional fibre, but averaging a hand and a half higher than the founding sire, Justin Morgan, and about one thousand and fifty pounds in weight.

In Canada, Morgan was for long a name more than a horse with which people were familiar. American settlers migrating to this country brought horses possessing one degree or another of Morgan breeding and held them in high favor, especially where roadsters were essential for long drives on both summer and winter roads. But by the time of the rush to settle western land, the Standard Bred was enjoying a great wave of popularity and eclipsing the older Morgan. Consequently, not many pure specimens of the breed were brought to Canada.

The first Morgan of which there is record in the West was the stallion Maximo, imported from Illinois in 1920 by C. H. Gilchrist of Manyberries. This one was a chestnut, fifteen and one-quarter hands high and nine hundred and fifty pounds in weight. Bred to range mares, the result was highly satisfactory and the owner went again to Illinois for a stallion and then to New Hampshire for a third one in 1945.

The last horse was regarded so highly that New Hampshire breeders bought him and took him back.

As time went on, the New England breed was going western, winning increasing attention from people who rode stock saddles and placed importance upon stamina, muscling, speed and intelligence. Many representatives of the breed did well in cutting competitions as well as in trail and endurance rides and new interest was born on both sides of the international border.

A group of supporters came together at Red Deer during the week of the summer fair in 1959 and formed a Canadian Morgan Horse Club, with William Unger of Calgary as the first president, Graham Bockus of Quebec as vice-president and Mrs. Peggy McDonald of Calgary—later Millet—as secretary. Pure Morgans continued to be registered in the General Stud and Herd Book of Canada and at December 31, 1960, a total of sixty-one horses of the breed had been recorded, fifteen of them in the single year, 1960. The new club found its best support in Alberta, British Columbia and Saskatchewan, but some interest in all provinces.

Still another breed of American origin, Tennessee Walking Horse, made its bid for support in Canada. For some reason, however, Canadians were slow in accepting. Horsemen saw and admired the running walk performance although not many were moved to become active breeders. But the Tennessee Walking Horse had a story to tell, one in which all horsemen should have found interest. Wanted in the Old South was a horse to carry planters on their plantations or wherever they might choose to go. Mild disposition and comfortable gaits were more important than speed. Stallions of various breeds were used on the hardy and free-walking mares settlers had brought with them from West Virginia and North Carolina. And in selection, natural tendency to the easy running walk was regarded as more important than pedigree.

What emerged was a sort with much of the refinement of the Thoroughbred and the gentle disposition and easy gaits of the mares. From the refining processes of time came the Tennessee Walking Horses with clearly defined characteristics. The color might be sorrel, bay, brown, black or roan but the height was generally fifteen and one-half hands and weight, one thousand one hundred pounds. Heads were sometimes plain with Roman noses but the Tennessee earned a reputation for intelligence and good temper. Backs were strong and feet tough and durable.

Clearly, the chief distinguishing mark was the running walk, good for seven or eight miles an hour. From his gait the breed took its name. It was four-beat performance with each foot striking the ground at a different time. But the stride was long, with hind feet overstepping the tracks of the fore feet by three to eighteen inches. It seemed like a gliding motion accompanied by pronounced nodding of the head and relaxed manner. Breeders insisted it was easy on both horses and riders.

The flat-foot walk and canter were not overlooked. Good representatives would do four miles an hour at the former gait and give a comfortable, "rocking chair" performance at the canter.

The horse qualifying for registration Number -1- in the Canadian Tennessee Walking Horse Stud Book was, quite properly, Chief Justice Allen, bred in Tennessee and imported by C. H. Gilchrist of Manyberries in 1941. This one was a chestnut, fifteen and one-half hands high and about one thousand two hundred pounds in weight.

But Chief Justice Allen's reception by Canadian record authorities was less than cordial. He was permitted registration in the General Stud and Herd Book and then the book was closed to the Tennessee breed, remaining closed for some years which meant withdrawal of official recognition in Canada. Ultimately the record book was re-opened and Chief Justice Allen's entry with registration Number -1- was confirmed. Registration Number -2- was taken by Granny Evans, first pure bred mare of the breed in Canada, one imported and owned by George Edworthy of Shagganappi Ranch, Calgary.

Tennessee Walking Horse registrations in the General Stud and Herd Book of Canada, up to December 31, 1960, numbered twenty-eight, with only four of them being entered in the twelve months of 1960. The Canadian interest was still more academic than real.

And Pintos were not to be ignored. While Palomino and Appaloosa strains were brought to breed recognition, friends of the Pinto were working toward the same end. The Pinto Horse Association of America was organized and incorporated under the laws of the State of New Jersey in 1956 and provided stud book services for approved horses from both sides of the boundary.

The Pinto markings—piebald, skewbald, spotted and mottled—were depicted in drawings in very ancient times and horses favored with the distinguishing colors were no doubt introduced to this continent by Spanish colonizers. The word Pinto comes from Spanish "Pintado," meaning "painted." Indians, with their love of color, helped to perpetuate the striking coats until horsemen of recent years seized the task of combining the markings with better quality.

Pinto markings were classified as Tobiano and Overo, the former being identified as a pattern with white as the base color and Overo with dark color as base. Canadians saw Pintos of both patterns from the pioneer years, many of them lacking refinement. But as a result of judicious crossing, some excellent specimens have appeared in showrings, most commonly in stockhorse, parade and pleasure classes.

The ideal Pinto, according to the Pinto Horse Association standards, should weigh about one thousand pounds, stand fifteen and one-half hands, possess all the qualities of a superior saddle horse and have a coat pattern with white and dark color divided about equally.

CHAPTER 34

Greensleeves and His Kind

G reensleeves was a hunter—big and handsome—and as western as a ten-gallon hat. An inheritance of true hunter type, plus many hours of patient training, took him from a remote farm in Western Alberta to win coveted championship honors under the bright Coliseum lights at Canada's Royal Winter Fair in Toronto. To the western-bred bay horse, more than one discerning judge pointed admiringly, saying: "There, look at the prominent withers, the deep thoracic development, strong back, flat bone, bold bearing and correct performance; that's the goal in breeding heavyweight hunters."

For people attending Horse Shows, the high-stepping Hackneys and lordly American Saddle Horses often aroused the most avid enthusiasm but for thousands of young people and old who ride the back trails for pleasure and health, a well-mannered and loyal hunter or hack is the "greatest horse in the world." That horse's breeding may be mixed— be completely foreign to the ideals of the purist—but in affording an elevated seat from which the world takes on a brighter appearance, the animal's contribution can be very great.

It's an uncertain line that separates the refined and reliable hack from the hunter but, in general, the latter is more of a working horse for long and hard rides, one expected to jump fences and other moderate obstacles encountered in a hunting field. Most hunter classes in the showring require performance on planned courses. Good hunting speed—neither too slow nor too fast—is about twenty miles an hour and judges look for even speed, always on the correct lead, with horse springing forward lightly, taking obstacles with rather flat arc-like jumps rather than throwing themselves into the air or making short hops.

Hunting with horses and hounds is an ancient occupation or pastime. In its earliest form the hunt was inspired by the need for meat or the necessity of killing destructive animals. In England, fox-hunting became a fashionable recreation, often demanding specific dress, expensive horses and, perchance, an Oxford accent. It was hard on foxes and sometimes hard on horses but the English riders loved it and established a code of hunting conduct adopted in widely scattered parts of the world.

In some parts of Eastern Canada, hunt clubs flourished at times and the hunter's "Halloo" echoed through Ontario countryside as a fox was sighted. In the West, the hunter type of horse with stamina and strength was always admired but hunting as organized in the Prairie cities had but fleeting existence.

Some western hunts would have shocked the well-groomed English participants. One at Lethbridge, recorded by the *Macleod Gazette* of December 5, 1889, is worth noting: "Lethbridge has gone wild over fox hunting. The first experience of this invigorating sport which the citizens of Lethbridge have enjoyed, was on a recent Sunday. A number of the wily doublers had been previously captured, and on this particular Sunday the town turned out almost en masse to give chase. As many as could get anything in the shape of an animal with four legs went to the meet mounted, while there was also a pretty liberal turn out of single and double drivers.

"Arrived on the spot, the foxes were let out one by one, and the pack of hounds—from Terriers up to Newfoundlands—let loose. Then the fun began. One prominent Lethbridge citizen who was driving, was overcome by intense excitement and, entering into the spirit of the thing, threw off his coat, and with a loud whoop, sprang out of the wagon and careered wildly over the Prairie in pursuit of the fox. It is not known whether he was in at the death or not. Another fox turned townward, followed by a wildly enthusiastic crowd, both mounted and driving, just as the children were going to Sunday School. The fever seized the latter. The fox darted across the railway tracks and the children joined pell mell in pursuit. Religiously inclined people felt much shocked and we hear the matter was reported to the police."

Indeed, many of the good hunter horses known in Western Canada never saw foxes and never followed hounds. But, without any thought of actually taking part in hunts, riders saw horses with hunter build and stamina as being the most suitable mounts for long and hard rides; and if the animals could jump hedges, ditches and wooden gates, so much better.

That no single breed was responsible for all the good hunters was quite evident. The massive heavyweight hunter, Copper King, exhibited extensively by the late Victor Sifton of Winnipeg, was said to be from a French Coach sire. Some of the good ones were from Standard Bred sires, but most of them carried one-half or more of Thoroughbred—like Onset owned by Robert Hutchinson of Regina, Ardeleno owned by Doris Littlewood of Calgary, and Pinnacle with three hundred prize ribbons and many championships to show for the four years after being purchased in 1956 by P. V. Ranch Ltd., Edmonton.

Some good ones were imported from Ireland and United States and some good ones were the products of Western Canadian farms. Of the home-breds, none had a finer record nor better story than Greensleeves which in 1959 won the $1500 Burton Canadian Hunter Stake over thirty-nine contestants at the Royal Winter Fair and second in the open heavyweight hunter class at the same show with entries from United States, Ireland, Argentina, Mexico and Eastern Canada.

Sired by the government-owned Thoroughbred, Warren-point, and foaled in 1949, Greensleeves, as a yearling, was Lady Joan Gordon's birthday present from husband, Lord Roderic Gordon, soon after they migrated to Canada and settled on a farm at Bentley. For the awkward colt, it was a most fortunate transaction, assuring good care and affection along with the varied experiences of farm life.

For a horse destined to national fame, this one's initial introduction to saddle and rider was most inauspicious and Lady Gordon could tell it well. It was during the crippling March blizzard in 1951. Country roads were hopelessly blocked and even snowplows were stalled in the heavy snow west of Lacombe. But notwithstanding obstacles, there were several reasons why somebody from Shady Spring Farm would have to make a trip to a neighboring farm. A secondary reason involved cream and butter which led Lady Gordon to announce that she would go, one way or another. Like good mixed farmers, the Gordons had been milking cows and selling cream but after days of blizzard, there was a huge supply of cream on hand and no way of delivering it to the creamery. The neighbor's wife made a proposal: "If you can get through to my place, I'll show you how to churn butter in the washing machine."

The only horse available was the green two-year-old and the plucky lady resolved to press him into service, noting to console herself that if she were bucked off, at least the new snow would provide cushion for the fall. She saddled the colt, overcame the natural opposition to bit and bridle, mounted and headed the mystified young horse into the deep snow. Greensleeves didn't know what to make of it but struggling in the snow was enough to partly take his mind away from bucking and bolting. "He did not submit easily," said Lady Gordon, "but I managed to stay on him and by the time we got to our destination, he was behaving fairly well."

Thereafter, Greensleeves was ridden regularly and later in that year he was selected for inclusion in the Alberta exhibit at the Royal Winter Fair where he placed second in a class of twenty-two crossbred hunters and fourth among twenty-four contestants in an open Conformation Hunter class.

But the showring is not all fun. On the way home from Toronto, the young horse went down with shipping fever in its worst form. "We very nearly lost him," Lady Gordon told, "and my husband and I spent four days and nights with him in his box stall and after careful nursing we pulled him through. It was at this time," she added, "that I realized how much Greensleeves meant to me as a pet and friend."

As a three-year-old, the horse appeared with the mature figure of a great hunter. He was the high ranking horse in Model Hunter classes that year although he did not take readily to arena jumping; he was the big country boy, terribly subject to "stage fright." But back on the farm his schooling was continued. There were hours daily of riding and jumping in snow or on summerfallow land and the big fellow became more reliable and lovable. With more shows, the "stage fright" disappeared and he grew to like the footlights.

"During the bad years of hail," his owner confessed, "when for three seasons in a row we had no crop and when the price of livestock dropped to rock bottom on account of foot-and-mouth disease embargo, Greensleeves became our only means of relaxation and the only thing we could afford to enjoy. I say 'afford' because he always paid his expenses and ours as well by winning consistently."

In the autumns of 1957 and '58, Greensleeves went again to the Royal Winter Fair, each time taking some top awards. But 1959 was his greatest year, winning, as he did, the Burton Canadian Hunter Stake. And the only horse to place above him in the open Heavyweight class that year was a United States entry for which the owners were said to have refused $40,000.

The great hunter went again to the Royal in 1960 but it was a year of near-disaster. As horsemen know, long freight hauls can be hazardous and early on this journey, Greensleeves contracted shipping fever. Obviously the attack was a severe one. A telegram brought a veterinarian to meet the train at a midnight hour in Winnipeg. The sick animal's temperature was then 106.5 degrees. His condition was critical. The best known treatments were administered but the Winnipeg veterinarian held out only a slight chance of the horse reaching Toronto alive. Discharging his duty, he notified the Animal Health authorities in Toronto by wire that an extremely sick horse was on the way.

It was clearly implied that if the hose were still alive upon arrival, it would not be allowed to leave the freight car. The Toronto veterinarian assigned to making an inspection and issuing a professional order, enquired about where he would find the car carrying the sick horse from Alberta and was told: "There's the horse trotting toward the barns right now." There was a hurried inspection. Temperature was checked and found to be near normal; the recovery had been spectacular and Greensleeves entered his classes and did some jumping performances which people who knew his handicap of sickness said was unbelievable.

Commenting in 1961, Lady Gordon, with unrestrained affection for her hunter, said: "He is now twelve years old, sound and happy and healthy and has a lot of jump in him yet. We will be showing him again. Meantime we will use him to 'pony' the young race horses and teach them good manners. His wisdom and sense rub off on the young ones and they love him for his power and calmness . . . Bless him, he not only gives us great happiness but he is indispensable to our operations and is completely one of the family and part of our lives."

CHAPTER 35

Barra and Buster

B arra Lad and Bouncing Buster lived in different periods but both were jumpers the western Horse Show patrons could never forget. Buster's crowd-pleasing ability was something to fill a seasoned politician with envy although Barra Lad was the greater performer. If asked to name the foremost jumper in Canadian history, most pioneer horsemen will say "Barra Lad," the sensation of the years prior to 1925.

Quite a few of the jumping marks made in early years are still impressive. Jumping at Calgary in April, 1914, Smokey, owned by D. P. McDonald of Cochrane, cleared seven feet— first western-bred horse to do it. Strangely enough, three visiting horses, The Wasp and Skyscraper owned by Sifton Stable, Winnipeg, and Blenheim owned by Calgary Real Estate Man F. C. Lowe—none of them bred in the West— jumped seven feet, four inches on the same evening program.

Another seven foot jumper of which horsemen speak with admiration was Rolla G. Kripp, a Thoroughbred owned and ridden by Ernie Bell who campaigned later with Scotsman. Then there was the Manitoba horse, Cerebos, which Thomas Sumner was reported to have bought at the Stockyards in St. Boniface for $35. At the Brandon Winter Fair in 1932, this one cleared at six feet, seven inches, and then the bars were raised to seven feet two inches. In the first jump at the higher level, the horse fell but in the second attempt, he went over and fell on the other side.

These were notable performances but Barra Lad's record surpassed them all by an astonishing margin. He was bred at

Colony Farm, Essondale, British Columbia, where many of the world's finest Holstein cattle were kept in later years. Sired by a Hackney and from a mare having Standardbred breeding, the foal was left an orphan at birth. There didn't seem to be much hope for him but the little fellow was bottle-fed and with the help of nurses at the hospital, was saved and thoroughly spoiled. That was in 1918.

Before any thought was given to the colt's future, men about the barns noticed him jumping logs and barrels instead of going around them. And before long, no gate was high enough to stop him. About this time, Scottish Peter Welsh, with a dealer's barn at the northeast corner of the Centre Street and Fifth Avenue intersection in Calgary, heard about the colt with unusual jumping tendencies and made an offer to purchase, sight unseen, for $150. The offer was accepted and the orphan colt was shipped express to Calgary. At once the colt's education was started with Louis and Josie Welsh as chief teachers. Taken to Eastern Canada as a three-year-old, Barra Lad was a surprise winner against experienced horses and Peter Welsh began to realize he had a potential champion.

At the Brandon Spring Show in 1922, the bay gelding with white muzzle brought spectators to their feet when, with fourteen-year-old Louis Welsh in the saddle, he jumped six feet, ten inches, to establish a Manitoba record. That was a Monday night and on Thursday night he raised his record to seven feet, one inch.

By this time the horse's peculiar disposition was becoming evident. In the stall he was friendly and when he was being exercised, he'd loaf along at three miles an hour. But once in the arena, the otherwise gentle horse became a fireball. "Just show him a jump," said Josie Welsh, "and he'd go half mad; there was no holding him." At a Brandon show, Louis Welsh, who usually rode Barra Lad, had an injury and it fell to brother Josie to take the horse over the jump. Josie was worried and asked Louis what he should do. The brother replied: "When you turn him to a jump, just grab a handful of mane and shut your eyes and let him go." Josie took the advice and said later: "I didn't know I was over the seven-foot bars until I heard the crowd roaring."

For the next three years, Barra Lad—15¾ hands and one thousand one hundred pounds in prime jumping condition—was a conquering hero at Canadian and United States shows. In a State of Washington show he distinguished himself by clearing the seven-foot jump in each of the seven days of the event.

On April 1, 1925, Calgary people saw The Lad jump seven feet, one inch in Victoria Arena. It was his last appearance in the home city. The climax in his career came soon after at New Westminster, by which time his name was a genuine box-office attraction. Six thousand people were present at the Horse Show arena at New Westminster Exhibition that night and what they saw was more by far than any could have anticipated. After a jump of six feet which the Prairie horse took with ease, the bars were raised to seven feet, then to eight feet, one and one-half inches. The measurements were made with obvious care by men who seemed to realize the importance of it all. The bars were at a level higher than any horse in the world had ever cleared.

Entering the arena, Barra Lad seemed untamed as usual. He champed angrily on his bit and tossed his head from side to side. The only thing on his mind, as always, was to locate the jumps and leap over them. With Louis Welsh, then seventeen years of age, in the saddle, the customary circle at the end of the arena was shortened and Barra Lad broke into a mad run toward the obstacle. With ears back, nostrils distended and muscles collected magnificently, the gallant horse leaped cat-like into the air. Front feet went over and momentarily it seemed he could not do the same with the hind ones. But with unbelievable co-ordination he pulled the hind feet close to his belly and was over without as much as a touch—eight feet, one and one-half inches—a world jumping record. The best previous record was eight feet and three-sixteenth of an inch, made in Chicago two years earlier.

The six thousand spectators stood and cheered in their astonishment. Every onlooker knew that horse history was being written right there. But the sequel was a sad one. As the great horse came down from the jump, he went on his knees and his distinctive white muzzle seemed to plow a furrow in the tanbark. Louis Welsh remained in the saddle and Barra Lad was at once back on all four feet. There was no particular reason to suppose that anything was seriously wrong. An enthusiastic crowd surged into the ring to be close to the Champion of Champions, but Barra Lad, even though severely shaken, was inviting no affection or intimacy—certainly not in the jumping ring which to him was always a place for serious work rather than play. He made it plain that spectators could keep their distance.

Barra Lad was taken back to his stall, given a good rub-down and his usual evening feed of rolled oats and bran. Generally he was hungry for his meals but this time he refused his grain and at once it was feared that something was wrong. And, indeed, something was wrong; in a matter of hours the great horse—greatest jumper of his time—was dead. The cause: internal hemorrhage. It was a sad day for the lovers of good and courageous horses. Fittingly, Barra Lad's body was given burial on the Exhibition Grounds at New Westminster, just outside the arena.

Bouncing Buster, horse of a different temperament, loved the bright lights of the showring. Crowds never bothered him; in fact, like a good actor, he was at his best when there was an audience. At the big Prince Albert Horse Show in the autumn of 1945, Buster was taken into the ring for familiarization jumps on the first morning of the show and, with very few spectators present, the old campaigner knocked down about every obstacle on the course. A reporter happened to be at the ringside and the evening paper disclosed his conclusion: "Buster's jumping days are over." But when the lights went on for the night show and bleachers were filled, the old horse never missed a jump and finished with another championship.

The Prince Albert performance led to a rumor that his owner, Gordon Williamson of Brandon, was giving the horse a pint of whisky prior to every jumping event. The rumor was taken seriously but investigation showed Buster to be a teetotaller. No stimulant except an enthusiastic cheering section was needed to make him jump.

Buster got his start on the Ronalane Ranch on the Bow River, west of Medicine Hat. His Thoroughbred sire was a son of the famous Yorkshire Lad and his dam carried Standardbred blood from a stallion called Vernon which J. D. McGregor sent from Brandon. In 1931, Walter Kane, cowboy and business man, bought four carloads of range horses in Alberta and shipped to Winnipeg. Among yearlings in the shipment was a bay colt later known as Buster.

About this time, Duncan McIvor from Selkirk, came to Winnipeg to buy some cattle. Said Walter Kane: "I'll sell you some colts that'll make you more money than cattle; I'll sell you three yearlings for $20 each and if you take care of them, I'll buy them back when they're old enough to work."

"That's a deal," said McIvor, "provided you'll come out and break them to saddle when they're old enough."

The colts—including Buster—were trucked to Selkirk. A couple of years later, Walter Kane, remembering his promise, drove to Selkirk and broke the colts to saddle, then bought Buster back for $125. At Mr. Kane's Cambridge Stable, the young horse was under the care of Josie Welsh, who had so much to do with Barra Lad, and he started Buster on a jumping career. As a jumper, Walter Kane observed, "The colt was a natural."

Years passed and in 1941, Buster was sold to Gordon Williamson of Brandon for $75. Now eleven years old and rated as an aged horse, he didn't seem to be worth any more. But the horse was worth more, much more, as time was to show. At this point, Buster became Bouncing Buster and from then until his death in his 28th year, Gordon and Lil Williamson were about the only people to ride him. Between 1941 and 1951, the aging horse went around the spring circuit of Horse Shows every year and attended many of the summer exhibitions as well. In the spring of 1947—then seventeen years of age—he was undefeated in the Knock Down and Out and High Jump classes at Brandon, Regina, Calgary, Edmonton and Winnipeg. It was a clean sweep.

Repeatedly people had been saying: "This will be Bouncing Buster's last year." But he came again and again and in 1951, despite his twenty-one years, won the jumping championship at Regina, Brandon and Calgary Spring Shows and tied for championship at Saskatoon.

Of course he brought many thrills to his owners, one of the best being at Calgary Spring Show in 1945 when he cleared sixty-two fences and other obstacles without a fault and won the Knock Down and Out class. In the first round of that contest, five famous jumping horses tied for top position, Huntsman, Gay Lad, Big Red, Royal Knight and Bouncing Buster. Each jump-off which followed eliminated only one horse. Huntsman and Bouncing Buster survived for the final test. Horses and riders were getting tired but the older jumper emerged as winner and after he had cleared his sixty-second fence that night, at heights up to five feet, ten inches, and won the trophy, Gordon Williamson wouldn't have taken $10,000 for him.

One thing about Bouncing Buster: he never refused a jump. He was game to try anything and give it his best. Horsemen loved him for his spirit. In height of jumps, he didn't and couldn't rival Barra Lad but in lifetime performance, no horse had more to show.

CHAPTER 36

A Cowboy's Horse

The cutting horse is a highly trained specialist—like a piano tuner or goalkeeper in human society—and often a high-priced one. A Texas horse seen in Western Canadian cutting competitions in 1961 was said to have been bought as a four-year-old for $50,000.

Most showyard contestants have been Quarter Horses, simply because animals of that breed seem to possess a special aptitude for western saddles and stock work, like Border Collies for sheep herding and Cocker Spaniels for flushing game birds. The fact is that cutting horses can be of any breed or any color. Morgans, Arabians, Thoroughbreds, Palominos, Appaloosas and horses of unknown ancestry have appeared as professionals in the cow country art of cutting. The cutting horse, it should be noted, is an individual more than a breed. In this instance, it is performance and that alone which counts.

Somebody said cutting horses are "born rather than made." The statement is only partly correct. No doubt the intelligence and disposition necessary for top performance are present as inherited characteristics; likewise, heredity will have something to do in determining the desired muscling, nimble feet and that all-important quality known as "cow sense."

But regardless of aptitude, no horse gains distinction without long and intensive training. Teaching begins lightly at about two years of age, calling for a patient rider and repetitious practise in running, stopping, turning quickly and pivoting.

The colt must be taught to neck-rein at a light touch, slide hind feet into position to stop suddenly and change leads appropriately at the gallop. In running, a horse leads naturally with the fore leg on the inside of the circle and any animal failing to change leads with change of direction is in danger of being caught off balance with all the dire consequences. Correct lead is important in all saddle horses but especially so in cutting horses where foot work counts for much.

The horse in training must learn to interpret the feelings of pressure from the rider's legs. In competitions, horses work without any perceptible guidance from riders—sometimes even without bridles or hackamores. At best, a horse doesn't reach a state of "finish" for two or more years. And the animal is not "finished" until able to work amid the glare and noise of a strange arena as well as in the quietness of home surroundings. The fact is that most horses selected for training never reach competition calibre, while those which do succeed, become highly valuable.

The competitive test consists of taking one protesting steer or heifer at a time from the herd in the arena and effectively blocking its eager attempts to return. Horse and rider enter the herd quietly and, having selected the animal to be cut out, the horse is turned to move it away from the other cattle. Then, when the segregated critter finds itself isolated from the herd-mates and makes a frantic attempt to return, the good cutting horse, with eyes fixed firmly upon the cattle victim, unwinds like lightning to frustrate every bovine plunge to achieve its purpose. It can be beautiful to watch as cutting horse displays the foot action of a tap-dancer, turning, twisting, leaning, blocking and ever in balance. The spectator will find it easy to agree that here is the finest of all examples of team work between a horse and its rider. And, if one may judge, the trained horses seem to enjoy the sport, enjoy outguessing the cattle against which they find themselves pitted.

Cutting horse competitions became popular in the '40s and '50s. In 1954 the Canadian Cutting Horse Association was formed and the increasing number of shows and entries after that date gave evidence of the rising interest. In 1961 there were fifty-five Canadian contest with $16,000 offered in prizes. Western Canada, by that latter year, was said to have more top cutting horses than anywhere outside of the Western States.

But it would be wrong to convey any idea of all cutting horses being frequenters of the showring. Horses of the kind were working expertly on cattle ranches long before competitive cutting was introduced. Like industrious back-country cowboys who never indulged in yodelling or glamorously colored shirts, they were indispensable at roundup time or whenever cattle were to be worked. Most of them lived and died on the job without ever seeing the inside of an arena or exhibition enclosure. But, worth their weight in mink coats to a rancher, those great horses of the range deserved the highest praise.

Indeed, thousands of those "skilled workers" served faithfully without ever becoming known beyond the home range. The first Canadian horse to be brought into the national or international limelight was a gelding called Keeno and he was nineteen years old—well beyond a normal span of life—before he left range routine on the Streeter Ranch at Stavely, Alberta, to indulge in the more frivolous activities of a public contest. The old horse was, in some ways, like a rancher who, after reaching retiring age, decided to travel and take part in the youthful pastimes he had missed in earlier and busier years. It appeared as a reckless adventure but the old horse brought one surprise after another and was finally hailed as the greatest cutting performer discovered in the Canadian Cattle Kingdom.

How was Keeno bred? The sire of the talented gelding, now a memory, was a Thoroughbred standing at Henry Sharples' ranch west of Claresholm. On the maternal side was Blackfoot Indian horse stock, mostly Mustang. It made for a fascinating pedigree: on one side an old English breed with speed and quality, and on the other, a long-time North American strain demonstrating the law of "Survival of the Fittest."

Keeno was foaled in 1927 and didn't attract any particular attention. Along with other Streeter Ranch horses of his generation, he was broken to saddle at three years of age although he received no special training. And until Keeno was in his twentieth year, nobody except the two Streeter brothers had ever thrown a leg over his well muscled back.

From the time of breaking, however, Allie Streeter suspected he had a "one-in-a-million" horse; but he was more concerned about day-to-day work on the foothills cattle ranch than in seeking showring glories.

There was nothing phenomenal about Keeno's speed, nor about his beauty. But his sagacity and determination in working cattle set him apart. Always he did a big share in the thinking when cattle were being handled, Allie Streeter said, and his technique was nigh faultless. "He was too smart for critters thinking they could cut back on him."

And at the age of nineteen, instead of being retired, Keeno went to the shows. The Nanton Horse Show of 1946 was the farthest the old fellow had ever been from the home ranch. Understandably, a horse of nineteen years would be "set in his ways," and he didn't like the fair. But even while registering his dislike for the strange surroundings, he won both stock horse class and cutting contest against the best in the foothills.

Streeter's friends were impressed and one said: "That horse is good enough for Denver. Why not take him there for the big show?"

But Allie Streeter wasn't convinced that a rising twenty-year-old should be taken anywhere except back to the ranch. The idea of hauling the ancient horse to far-away Colorado was quickly dispelled. Along in December, however, Streeter met up with W. A. Crawford-Frost of Hereford fame and was persuaded to make the bold adventure, take Keeno to what was admittedly one of the strongest competitions in the world. The formal entry was transmitted to Denver by telegram and on the day after New Year's, 1947, Allie Streeter and Hal Sears loaded the horse in a trailer behind the former's car and headed southward.

Keeno was on wheels for the first time in his long life and didn't like it, didn't like leaving the grassy hills he knew so well and heading into the unknown at forty miles an hour. He was nervous, worried and annoyed. But after days of travel, men and horse arrived at Denver, forty-eight hours before the contests were scheduled to start on January 9.

First there was the elimination contest, with twenty-seven contestants—twenty-seven of the best stock horses on the continent and most of them experienced under the distracting lights of a showring. Eliminations reduced the field to eighteen and Streeter and Keeno were "still in." So much, so good. For that two-minute period during which the Alberta horse was officially under the observation of judges, Keeno managed to hide his uneasiness about the strange and gaudy surroundings and worked well—extremely well for a newcomer to the big city. The old horse had probably worked more cattle than any two other horses at the show but never was he exposed to so many hand-clapping spectators and every time the crowd cheered, Keeno naturally wondered what it was about and momentarily his mind was off his work.

In the next competitive round, contestants were reduced to twelve, then to eight. The Alberta horse and cowboy were still in the race and when the winners were finally determined, Keeno was in seventh place. Under the circumstances, it was seen as one of the most notable triumphs in the history of those sturdy little horses which carry stock saddles.

And when Keeno and Allie Streeter arrived back at Nanton, ranchers, farmers and town people united at a banquet to celebrate the success and do honor to a cowboy and his horse. A presentation was made and with the gift went an inscription: "To Allie Streeter of the Nanton-Stavely district for the excellent showing made by him and his horse, Keeno, in the stock cutting contest at Denver, Colorado, U.S.A., January 9, 1947, against the best on the continent. Nanton Agricultural Society and Nanton and District Board of Trade."

Back home on the range, Keeno was ready to forget the bright lights and high living; there was work to do and he would settle down to it as though he had never been away. At the time of the horse's twentieth birthday, Allie Streeter could say: "He's as sound as a bullet and still likes to buck a little when you first get on him."

The adventure to Denver had added glamor to Keeno's life but he was first, last and always a cowboy's working horse, reliable, skillful and tireless—like thousands of those faithful and indispensible animals which assist in the cattle industry and rarely leave the home ranges.

CHAPTER 37

Respect for the Buckers

In homestead communities where cowboy influence was absent, the broncho with an addiction to kicking or bucking was regarded as the lowest form of horseflesh. It was the troublemaker in a team, the horse most likely to demolish a buggy and the one no ordinary sodbuster cared to saddle. There was nothing good about the rebel. Being the "bad boy" of the stable, this one was always the first to be offered for sale or trade. No homesteader could have anticipated the coming age of rodeos and a time when hard-kicking horses with fighting spirit might buck their way to fame for themselves and fortune for their owners. To have suggested that such outlaws might one day outsell more amiable stablemates would have seemed fantastic.

In the ranching country, things were different; even in the pre-rodeo years bucking horses were able to command some respect. The "bad" horses were not always salable but, up to a point, they had entertainment value. No rancher could be bothered with many of them but it seemed worth while to keep at least one around to test local skills and help in humbling conceited cowboys who happened to drift that way.

According to rangeland verse: "There ain't no man what can't be throwed; And there ain't no hoss what can't be rode." It wasn't surprising, therefore, that Sunday afternoons during roundups found men and selected "hosses" being put to the test.

In the course of time, rangeland communities developed local pride in the violence of their best buckers. In the

Medicine Hat countryside, for example, cowpunchers talked boastfully about Scarhead and Rooster, horses which never failed to make life difficult for men who tried to ride them. Rooster was a J. D. McGregor horse and everybody on the roundups in 1910 and '11 remembered the chestnut with the explosive disposition. In harness, Rooster behaved tolerably well but everybody was aware of the dynamite packed in his legs when he decided to buck.

As a harness horse he was used in the team delegated to haul the chuckwagon and there was a June morning Rooster staged a show which spectators like George Armstrong and others could never forget. The chuckwagon team was about to be hitched. One tug only was hooked when something disturbed the temperamental Rooster. He began to kick as only Rooster could. The chuckwagon faced possible destruction until the iron end of the singletree came loose, leaving the bucking horse in the clear. But the horse's display of rebellion against harness and saddles did not subside.

"It was beautiful to watch," said William Wilde who remembered all the details. "That horse sunfished, jack-knifed and did about everything a horse could do, and then began to peel his harness. You wouldn't believe it possible but he did it methodically."

First the bridle was jerked off; the breeching went next; something happened to the bellyband and backpad and they fell to the ground; then the hames and tugs were dislodged and, finally, with head close to the sod, Rooster shook the collar off over his head and then was as naked as when he was foaled. Only when the last shred of harness had been dislodged did Rooster end his bucking.

"Yes, it was a beautiful performance," the cowboy spectators agreed, and even the trouble of making repairs to broken harness seemed a small price for the thrill of witnessing such a finished display of versatile bucking.

Gradually, as rodeos became popular, there was reason to believe that Canadian-raised horses possessed a certain superiority in bucking ability. At least some of them were taken to the United States to make rodeo records and win international applause. One to become famous in the neighboring country was Fox, of which a cowpoke of the old range said: "That horse could unload anybody who got on him and kick the seat of his pants before he struck the ground."

But Fox wasn't in all respects a bad horse. In a stall, he was gentle and in harness, quite reliable. He was used on scraper work in excavating the basement for the Hudson Bay Store and the First Street subway beside the Palliser Hotel in Calgary and anybody seeing him at work would never suspect the rebellion which the feel of a saddle could kindle within him.

Fox was bred and raised near Gleichen, foaled in 1908. At first there was no reason for his owner, Tom McHugh, to take any special notice of him. He was just another broncho colt, sorrel in color and fairly heavily built. At two years of age he was sold to Frank McHugh and then Jack McGillis broke him—if it could be said the horse was ever really broken. McGillis vouched for it that Fox acted quite domesticated in harness but was ready to buck every time a saddle ever touched his back.

After being the downfall of almost all who tried to ride him in Alberta, Fox was taken across the border and, with name Reservation, was bucked in New York in 1916. There, as in Alberta, he left the best riders sitting on the ground. Most rodeo patrons hadn't seen anything quite like him.

Canadians saw him again at the Victory Stampede in Calgary in 1919 when Guy Weadick was trying to duplicate the successes of 1912. Fox was at his best and, unseating one champion rider after another, was the sensation of the infield. Instead of becoming tired, Fox became rougher and tougher as the week wore on and among those meeting downfall as he kicked toward the sky was the great rider, Emery Le Grandeur.

The Victory Stampede appearance was the last in Canada for Fox. Soon after, he was shipped to new owners at Pendleton, Oregon, where he was entered with another change of name, No Man's Land. It was there that the great horse—always Fox to Canadians who knew him—ended his days, rating a hero's funeral and gravestone.

The pioneers in rodeo talked admiringly about Fox, Bassano, Tumble Weed, Alberta Kid, Grave Digger, Cyclone, Bay Dynamite and others but most would agree upon Midnight as the bucking horse of them all. It was an opinion shared by Pete Knight of Crossfield, four times winner of the world championship for bronk riding and on his way to a fifth award when killed under a bad horse in California in 1937.

This bone-bruising black gelding was bred and raised near Fort Macleod. His breeder was James Wilton McNab, born on the Horseshoe Dot Ranch beside the Belly River. One of Jim McNab's boyhood friends was Tom Three Persons who lived on the nearby Blood Reserve and distinguished himself by winning the world championship in bronk riding at the Calgary Stampede of 1912. As soon as he was old enough, Jim McNab was ranching in partnership with A. W. Brusselle in the Porcupine Hills, using the doorkey brand. There Midnight, from a mean-tempered Thoroughbred mare and a range stallion of Percheron and Morgan breeding, was foaled in 1916. But by this time, Owner Jim McNab was overseas with the Canadian forces.

After being given the ranch brand, the black colt ran on the range until McNab's return in 1919. Seeing the sturdy black three-year-old for the first time, the returned man fixed upon the name, Midnight, and quietly set about to break him with the idea of using him for general saddle work on the ranch. The young horse responded reasonably well but it was soon observed that he had a dual personality and was capable of dumping the old ranch hands with ease.

In 1924—the year Fort Macleod was celebrating its 50th anniversary—Jim McNab undertook to furnish horses for the Calgary Stampede. Midnight, then eight years old, was taken along to his first big-league tests. With a flank strap to aggravate him, he was spectacular from the very first time out of a bucking chute and by the end of the week had bucked off every cowboy who drew him.

About this time, Peter Welsh of Calgary was assembling horses for a travelling rodeo and determined to get the best buckers in Western Canada. Midnight was his first choice and he bought him for $500, then got Tumble Weed, a horse bred by Joe Laycock of Okotoks, and good enough to be reserve champion to Midnight at the Calgary show. Adding Bassano, champion in 1923, Welsh figured he had the three best bucking horses in the world.

Still buying for his Alberta Stampede Company, Welsh acquired another famous black gelding, one found to be so close to Midnight in bucking performance that he deserved the name, Five Minutes To Midnight. This one, with storybook beginning, came from the Cheadle district, east of Calgary, and gained the first public attention as an unattractive stray colt with annoying skill in jumping farm fences. Farmers finding him in their crops tried to catch the little stray and when they couldn't get a lariat on him, they threatened to shoot.

Finally, the young outlaw was herded into a local pound and from there was sold for $3 to a man who wanted a saddle horse for his children. But this was no horse for children and after fighting bits and bridles and saddles and proving his rebelliousness, he was bought for $75 by Peter Welsh who discovered exactly what rodeo promoters were combing the country to find.

During the next couple of years, the two Midnights made life extremely difficult for contesting cowboys in Western Canada and in 1927, both were sold to Vern Elliott and Eddie McCarty, rodeo suppliers of Wyoming and

Colorado. At once the two Canadian-breds became the outstanding performers at major American rodeos, capable of unwinding the most devastating pitches seen in any arenas on that side of the line. The two horses campaigned together for some years and then, in 1933, the original Midnight—seventeen years of age—was formally retired. It was at Cheyenne and Turk Greenough won the riding championship. As a parting gesture, it was arranged that the cowboy champion would ride the retiring bucker champion in an after-the-show contest. Spectators said it was one of the old horse's best displays and he promptly unloaded the rider. Pensioned off, Midnight enjoyed all the freedom and luxury the McCarty and Elliott ranches could offer and at his death a headstone was erected to mark the place of burial. On the stone was a verse:

"Under this sod lies a great bucking hoss;
There never was a cowboy he couldn't toss.
His name was Midnight, his coat black as coal;
If there's a hoss Heaven, please God, take his soul."

The other black, Five Minutes To Midnight, was given a similar opportunity to enjoy some years of retirement and died on Vern Elliott's Colorado ranch in 1947, age twenty-seven years. A short time before his death, owners saddled him and assigned a good rider to see if soft living and leisure had changed the old bucker. But the horse left no doubt in anybody's mind; with his former fury, he exploded from the chute, threw his rider as of old and bucked all the way down the field. This horse, once a three dollar colt and for which, at his prime, Elliott and McCarty were supposed to have refused $10,000, was still a champion.

It did seem convincing that Western Canadian soil imparted an extra bit of spirit and kick to its rodeo horses and the good ones came to be seen as specialists, much as roping horses, race horses and parade horses were specialists.

A visitor enquired if it was correct that the horses he saw performing so vigorously at Calgary Stampede were really fed on "buckwheat and wild oats." The answer was: "No, these bronks raised in the buckbrush never need anything from a feedbag."

Said the same shortgrass philosopher: "Bucking horses aren't necessarily bad ones. They're just non-conformists and I admire 'em."

CHAPTER 38

Everybody Loves a Pony

When a pony sells for $85,000 and another for $55,000, buyers leave no doubt about interest and eagerness. For some years after the Second World War, the little fellows were rather consistently outselling the big ones.

Ponies, of course, never had trouble in making friends. Young owners loved them. Anything as dear to little hearts could not be forgotten even in bedtime prayers. It was the repeated supplication of a certain little girl whose black pony went by the name of Molasses: "God bless Molasses and Mummy and Daddy—but don't forget Molasses."

Children not so fortunate as to have ponies thought of them longingly, hopefully. For many years, ponies were the most popular of all draw prizes on Childrens' Days at Canadian exhibitions. There the introduction of a lucky boy to his new pony left no doubt about it being the biggest moment in his life.

When a draw was made for a pony at a morning show for boys and girls at Saskatoon Exhibition in 1944, the lucky number was announced and out of the grandstand crowd of eight thousand youngsters a lad of eleven years marched to claim his prize from the donor, Fred Mendel. With a smile of joy completely out of control, the boy mounted to the platform. Then, before taking the new halter shank in his youthful hand, he reached into a pocket and produced three lumps of rationed sugar for his new pet. Not only had he come hopefully to the exhibition but he had come prepared. From a member of the platform party was heard a whisper: "Great is thy faith."

Were it not for certain practical problems in keeping them, there would be equine miniatures in every back yard where children reside. And in a mechanical age, more ponies in more back yards would be "good medicine" for those young people.

Technically, ponies are any members of the horse species which, at maturity, stand not over 14½ hands. They are the little horses with personalities inviting childish affection. Most of the pony breeds seen in Canada and United States had their origin in the British Isles where no fewer than nine developed. Best known was the Shetland, most diminutive of the pony breeds. Specimens of the old "Sheltie" strain have been called dwarfs and runts but such has not detracted in any way from public interest and the Shetland continues to be popular, not only with children but with adults who classify as hobby breeders.

For how many hundreds of years these small ponies lived on their native Shetland Islands, lying to the north of Scotland, nobody can be certain but some historians say "at least twelve hundred years." With cold winters and sparse vegetation, living was never easy in those parts. Usually the ponies ran throughout their lives in the open and often they had to depend for winter feed upon seaweed picked up along the coast. In the course of many generations, they adapted themselves rather well to the harsh environment. Hardiness became a leading characteristic and, as horsemen have observed, the long and heavy winter coat of hair—resembling fur about as much as hair—has been an effective means of protection.

From their bleak islands the Shetlands have gone to nearly every country in the world. Their small size coupled with heavy muscling made them acceptable for draught purposes in small quarters and many were worked in Old Country mine pits. On Scotland's hillsides they found use in carrying packs. But west of the Atlantic, it was as children's pets and mounts that the Shetland found the place it seemed to have been destined to fill. Many of the country's expert riders started in tender years in a saddle less than twelve hands from the ground.

It didn't mean that the Shetland was in all respects the most ideal mount for young riders. Trot and canter in the traditional type were rough gaits and although the typical breed representative was intelligent, it could be annoyingly set in its ways—in other words, stubborn.

But the Shetland is a reformed creature—in body conformation and action at least. The original or Island Shetland was a thick set kind, best described as a miniature Percheron. In the showring, the more dwarf and chunky, the better judges liked him. He had far more middle and muscling than he needed but was often short of quality. The height maximum was 11½ hands and there was no minimum. It was impossible that anything having such squat conformation could excel in action. Indeed, there was little good that anybody could say concerning the lazy-footed trot and canter in the older type of Shetland.

But much was to change. No breed of livestock has been transformed more completely. Specimens of the old draught type in miniature still exist but hobby breeders, especially in the United States, demanded a more stylish pony with flash and action. The ponies commanding high prices at sales in recent years have been those with high heads, trim necks, refined bodies and quality bone, and able to step out like little Hackneys. About all that the new North American Shetland appeared to have in common with the old Island type was its restricted size. The maximum height remained at forty-six inches or 11½ hands, with forty-three inches considered as maximum height for yearlings and 44½ inches for two-year-olds.

How was this new, proud-stepping show type in Shetlands achieved so quickly? Selection would account for considerable but many breeders hint at infusions of the blood of pony type Hackneys. There is no question about the modern show-type Shetlands as displayed with overgrown tails and heavy shoes being graceful and beautiful. They may retain some sturdiness of body but they are far removed from the pluggy ponies of other years, also far from the docile specimens whose slow rate of speed was just about right for young drivers.

The tremendous upsurge in breeding and selling of ponies directed attention to other breeds, Welsh, Dartmoor, Hackney, Fell, Highland, Exmoor, Viking, Iceland and others. All these have been imported to Canada although not all have survived in the pure state.

Welsh ponies such as lived on the mountains and moors of Wales for centuries have been brought to Canada from time to time since the beginning of settlement. As pedigreed ponies they did not become numerous but thousands of "half-pint" ponies standing twelve to thirteen hands, well furnished with utility and described as "part Welsh," have been the indispensible mounts of boys and girls who were too big for Shetlands and not ready for larger horses. Being of dual purpose type, they were well suited to both harness and saddle. And, like all the breeds of British ponies, they were of a hardy kind, capable of adapting quickly and completely to Canadian conditions.

Through the years, parents seeking children's ponies other than Shetlands, have turned most commonly to the Welsh, concluding that here was a breed with pony personality and yet a fair measure of horse character in the manner of carrying a saddle.

The pioneer band of Dartmoor ponies in Canada was imported to the E. P. Ranch in the foothills in 1920 by the ranch owner at that time, Edward, Prince of Wales. It was while the Prince was touring Canada and paying a brief visit at George Lane's Bar U Ranch that the royal guest fell in love with the adjoining property and resolved to own it. In due course the purchase was completed and in the following year pure bred cattle, horses and sheep were imported for breeding purposes. Some famous animals like the

Thoroughbred stallion, Will Somers, and Shorthorn bull, King of the Fairies, were brought to the ranch. And the Dartmoors, regarded as an experiment, did well in their new surroundings. Later, an Arabian stallion was imported from England and from crosses of Arabian on Dartmoor made at the ranch came some of the finest pony hacks seen in Canadian show rings. One of those crossbreds, Dixie Belle, foaled in 1931, was exhibited with an almost unbroken record of successes by Mrs. Allie Steinman of Saskatoon. That pony, at the age of thirty, was still living and active, testifying to an obvious pony characteristic, that of long life.

Other breeds were introduced. Representatives of the Fell breed, having an ancient association with the North of England, were brought by Dr. Howard S. Mitchell of Montreal. Here was a pony with somewhat more size than the average for British breeds, being usually 13½ hands.

In 1958, Canadians met the Viking, a comparatively rare breed from the Island of Gotland in the Baltic Sea. The Canadian importer and owner, Knut Magnusson of Fogelvik Farm, Innisfail, Alberta, estimated the world population of Viking ponies to be not more than one hundred and his Alberta group was seen as the biggest outside the native island. In 1960, Mr. Magnusson imported two more stallions and, strange to relate, obtained one with Palomino and one with Appaloosa colors. The additions brought the Innisfail band of ponies to twenty-two.

Most text book writers missed the Viking and it wasn't much wonder because of its isolation on a small island. But it appeared to possess some definite characteristics: an average height of 12¼ hands, good dispositions, admirable adaptability and extreme hardiness.

With so many people enquiring for ponies, it was natural for enterprising stockmen to be looking for something different and in 1959, the Iceland breed made its entry to this country. Ponies of the breed were said to have occupied the native

Iceland for almost a thousand years without any outside influence. No doubt they were Celtic in origin and thus remotely related to Highland and other British pony breeds. The importers were westerners prominent in the raising of Hereford cattle, Tom and Harold Lees of Arcola, Saskatchewan, and John and Perry Minor of Abbey, Saskatchewan, and Brooks, Alberta. Thirty-five of the Iceland ponies came in 1959 and more in 1960. They made their first appearance in the Canadian Stud Book in the latter year—all seventy-three of them.

The Canadian Pony Society was organized in 1901 and incorporated under the Live Stock Pedigree Act in 1908. Shetlands, as most horsemen would expect, have been consistently far ahead of any other breed in numbers entered for registration with the National Live Stock Records. Up to the end of 1960 registrations included three thousand seven hundred and sixty-four Shetlands, eleven hundred and twenty-one Welsh, seventy-three Iceland, forty-six Dartmoor, twelve Highland, eleven Fell, seven Polo and three Exmoor. In the case of Dartmoor and Polo, registration numbers have not changed since 1935.

At the time of writing, Ontario could claim the greatest interest in ponies and pony breeding. Of the seven hundred and two ponies of all breeds registered in the Canadian Pony Stud Book during the single year, 1960, more than two-thirds or five hundred and six of them were entered by residents of Ontario; Saskatchewan was second with eighty-four registrations, then British Columbia with forty-five, Alberta with thirty-seven, Quebec with eighteen, Manitoba with nine, Prince Edward Island with two and Nova Scotia with one. Significantly enough, pony registrations in the year were exceeded in numbers by two horse breeds only, Standard Bred and Thoroughbred.

CHAPTER 39

Horses and Art

W hen Charles Beil of Banff—one of Canada's foremost artists and sculptors—was seen walking with perceptible stiffness, he explained submissively: "Guess now that I'm in my '60s, I ought to quit riding those bucking bronchos; but it's my fun." Needless to say, the man wasn't typical of the artistic set. But, like Charlie Russell, Frederick Remington, Will James and scores of others—even Leonardo da Vinci—Beil was a horseman before he became an artist.

The connection between horse and art is a very old one and it's easy to understand. No other animal was more successful in capturing human loyalty and affection and the relationship found expression at the hand of the artist. Throughout the ages, horses were favorite subjects for sketches. Primitive man made crude drawings of them on cave walls and modern man found no better subject matter. Over and over again, love of horses and admiration for their matchless lines brought inspiration leading to songs, poems, stories, paintings and models.

Charlie Russell, whose pictures of horses, cowboys and other living things on the fading frontier won international applause, admitted that an inherent fondness for horses was the main reason he started sketching. This man, the best known of cowboy artists, was not a Canadian although he was frequently on the Canadian Prairies and, like migratory birds, was as much at home on one side of the boundary as on the other.

Certainly, his scenes were as thoroughly understood and appreciated in the Canadian West as in the State of Montana. The picture bringing his first fame, "The Last of 5000," was done in response to a letter from ranch owners enquiring how the cattle were wintering. It was the fateful winter of 1886–'87 and range animals were dying by the thousands on both sides of the boundary. The emaciated old longhorn cow in the picture, about ready to lie down and give her shrunken muscles to the coyotes lurking in the background, told a story that Canadians understood very well.

As early as 1888, Russell, a carefree young cowboy, spent several months on the Blood Reserve, south of Fort Macleod, and on other occasions visited with Phil Weinard of High River and George Lane of the Bar U Ranch. Quite a few of Russell's early sketches were inspired by his Canadian experiences and Canadians grew to love the boldness, action and colors in his pictures. Here was a man painting for horsemen as well as for connoisseurs of art.

When Russell died in 1926, the person who led the late artist's saddled but riderless horse behind the horse-drawn hearse was his protege and friend, Charlie Beil. There was a big difference in ages but otherwise the two Charlies—both princes of the Bohemian type—had much in common. Both began as cowboys; both retained undivided ranchland loyalties; and even in the way they wore their western hats there was resemblance. And after Russell's death, his mantle seemed to fall squarely upon the shoulders of the younger man, who later adopted western Canada and added greatly to Canada's cultural riches.

Charlie Beil was born in Colorado in 1894 and was left an orphan at an early age. Shifting for himself became a matter of necessity and he went to sea, sailed around the southern tip of South America. But it didn't take long to prove that the life of a sailor wasn't for him. Faking his age, he got into the United States cavalry and there received an introduction to horses and saddles, convincing him that the "weather deck" of a horse was far better than anything a ship could offer.

Out of the army, he drifted westward, drove oxen, worked the jerk-line on big horse-drawn outfits hauling freight over primitive western trails, and became an itinerant cowboy. As he worked his way through range country between California and Nevada, he found himself filling idle hours by sketching—usually horses. He said facetiously that he couldn't read or write very well so started drawing pictures to make himself understood. Sometimes the picture was on the flap of a tent, sometimes on a barn door, sometimes on the face of a big rock. These works of art didn't arrest more than local attention but, later, when Beil found himself out of work and out of money in a Nevada city, he tried making pictures for sale. He would paint and one of his equally bankrupt friends would try to sell the result. But the artist's name was unknown and trying to find purchasers for pictures by an unknown artist was like peddling hotdogs at a vegetarian picnic.

As good fortune would have it, however, Beil met up with Charlie Russell, met him at Glacier Park where the younger man was working as a guide in 1920. Attraction was instantaneous. Both liked horses and both liked searching for Nature's secrets. Said Russell: "A machine will show you the man-made things but if you're to see God's own country, you got to get a horse under you." Charlie Beil agreed and years later observed: "Horses did a lot for me; guess I'll ride 'em and sketch 'em as long as I live."

Russell recognized talent in the younger man and encouraged him to give more time to his painting. The advice led to a decision on Beil's part to make a career of art. One thing led to another and he began modeling in clay. Sculpture offered a good means of expression and clay led to the more difficult but more enduring bronze.

After Russell's death, Charlie Beil realized a need for some technical training and in 1928 enrolled in the School of Art at Santa Barbara, California. A special interest in bronze casting developed and before long this student, still walking and talking like a cowpoke, was becoming an expert in casting by the Cellini or Roman method, a technique which Beil had to re-discover practically. At least he had to work out a formula that would permit him to carry the process to completion under his own roof.

The steps in that ancient process consisted of first creating a model from plasticine and from it making a plaster cast or master cast. From the latter a gelatine mold was made and in it was cast the wax. Over the wax model, another mold was made and then by exposing the figure to high heat, the sculptor could melt away the wax, leaving a space into which the molten metal could be poured. But it was not as simple as it sounded and a single specimen could take weeks to complete.

In 1930, Charlie Beil wandered into Canada and visited Banff—for no particular reason. But he liked what he saw. Banff appeared as an artist's paradise; the scenery was magnificent; the mountain resort people were friendly and there were enough horses and stock-saddles around to make him feel at ease and at home. He stopped to fashion some figures and ride some mountain trails, and the longer he lingered, the stronger became the attachment. Then there was a romance and Charlie Beil married the daughter of Pioneer Louis Luxton.

Banff became home and Beil became a busy man—at least as busy as he wanted to be. He made it clear that he had no intention of becoming so occupied in his workshop studio that he couldn't tramp into the mountains or go fishing now and then, or ride Gene Burton's range at Medicine Hat or help Dick Cosgrave with a roundup. "He's a lucky man," said Beil, perhaps thinking of himself, "if he can make a living doing the things he likes."

But more and more figures modeled by Beil were being looked upon as treasures. Each year he furnished the majority of coveted trophies offered by Calgary Stampede, including the miniature four horse team for the winner in the chuckwagon events. How long would it take to turn out a model chuckwagon with four dashing horses? To that question, he replied: "I'd be lucky if I did it in a month and a half."

A bronze figure of a cowboy and his horse was modeled and cast to be a gift from the Kiwanis Club to the late Viscount R. B. Bennett. It is known that the recipient looked upon this as one of his most priceless possessions, becoming one of few art treasures specifically mentioned in the Bennett will and withheld from sale after his death. A bronze bucking horse was presented to Her Majesty, the Queen, and a similar model was given by the city of Calgary to Governor-General Georges Vanier and Madame Vanier on the occasion of their first official visit across the West.

When Banff held its Winter Carnivals, it fell annually to Charlie Beil to fashion the huge prairie buffalo figures—seventeen feet high—in ice. Then there was always the fear of a chinook wind coming to reduce the sculptored masterpiece to a puddle of very common water. And one of Beil's important contributions to art was in the recovery of some Charlie Russell clay models, giving them permanency in bronze.

There was one thing very evident about Beil's horses, whether on canvas or in bronze: they were correct to the last detail. Having studied horse anatomy through the many years of working and riding them, he knew exactly what a hock should be like and what constituted a good foot, pastern and ankle. "But horse personalities," he said, "are all different, just like humans. They're worth studying."

But notwithstanding cultural triumphs and continental acclaim, Beil remained the modest fellow who liked most of all to talk about horses or, perchance, his mule. That mule became famous too. Following the Calgary Exhibition and Stampede of 1954, the trick mule which had been the property of Rodeo Clown Slim Pickens, was presented to Dick Scholten of Medicine Hat and then to Charlie Beil. Before long, everybody in Banff knew Charlie Beil's mule and could say something good or bad about it. One story, for what it was worth, described the artist riding the mule to the post office and having the unpredictable animal decide to sit down on the main street, right in the line of traffic. Nothing the owner could do would induce the former trick mule to get up and, as the story was related, it was necessary to call Slim Pickens by long-distance telephone in California to find out what technique was employed in grandstand circles to induce a performing mule to abandon a sitting position.

Speaking to a Calgary audience some time later, Charlie Beil said he was engaged in a couple of research projects, trying to find, first, why you can keep a mule for two years before he makes up his mind to kick you and, second, why a branding iron affects the flavor of beef; dwelling upon the latter point, he asked: "Why does beef taste better when it has another man's brand on it?"

Quite obviously, this man was no run-of-the-mill artist. With the accent of the West on his words, he could tell a good story as he could paint a good picture. Displaying the skin of a rattlesnake he shot at Gene Burton's ranch, he explained: "It was lucky I had my gun. It took three bullets—the rattler swallowed the first two."

Yes, the mantle of Charlie Russell just seemed to fit both the artistic instincts and the cowboy personality of Charlie Beil. "You see, we both loved horses," he repeated. "Now, I want to capture the story of the North American cowboy and his horse as they moved north into this country. Guess I'm still a cowboy at heart. I'll die that way, just like old Charlie Russell."

But Charlie Beil captured more than the story of horses on the frontier; he captured the rhythm and beauty of God's noblest animal creatures, creating art treasures being sought ever more eagerly by collectors in many parts of the world.

CHAPTER 40

Thanks Pal

At least once in Canadian story the name of a horse was proposed for candidature in an election. It was intended as an expression of gratitude to the horse and it happened at Calgary in 1884 as the seeds of an internationally famous exhibition and stampede were being planted. An agricultural society was formed in August of that year and there was enthusiasm to hold a fair. But the infant society had no property on which to establish a fair grounds.

As fate would have it, A. M. Burgess, deputy minister of the Interior, came to the Bow River Valley to inspect federal lands and while riding a strange horse in the vicinity of Fish Creek, had the misfortune to be thrown and suffer the multiple indignities of fractured collar bone and various painful bruises. As though it had been planned, Major James Walker, a leader in the Agricultural Society movement, came that way with team and wagon and mercifully rescued the injured man from Ottawa and took him to the Walker home.

While the high-ranking civil servant was recuperating and still in a hopelessly poor position to refuse a benefactor's request, Walker explained the Agricultural Society's need for a site for a fair grounds and pointed to some Crown Land beside the Elbow River. Before leaving the hospitable home to return to Ottawa, Burgess went with Walker to inspect the land and promised to do something about making it available at small cost. A short time later, the Agricultural Society bought 94 acres at $2.50 an acre—a total of $235 for what is now Victoria Exhibition Park in the heart of a big city.

An editorial writer, quite unimpressed by the calibre of men about to be nominated to represent the constituency in the Territorial Assembly at Regina, and very much impressed by the important part played by the local horse in detaining the deputy minister and thus getting the land for a fair grounds, had a proposal; he suggested this horse with proven record of service to the community might be the best representative.

Horses have been special guests at Rotary Club luncheons and they have been elected to honorary memberships in service clubs. Titanic, a champion Palomino stallion, was chosen to be an honorary member of a Chamber of Commerce in California.

Quite fittingly, some of the great horses have been immortalized one way or another—Man o' War, for example, the Old Grey Mare, a Halifax pony called Flash, and Captain Stanley Harrison's warhorse, to mention a few. The song about the Old Grey Mare, long a favorite with soldiers, students and others, was inspired by the performance of a transport animal in a Texas unit of the Southern Army during the Civil War. After a long march, soldiers were taking some sleep when the old mare, hitched to a cart loaded with pots and other cookhouse utensils, received a sting from a bee. Convulsively, she burst into a wild bucking performance in the middle of the camp. The sudden turmoil along with rattle of pots and pans brought the soldiers to their feet and reaching for guns, believing the enemy was attacking.

Among the Texas soldiers was James August Bailey who composed the marching tune and words. The displacement of horses accompanying a mechanical age, of which the song's author could not have known, seemed to give more meaning than ever to the words: "She's not what she used to be." But to many people with pioneer experiences, the song brought memories of some particular old greys whose records of service as school ponies or roadsters or work horses deserved lasting thanks and praise.

Flash, to use another example, was a western-bred bay with white stockings. Taken to the East, Flash became an institution and a favorite in the Halifax Junior Bengal Lancers. In 1959, at the age of thirty-one, the pony was officially retired at the Hants County Exhibition; but Flash was not to be forgotten. Too many young people had feelings of affection for the old horse to allow him to be forgotten.

As a reminder, the Oland and Son Perpetual Trophy was offered for Intertownship Team Jumping, "In Memory of Flash," the little westerner, 14½ hands high, which helped to teach successive generations of children to ride. Through many years, in carrying strange and inexperienced youngsters, Flash had never made a move such as might have constituted a danger; if a child fell off, Flash stopped and waited for the young one to wipe tears from eyes and get back in the saddle. Many of the youngsters who became good horsemen and horse-women acknowledged their debt to Flash and, after retirement, the old horse was assured of good grass and the best of care as long as he lived. At the age of thirty-three, he was still in good health and enjoying Nova Scotia gratitude.

On farms and ranches, gratitude was not totally lacking. In farm practice before the age of tractors, horses received their regular rations first, then men took their meals. Cruelty and injustice occurred, yes, but there was more feeling for work horses than men talked about. Horse blankets were carried when winter teaming had to be done. And placing a frosty bit in a horse's mouth was an unpardonable sin.

Perhaps the feeling of partnership between man and horse reached its highest point on the range. A cowboy without a horse wasn't much of a cowboy and he knew it. Walking came to be regarded as something of a disgrace and the old cowboy avoided it as much as he would a contagious disease. Sheepherders and sodbusters could walk to their hearts' content but no self-respecting cowboy wanted to be caught afoot. A stock saddle offered a seat of honor and dignity just as a horse offered a companion and men of the range shared at least some sentiment with Genghis Khan who wanted nothing better than mare's milk for his food, a tent for his palace and a saddle for his throne.

When those old time cowboys took to other occupations, their affinity for saddle horses didn't end. If a former cowboy's job was in freighting, he rode a wheel horse and when he went farming, he rode a saddle pony behind the harrows.

When one of those horse-loving cowboys settled on a farm and was obliged to go regularly for the mail, he always walked farther to catch his saddle horse than would have taken him to the post office. "It's just the principle of the thing," he was known to say.

Rather than tie to a hitching post, that same old cowboy preferred to take his horse inside and ride to the hotel bar. He wasn't alone in that. A man like Rancher Jack Morton of Rosebud, might buy the first drink for his horse and the second for himself. One Prairie bartender, knowing the cowboys who regarded their horses as their closest friends would ride to the bar anyway, decided to erect a sign: "Horses Welcome."

There could be no doubt; men on the frontier found companionship and pleasure in their horses. A bachelor homesteader confessed he might have forgotten his native tongue had it not been for talking to his horses. Talking to a horse seemed much less a symptom of mental disorder than talking to one's self.

When selling at Malcolm McGregor's Polled Hereford dispersion at Brandon in June, 1949, Auctioneer Arthur Thompson told of visiting Kentucky and breaking a journey to see Man o' War. An elderly Negro, obviously proud of his charge, led the famous Thoroughbred stallion out for inspection. To make conversation, Thompson asked what price the horse might have brought if sold. "Two-thirds of a million dollars," was the reply. Then a son of Man o' War was led out and, to a similar question about price, the reply was "one-third of a million."

Pursuing the subject, Thompson asked: "Don't you think you'd rather have a million dollars than those two horses?" The old man shook his head. "No sur," he said, "I could do with a few mo' dollars, but even a million of 'em couldn't give me as much pleasure as that ol' hoss. Why, Man o' War, he's got life an' spirit; an' he an' I are friends. No, I wouldn't sell my friend fo' a million dollars." The old man was grateful for a friendship.

Another of those old horses to come prominently into the public gaze, carrying man's gratitude for work well done, was Old Buck who died in retirement at the Union Stockyards, St. Boniface, in 1948—age forty-one. He was a buckskin, foaled on a Wisconsin farm in 1907. At the age of eight he was bought for use at the stockyards in South St. Paul and there he received his primary education in the operation of a livestock market. He carried commission men up and down the alleys, sorting beef and directing cattle traffic. Then, after four years, he was an immigrant to Canada, coming to St. Boniface as an experienced stockyards worker.

In 1921, when Buck was fourteen-years-old and considered "aged," he was bought by Weiller and Williams Company at the St. Boniface yards and continued year after year to work around the pens until somebody observed that he probably knew as much about grading and sorting cattle as many of the men in the business. He learned all the tricks in "cutting," could block a steer's retreat and when a bull threatened to become ferocious, Buck could pivot and deliver a well-directed kick between the animal's eyes. That's the way it was until 1937 when it was decided that Buck, at age thirty, should be retired.

William McGugan of the Weiller and Williams firm heard of a farm at Headingly where Buck could live out his years in comfort. Amid mixed feelings, the horse was led away. Some years passed. There had been no report about the old horse but Mr. McGugan, when driving on the city's outskirts on a summer evening, noticed a thin horse carrying a boy and shabby saddle. There was something familiar about the mount and McGugan stopped. Sure enough, here was his old friend Buck and the horse pressed its nose against the man's face.

The boy admitted he had hired the horse from a riding stable. To that stable went McGugan and there confirmed his suspicion: the old horse had been sold to the riding stable and was obliged to work again. McGugan was angry. In order to regain possession, he bought the horse back, there and then, for $35 and instructed about delivery at the horse's former box stall at the stockyards.

Back at the yards, Buck felt entirely at home and perfectly happy. At the Winnipeg Horse Show in May, 1946, Buck, then thirty-nine years old, was a special guest and five thousand people cheered when he was presented. But he had never been much for publicity and didn't care for it. Right after being returned to his Horse Show stall, he slipped his halter and made a hasty departure. Searchers found him moving quickly through city streets, trying to discover the shortest route back to his private quarters at the stockyards where he knew the best hay and oats were for him as long as he lived.

It was a further expression of something deep within the human frame, a feeling of debt and gratitude and fondness. It was proof that even a mechanical age will not rupture an association embracing the full scope of history. Cold steel cannot satisfy all of mankind's needs and today the horse renews its hold upon human hearts. More people than ever share a hope expressed by the late Will Rogers that there'll be some horses and saddles in Heaven. The drum-like sounds of hoof-beats would be the perfect accompaniment for the melody of harps.